MY CENTURY

A Memoir of War, Peace and Pioneering
in the Emergency Room

Kristaps Juris Keggi, M.D.

ISBN: 9798846270367

Cover design by: Marisa Dragone
Cover photo: Kristaps arriving in America by brother Juris Keggi
Printed in the United States of America

*In memory of Julie, unmatched wife, mother,
grandmother - golfer and gardener.*

FOREWORD

By Senator John Barrasso

For the last 60 years, every orthopaedic surgeon who trained at Yale was influenced for the better by the life and work of Kris Keggi.

I was fortunate to be one of them.

By the time I was assigned to train under him at the Waterbury Hospital in 1982, he was a larger than life figure.

Based on his reputation, surgical skill and imposing physical prowess, being a resident under Dr. Keggi could be both intimidating and inspiring.

Every orthopaedic resident wanted to be with him and wanted to be like him.

He inspired confidence in his patients, the hospital staff, and the surgical residents privileged to work with him.

He made you want to excel and convinced you that you could.

Kris made it clear that to succeed in surgery both speed and skill were necessary.

You could not be slow and you could not be sloppy.

The impact Kris has had on the profession, and the lives of his patients as well as the doctors he's trained is forever lasting.

For me, it has turned into a 40-year mentorship and friendship.

As you will discover in the pages that follow, Kristaps Keggi is the epitome of the American dream. He was born in Riga, Latvia, and as a boy, with his family, he survived World War II through a series of diversions, adventures and spectacular escapes. At the war's end, the Keggis avoided Russian Soviet rule and the spread of Communism by boarding a refugee ship bound for New York City and a new life. He attended high schools in Brooklyn and Greenwich, CT, and then Yale College, Class of 1955, and Yale School of Medicine, graduating in 1959.

Eight years after he arrived in the U.S., while in medical school, he volunteered for military duty, commissioned as a second lieutenant in the U.S. Army, eventually joining the Army Medical Service and Medical Corps. In 1965, he was shipped to the war in Vietnam, where he was the orthopedic surgery chief in the Third Mobile Army Surgical Hospital, better known as MASH. His was the first MASH unit to deploy to Vietnam, where the action in the expanding war was steady and fierce. The Third MASH supported the 173rd Airborne Brigade, the 1st and 25th Infantry Divisions and many other units. His two years of active military duty finished in 1966 and he resigned his commission with the rank of captain.

Kris's service did not stop after Vietnam. His battlefield experience - dealing with whatever came into the surgical tent on a given day - sharpened his skills. He would go on not only to perform countless surgeries but also to train generations of orthopaedic surgeons and win worldwide acclaim for orthopaedic education and innovation. He famously pioneered and popularized the less invasive anterior surgical approach now widely used for total hip replacement. His influence has been enormous. I credit much of my success as an orthopaedic surgeon and in life to my training under Dr.

Keggi.

Perhaps most notably, Kris is the founder and president of the Keggi Orthopedic Foundation and Orthopedic Exchange Program between the United States and the former Soviet Republics which is now the Yale University Keggi Kimball Fund for International Orthopaedic Education. The program has fostered hundreds of fellows in exchanges in Latvia, Russia and other countries in Europe. He even mentored Valdis Zatlers, the former President of Latvia and a fellow orthopedic surgeon. I had the occasion to meet Zatlers during a congressional trip to Latvia and was proud to stand with him as a President and a U.S. Senator who'd both been influenced by Kris's training.

He has published more than 135 scholarly articles on orthopedic medical treatments. He was the senior author of the seminal American Academy of Orthopedic Surgeons instructional course on "Early Care of Severe War Wounds" on how battlefield wounds should be treated. The list of his charitable endeavors and honors and scholarly society memberships is nearly endless.

And yet he has found time for a full life outside his profession, one that after the recent loss of Julie, his beloved wife of more than 60 years, he continues to enjoy with his three daughters, their spouses and five grandchildren. Along the way, he's run marathons, rowed competitively, golfed enthusiastically, vacationed impressively and remained keenly observant and opinionated about the country's shifting political landscape.

Upon reading these memoirs, I think you'll agree with me that Kristaps Keggi embodies everything – all the good - our country stands for. Every opportunity he has been given in the U.S. he has given back in full. His own mentor at Yale, Dr. Wayne Southwick, used to utter the words that would follow him through the rest of his life as a source of encouragement:

"You can do it, Kris."

And so, as these pages make clear, he has.

ORIGINS

Kristaps Juris Keggi. I am the second of four sons born to Dr. Janis and Ruta Berzins Keggi. Kristaps is the Latvian version of Christopher, patron saint of Riga, the capital of Latvia. His statue stood for several centuries at the gates of his city. Juris is "George," the saint and dragon slayer. Typically, Latvians have only one first name, but my parents could not settle on a single name, so I was given both Kristaps and Juris. Kristaps was my mother's choice, the name of one of her father's brothers, while Juris, my father's alternative, was given to the second born son in Orthodox Christian Church tradition. The family name of Keggi is Estonian. My paternal great-grandfather is said to have gotten into a family inheritance dispute and as a result of it exited Estonia to settle in Latvia, marry a Latvian woman and start a Latvian family. On my Latvian maternal side, the family name is very common, Berzins meaning "small birch tree."

I am Latvian, a descendent of tribes that migrated 2,000-3,000 years ago from somewhere near India to what is now Latvia. However. I am certain that there are Livonians, Estonians, Finns, Germans, Prussians, Saxons (Teutonic Knights), Danes and Swedes in my ancestral pool. My DNA report reveals no surprises, my genotype corresponds to the Northern German and Finish varieties. My father was especially proud of his ancestors from Northwest Estonia and the Island of Saarema. During a visit to this corner of Estonia in the summer of 2019, I asked a university student who was working at the front desk of our hotel if she had heard of the Keggi family. She had not, but within 15 minutes found it on her computer and produced three pages of Keggis from the region, some dating back to the middle of the 17th century. Saarema, meanwhile, was the stronghold of the Eastern Vikings and is said to have been the last place in Europe to be Christianized. Apparently, the Eastern Vikings or pirates, as they were called at the end of their era, were crafty sailors able to hold off any attacks by sea. Their independence and pagan ways came to an end only as a result of a very cold winter that allowed the Christian Teutonic Knights to finish their "missionary" work by riding their horses across the frozen sea.

Our "Estonian Keggi" father loved to tell us stories of the Estonian Saarema Vikings sailing to Sweden for plunder, but we also knew that the Swedes visited Saarema for their turn at plunder, too. These stories were meant to emphasize the hardiness of these ancient tribes and how fortunate we, the descendants, were to have some of their genes to face the problems in our own times.

My mother's side of the family came from the Western part of Latvia known as Kurzeme or Kurland (in German). The Baltic tribes in this area were primarily interconnected with those in Lithuania and East Prussia. Interestingly enough, there is also an anecdotal family connection to Immanuel Kant, one of the most influential philosophers of all time. My maternal great-grandmother came from an area close to East Prussia where he had lived and his name was inscribed in her dowry when she came north to be married to our maternal great-grandfather in Dzukste, Kurzeme. There may also be some residual genes from the Livonians (Livs), tribes related to the Ugro Finnish group, who preceded the Baltics in what is now

Latvia. The land had also been criss-crossed for centuries by Germans, Swedes, and Russians after their victorious Great Northern War in the 18th century.

Born in 1907, my father's first seven years of life were spent in Latvia, but when World War I broke out, the family escaped to Russia to avoid the carnage raging at home. During those years, his education was Russian, and for the rest of his life he was fluent in Russian and familiar with all of their customs. My mother felt that when she first met him, in 1929, he had a Russian accent and manners. With or without an accent he'd always been number one in any class he attended. The straight A's on his report cards seemed boring and repetitive to those of us with lesser performance. It was a level of academic excellence that he carried through his years at the University of Latvia and in surgical training with Professor Paulis Stradins, the Chairman of Surgery at the University of Latvia, who had been a student in my grandfather Berzins' school before World War I. Having had his medical training in St. Petersburg, Russia and the Mayo Clinic in Minnesota, Prof. Stradins was one of the great surgeons of his era. He thought my father should pursue an academic career, and after the completion of his surgical training in Latvia sent him to visit some of the major surgical centers of Europe and spend a year in Copenhagen doing research on tissue cultures.

My mother, born in 1910, had spent the chaotic years of WWI in Estonia and, upon her return to Latvia, received a degree in education and pursued a teaching career until it was interrupted by the arrival of four sons. Her paternal grandfather was born into serfdom the early 19th century, but, when freed, his children quickly rose to successful lives as farmers, teachers and writers. My grandfather, Ludis Berzins, pursued an education in theology at Dorpat University in Estonia. He became

3

an ordained Lutheran minister who baptized, confirmed, married and buried almost four generations of family members. But most of his life was dedicated to education and the study of Latvian culture, folklore and linguistics. He was the founder of a major secondary school in Latvia before WWI, said to have been the first boarding school in Czarist Russia. The school was totally destroyed during the war, but my grandfather's career in education resumed after Latvia achieved its independence in 1918. He was a longstanding director of the Latvian Teacher's Institute and Professor of Latvian Folklore and Philology at the University of Latvia. He was the author of many publications and books on these subjects. He was also a poet and wrote many hymns found in the Latvian Lutheran Church Hymnal.

My parents met in 1929 at the University of Latvia, where father studied medicine and mother was headed for a doctorate in education. They married soon thereafter. I was born on August 9, 1934, and was the second of four sons, they being in birth order, Janis/John, Kristaps/Christopher, Andrejs/Andrew and Ludis/Louis. Shortly after my birth, my mother and brother Janis joined father in Copenhagen where he was doing his research on tissue cultures and I was left with our maternal grandparents in the house they had recently finished in Jurmala . I am sure it had no negative effects on my future, and in all photographs of that period I look blond, pink-cheeked, fat and happy. My first five years of life in a free, independent Latvia were as uneventful and happy as they might have been in Sweden, Denmark or America. It was a time spent with grandparents on the beaches outside of Riga, sledding in winter snow, and being rewarded with chocolates and candy for good behavior. One of the most memorable events from those early years was my first visit to a movie theater to see

Walt Disney's "Snow White and the Seven Dwarfs." There were very few cars; you went by horse-drawn carriage in the summer and horse-drawn sled on the snow-covered roads in the winter. The only member of our family who had a car was mother's brother Andris who was working for his father-in-law, one of the wealthiest men in Latvia. He later died in one of the cattle cars meant to deport him and thousands of other "enemies of the State" to Siberia. The story told about his arrest and deportation is that when the Communist militia came to get him, he was having his morning breakfast. He was given a few minutes to pack a bag, but he chose to finish his coffee and then be loaded onto the train with no more than the "shirt on his back." He was dead long before getting to his Siberian concentration camp.

Brothers Janis, Kristaps, Andrejs and Ludis with Uncle Ansis Berzins; rear: Ludis and Minna Berzins, mother Ruta and Aunt Antra Berzins. 1939 or so.

THE WAR COMES

My carefree youth came to an end in 1939 when Russia and Germany signed the infamous Molotov-Ribbentrop "non-aggression" treaty, allowing the Germans to take western Poland and giving "carte blanche" to the Russians in eastern Poland and the Baltic states. The agreement was signed in August 1939, and a few days later, on September 1, the Germans marched into Poland and the Russians started the occupation of the Baltics and eastern Poland. For us, it was the official beginning of World War II. I was five and remember mother listening to the radio, crying and telling us about war. It had very little meaning to me, but the fear and emotion she was expressing was memorable. The Russian Red Army arrived without any resistance - all of a sudden, they were there. The first Russian soldier I saw was a few blocks from our home in Aluksne. There he was, in broad daylight, disheveled, drunk, in the middle of the street, spraying urine all over himself and the ground around him - the ultimate hero, taking charge of a conquered land, penis in hand.

The year of the so-called first Communist occupation of Latvia (1940 - 1941) came to be referred to as the "Baigais gads" - the year of horror, year of terror, year of fear and year of suffering. There were executions and individual condemnations to labor camps, followed by the systematic deportation to Siberia of thousands of people, starting in June of 1941. Latvian officers who had been incorporated into the Red Army were ordered to report for special maneuvers in eastern Latvia where they were shot and buried in mass graves, a scenario identical to the fate suffered by Polish officers in the Katyn Forest massacre. Anyone with an education and potential political influence - teachers, ministers, lawyers or physicians - were considered enemies of the state to be dealt with by execution or deportation. Mother's youngest brother Ludis, who had a bleeding stomach ulcer, was doing his compulsory military service when he was condemned to 10 years of hard labor for reporting to duty a few minutes late. He was deported to a concentration camp in Northern Siberia where he died less than a year later. Another brother, Janis, one of my godfathers, had been a student of theology and was doing his military service in the Latvian Army when the Russians arrived. He was switched to the Red Army and was a junior officer in one of the Latvian Red Army units soon ordered to report for those Katyn-like "maneuvers" in Eastern Latvia. He sensed trouble and fled to safety among the guerrillas in the forest, thus escaping execution. After fighting with these Latvian guerillas and later the German commandos near Stalingrad (Brandenburg Brigade) and the Latvian Legions in Russia and Latvia, he ended up in the infamous Riga central prison. His exact place of death remains undetermined. He may have been executed in Riga, but the most likely scenario was death in a collapsing mine shaft in Siberia, as vaguely reported 20 years later by a survivor of that camp. Uncle Janis was one of my childhood heroes and has remained one ever since.

My grandfather Ludis Berzins, pictured here with my grandmother, Minna, my mother, Ruta, left, and aunt Irene Berzins, may have escaped Communist deportation by being hospitalized with a broken femur.

Our maternal grandparents may have escaped the deportations of June 1941 because Grandfather was, at the time the Communists were making up the list of those to be deported, in the hospital with a broken femur. Our young family in Aluksne similarly escaped because the Communist mayor of the town was ill with gallbladder problems and Father was the only one who could take care of him.

We children were spared those stories and were sheltered from the fear and terror our parents lived with, but I do remember how strange it was that we were told to keep secret our Christmas celebration, including Christmas carols and the Christmas tree we had in the house. I was also puzzled that my father, mother and older brother did not show any enthusiasm for the images and symbols of Communism that were a constant presence in my school and, in their own way, earned me academic honors. I had learned reading at age four. It had been a simple process of starting with the letters on the front cover and first page of "Kristaps Robins and Vini Pu" and knowing how to read by the end of the book.

Even though I was a year or two younger than the rest of the children in the first grade, mother felt I was ready and that was that. I was going to school and doing the work, but there was another boy who had better grades. As we were approaching the end of the school year the new political indoctrination process came into play. We could add extra points to our grades by doing something in support of Communism. It was an opportunity six-year-old Kristaps could not ignore, and a large poster celebrating Lenin, Stalin and Marshal Voroshilow was the result. It was worth the extra points and placed me first in the class. I brought the poster home and fixed it to our bedroom wall. Janis teased me about it, but my parents did not dare say anything. Interestingly enough, one of the most celebrated Communist heroes was Pavlik Morozov, a 13-year-old boy who reported his parents to the State for their unacceptable counter-revolutionary talk at home.

That is the way it worked for me in first grade, and in later years I was able to witness it at all levels of the Communist society. As a mediocre surgeon but good Communist you moved up in the privileged world of special stores, cars and housing. If you were outside of the system, your job as an excellent surgeon was to make your Party comrades look good and hope for an occasional handout of material favors. Sometime later, my father's sister, who had remained in Latvia, occasionally sent us a carefully worded letter reporting the family activities but stopped writing when her daughters were hoping to go to medical school. Any type of contact with the outside world could label you an enemy of the State, disqualified to a higher education. Contacts with anybody in the West could be a major risk to their education and lives.

Many years after that, as I started to visit, teach, operate and run an academic exchange program in Latvia and the rest of the Soviet Union, it was obvious that many of the surgeons I was dealing with were probably cooperating with the Communists at every level and telling the KGB anything they wanted to hear. They lived double lives and since early childhood had learned their family lives had to be hidden from the official outside world. Almost all the Latvians I encountered who had survived and were successful within the Communist system were experts at switching from the one life to the other. When dealing with the KGB they were model Communists, when talking to me they were telling me how liberal they were. This agility, a necessity for survival and sanity, also made them expert liars on any subject who could look you in the eye and, without the slightest hesitation, change in posture or facial expression tell you lie after lie. As a first grader under Communism, I was on that track and was learning the road to success in that world. Being the son and grandson of enemies of the State, my chances of escaping summary execution or Siberian deportation were remote, but I was learning the tricks of survival.

As children we were sheltered from most of the horrors of that first year of Communism in Latvia. Some of the strange happenings such as the secret Christmas, the Communist poster, the Russian soldier and the Latvian soldiers now wearing Russian uniforms were confusing, but most of the days were uneventful. With the exception of mother's crying about the war, we children did not experience it until suddenly one day there was panic in the Russian ranks. The Russian soldiers and their families were packing and leaving in a great hurry by truck, horse-drawn carriage and overloaded bicycles. Then came rifle fire and explosions. The Latvian anti-Communist guerrillas, my godfather Janis among them, the Latvian soldiers who had deserted from the fleeing Red Army, and the local citizenry were fighting for control of an ammunition depot on the outskirts of town. Father was also involved, and our house became an armed camp with a machine gun on the balcony and rifles with boxes of ammunition and hand grenades at the doors. The spur to this activity was that the German invasion of Russia had begun. The Molotov-Ribbentrop Treaty was no more. It was June 22, 1941, only eight days after the first mass deportation of Latvians to Siberia, with over 15,000 taken away, or close to 1 percent of the population.

The main thrust of the German attack was from Poland to Leningrad, threatening to trap the Communist troops, NKVD/KGB secret service operatives, political leaders, Russians and their sympathizers in Latvia. That threat was very real and it was the reason for the Communists' chaotic rush to the east. The Germans did not arrive in Riga until July, and those of us in Aluksne, the northeast corner of Latvia, did not see them until a bit later. During that period of time, late June and early July 1941, every able Latvian male was pursuing the fleeing Russians. Everybody was up in arms, in the true sense of the word, ready to go after the Russians. Uncle Janis, who was with the Latvian guerillas, was involved in these skirmishes, sustained a gunshot wound to the scalp and was thought to be dead, but he survived and was soon able to row a boat across the Daugave River to inform the advancing German military units that the Russians had left Riga and they could march into the city without any preliminary bombardments or artillery barrages. He was accompanied on this heroic mission by one of his Lettonia fraternity brothers, who somehow survived the war and concentration camps to tell me the story when I first started going to Latvia in 1987.

There was a sense of disappointment when the Germans disarmed the Latvian militias, indicating they did not need any help in handling the fleeing Russian hordes. That soon changed as one of the coldest winters on record set in and the German armies were stopped outside of Leningrad and Moscow. Within a few months after the Germans lost the dramatic battle for Leningrad, the situation reversed. Now, every able-bodied Latvian male of military age was to be put into active duty. Since only Germans could be in the Wehrmacht (regular army), all the new recruits were placed in "Foreign Legions" under the command of the Waffen (Combat) SS, as opposed to the Nazi Party SS, their execution squads and concentration camp units.

Even before these mass mobilizations, some of the Latvian soldiers and officers who spoke German and Russian had been kept on by the Germans and assigned to military units such as the Brandenburg Brigades (special, long range patrols for combat and scouting behind enemy lines). Uncle Janis was one of those who found himself fighting the Russians near Stalingrad. He was, in less than two years, a junior officer in the armies of three countries – first Latvia, then Red Russia and now Germany. He survived Stalingrad and was among the first to become an officer in Germany's Latvian Legions, fighting in Russia and on his ancestral lands in Latvia. Later, at the time of the German capitulation in May of 1945, he was one of the most highly decorated officers in those units. I remember him on leave in Riga during the summer of 1944 in his Obersturmbandfuehrer (senior leader of attack units, probably the equivalent of Captain in the American Army) uniform with its combat badges, four " Purple Hearts," Iron Crosses of the Second and First Class and the Deutsche Kreutz (said to be the equivalent of the Ritter Kreutz, the highest order of the historic Iron Crosses). Impressive to all, but more than impressive to his 10-year-old godson.

In Aluksne, near our home, there was no combat except for some firefights near the ammunition depot. I remember seeing, from our second story windows, some soldiers running around, hiding behind trees, expecting Russian counterattacks, but the Russians had vanished without any exchange of fire. Our house was fully armed as a result of my father's participation in the assault on the ammunition depot outside of town, but none of the rifles, machine guns or hand grenades we had on our balcony and at our doors had to be used. Not so far from us, the old highway from Riga to Pleskau and Saint Petersburg (Leningrad under the Communists) was the scene of heavy attacks on the fleeing Russians by Germans from the air and Latvian guerillas, godfather Janis among them, on the ground. For months after the retreat of the Russians, that highway was littered with burned out trucks, cars and a variety of other military vehicles, all of them fascinating in our young eyes and imaginations.

In spite of 600 years of oppression by the German Teutonic Knights and their descendants, the Germans had been welcomed as liberators throughout Latvia. The Russian Communist regime, during its one year in power, had been brutal and tens of thousands had been its victims – imprisoned, shot or deported to Siberia. I do not remember any large German units marching into Aluksne, but by the fall of 1941, when we returned to school, the red flags had been replaced by German swastikas. Instead of singing the "L'Internationale" (the Communist anthem) we were now singing "Deutschland uber Alles" (Germany over all others) while the hymn "Dievs Sveti Latviju" (God Bless Latvia) was relegated to home behind closed doors. We were all shown graphic exhibits of Russian/Communist terror and its victims. The photographs of the bloated corpse of a well-known

Latvian general and the mass grave of lesser men and women still haunt me. We also had heard by now of the tragedies such as Uncle Ludis' death in the Siberian labor camp, the deportation of relatives and the execution of some family friends.

The Germans had arrived and even though there were no major military activities around us, Aluksne was an administrative center for their troops in Russia. We got to know German officers who were housed with us. They were with the logistical units of the forward moving (forward at first, backward later) combat units. They were polite and gentlemanly, having been teachers, accountants or similar professionals before being called to active duty in the Wehrmacht. Major Eierman, a teacher in civilian life, was one of them. His stay with us was fairly prolonged and became a true friend who, when we later were forced to flee from the return of the Communist Russians, would help us get to Germany and his home in Freiburg. After his stay with us he was ordered into a combat zone, where he came close to being killed when his car was blown up by a landmine. He survived but suffered a major spine fracture which disqualified him from further active military service and returned him to his teaching job in Freiburg. Father and Mother stayed in touch with him by letters and telegrams, and when the time came for us to flee Latvia, he promised us refuge with his family.

The Germans had been lifesavers for most of us, but their handling of the Jews throughout the country, and our town in particular, was truly frightening. The Einsatz Units, whose mission was the extermination of Jews, arrived in Aluksne several weeks after the Wehrmacht during the summer of 1941. In one day, they rounded up all the Jewish families that had not escaped to Russia and shot them less than a mile from our house. I remember the sounds of the shots and a tragic scene, involving Father, we witnessed from the second-story windows of our house, which was next to the hospital building. As the shooting was going on, a truck pulled up to the front of the hospital looking for a Jewish woman who had just given birth. Father, who was the chief surgeon and director of the hospital, would not let the armed men into the hospital. They knocked him over, pushed him aside, found the woman, dragged her and the baby into the truck and headed in the direction of the shots we'd been hearing. The massacre of these people was known to all of us. When I visited the area 50 years later, I asked about the grave but was unable to get clear answers. There is, however, a monument in the center of the town in memory of these executed Jewish families. The episode left me, as a seven-year-old, with recurrent nightmares of firing squads, rifles pointed at me and bodies in a mass grave. It was disturbing to think of some of these families who had been guests in our home, who had come to greet us at Easter/Passover time with gifts of matzos, now at the bottom of an unmarked pit. I still have a first-grade class picture which includes a Jewish girl with long dark hair. Her image is a haunting one. The shooting was carried out by the German Einsatz group, but local Latvian boys were involved. Shortly before the arrival of the Germans, a group of boys in the upper classes of our school, 15 to 18 years old, who had joined guerrilla bands had been caught by Russians on the outskirts of our town. They had been tortured, mutilated, killed and left dead in a field. When the Einsatz Unit arrived, it blamed the fate of these boys on "Jews" and were able to get some of their friends, after appropriate alcohol consumption, to participate in the identification and massacre of the entire Jewish population.

It is also haunting to remember that, for a few

days, one way or the other, our family, as "enemies of the Communist State," could have come to the end of our lives in that same grave. It's worth repeating that we'd escaped deportation or execution during the last weeks of the Russian occupation because my father was the only surgeon in the area who could take care of the Communist mayor's gall bladder attacks.

In school, my second grade, we had switched from the Communist left-fist salute to high-held rigid right arm and "Heil Hitler!" Reading, writing and arithmetic continued, but there are times I wonder about the effectiveness of this education in the midst of the changing times, its horrors and the propaganda that went with it. Would an uninterrupted, smooth education in a small Connecticut town have made me a better person? Would I be more effective in writing this "autobiography" if my education had not been disrupted by war, fear, famine, "cultural" changes from Latvian to Russian Communism, to German, to French and finally American?

The school we attended under Latvians, Russians or Germans was different from what I saw many years later with our children in New Haven and Middlebury. We all wore uniforms and caps that identified us as primary school students. The boy's jackets were black and had stiff collars. The girls had dark dresses with white aprons. The bright kids sat in the first two rows, the girls in the first, the boys in the second. You were not promoted to second grade unless you knew reading and arithmetic, and there were boys in the back rows who just sat there waiting to reach the age of thirteen when they would no longer be required to waste time in school, could return to their farms and the simpler life they knew well. Most of the "good" girls in the front row had long blond hair in neat tresses and their tips presented a major temptation to be dipped into the ink wells of the second row. I was a second rower but managed to stay out of that bit of trouble, being the "good boy" I was.

Another interesting activity during that first year after the Russian departure was the collections of weapons, hand grenades, flares and ammunition that could be found throughout the town and surrounding countryside. As a second-grader I was not involved, but 10-year-old bother Janis had a box full of the "stuff" which he kept in our bedroom, under his bed - until discovered by Father, who, after the appropriate spanking of poor Janis, decided to have a little fun of his own. It was the fall, and in our garden there were pits in which dead branches and fallen leaves were being burned. Father decided to put on a show of fireworks and in the late afternoon, as it was getting dark, dumped Janis' box of grenades, flares and ammunition into one of these smoldering pits. We were allowed to watch it from the second story of the house, about 20 or 30 yards away. Father barely had time to hit the ground a few yards from the pit before the show went on - it was momentous for all of us to see and for brother Janis well worth the spanking he had received.

But always, the war loomed. There were military planes on the frozen lake in front of our house and boys were conscripted as trench diggers who would progress to the infantry by the time they were 16, or big enough. At one point during the summer of 1944 we had to hide 12-year-old brother Janis in the cellar of the house, as German patrols were in the area looking for new troops. Words of indoctrination, different anthems and flags give you much to think about, but approaching artillery fire is real, understandable, and a threat to life that requires action.

After stopping the German advance at Leningrad, it took the Russians a while to regroup, but by the winter of 1943-44, they were attacking, and the Germans were being pushed back to the West. We were still at home in Aluksne. As the Russians made their advances, the fighting came closer and we could hear artillery fire all day and at nighttime could see flashes of light along the eastern horizon. It was relentless. By early spring, Mother, my three brothers and I departed to Jurmala to stay with her parents. Jurmala is on the Baltic Sea, just west of Riga. Father stayed in Aluksne and continued to operate until July of 1944, but when the Russians were less than three miles from town, he got on his bicycle and rode over 200 kilometers. in one day to join us in Jurmala.

Aluksne was taken by the Russians shortly after father's departure and there was no question that it would be only a matter of time before all of Latvia was to be in their hands once again. Based on their brutal actions in 1940 and 1941, we were certain that falling into their hands meant for us execution or deportation to Siberia. Our only chance for survival was escape to the West via Sweden or Germany. The western allies had landed in Normandy in June and were moving east, in the direction of Germany. They were also marching north from Italy. Father and Mother were keeping up with their progress by listening late at night to the forbidden news broadcast by the BBC. As children, we pretended to sleep but were very aware of the British broadcasts and how they differed from the German propaganda news. Hitler was talking about how well the war was going and the introduction of new secret weapons, but we thought the likelihood of a German victory was nil. Some of his secret weapons, such as his V-1 and V-2 rockets, were operational and causing havoc in London. In addition, his first jet fighters were leaving their mark, but his ultimate weapon, the atomic bomb, had not materialized. The Germans were not a threat to us. The Russians, however, were. Our salvation lay in the West. My father's first plan was Sweden, but his alternative was the western part of Germany once it had been liberated by the Allied Forces. We had to get there. Staying in Latvia under Russian-Communist rule was not an alternative.

ESCAPE

One of our very unrealistic hopes was that, no matter who the victor or loser was, at the end of the war the Civilized World would return the Baltics to their independence and we'd be able to return home from Sweden, Germany or whatever other safe haven we might have reached. That had been the case after WWI, when my mother's family had escaped to Estonia and father's to Russia. Once peace was declared, both families returned to their Latvian homes. There were even a few in our midst who thought Germany was on the verge of surrender and that we'd be back in Latvia by the Christmas of 1944. We obviously did not know about the Stalin/Roosevelt/Yalta agreements that left Eastern Europe in the Russian zone of influence that would have put an immediate end to our flights of naïve imagination. To Roosevelt, "zone of influence" meant economic aid and restoration of democracies. To Stalin, it meant total control of the area and Bolshevism in its most brutal form. The Yalta agreements have been studied and discussed from all historical and political perspectives, but as victims of this pact, we tend to see Roosevelt as ill, counselled by his pro-Communist advisors, and giving in to all of Stalin's demands. Those of us given up to Stalin have long been very conscious of the tragedy of this agreement.

Sweden, fewer than 100 miles across the Baltic Sea, represented hope, and, with a little luck, could be reached with the help of Latvian fishermen and their boats. Thousands of Latvians had done it, but it was risky and expensive. It was a consideration. Mother had spent some summers in Sweden, spoke the language and had Swedish friends. Father had spent a year in Denmark, was familiar with the country, its people and some of their surgeons. It made sense to give it a try.

By this time, our entire family was in our grandparent's house in Jurmala, on the beach west of Riga, separated from Riga itself by the Daugava and Lielupe rivers. We were very aware of the approaching Russian armies, and during the summer of 1944 a column of their tanks had broken through to the Gulf of Riga only a few miles west of us. Soon after, we were encircled by Russians. We heard their steady artillery and rifle fire. Chaos set in as everybody scrambled to get to Riga and somehow escape by ship to Germany. Our family tried to get on the last train to Riga, but when it reached the station where we and hundreds of others were waiting, it was absolutely packed. We were able to push Grandmother, one of our aunts (Antra) and her four children (all under the age of 10) into what little space there was. The rest of us - Mother, Father, Grandfather, my brothers and I - were left on the platform to await our fate. Throughout the days of fear and horror that followed, Father and Grandfather were amazing in keeping all of us calm and safe. As a surgeon, my father was constantly considering alternative plans of action. As a theologian, minister and man of God, my grandfather, with utmost faith, prayed with us and put himself in the hands of the Lord. We left the railroad station, went home and, to everyone's surprise, a few days later the Russian tanks were counterattacked and destroyed. Grandmother, Aunt Antra and her children returned from Riga and we could start contemplating new plans of escape.

My father Janis, here walking in Riga in 1938 with me, older brother Janis and Grandfather Berzins, later performed miracles to keep our family safe.

Another memory from that summer of 1944 was the desperate efforts of the losing German army to build up its fighting strength by enlisting what seemed like the youngest of boys. My brother Janis had to hide in the cellar to avoid being taken by the German military police for trench digging duty. The official word was they would not be taken under the age of 13, but in practice, if you were big enough, you were good enough. Janis was a "big 12" and had to be hidden in the cellar while this desperate recruitment went on. We knew several boys who were taken for trench digging duty and rapidly graduated from the shovel to a rifle. The most interesting of these boys was one we later came to know in Germany. He had gone from digging trenches (1944) to being a rifleman in combat with the Latvian Legions in Germany (1944-1945) and had been lucky enough to reach the

Western Allies and surrender to them. But he didn't like their prisoner of war camp, and when the French Army came asking for volunteers, he joined their Foreign Legion to fight in Indochina (1945-1949). He was only a few years older than we were, but his stories covered several lifetimes. My most vivid recollection of him was his reply to my question of how he was able to survive more than five years of both heavy combat in Germany and what is now Vietnam. His answer was, "Always let the other guy go first." This cynical response didn't fit with the medals for heroism he'd been awarded by the Germans and the French.

Of course, equally sad as being forced to fight with the Germans at 14 or 15, was the induction, at the same age, into the Red Army as soon as the Russians had control of the land and its population. These pediatric-age "soldiers" were then sent into action as cannon fodder in human-wave attacks against the Germans or in some notably tragic encounters, such as the Christmas battles near Dzukste in 1944, when they were forced to charge their Latvian brothers in German uniforms. One of these young boys who had survived the war with the Latvian/German Legions was to reach New York at about the same time as our family and was in our church, our folk dancing group and choir. He was in his early twenties and was drafted into the American army as soon as the Korean War broke out in 1950. Since he was tall and strong, he was assigned to man a heavy machine gun and was soon killed in action. As with so many other Latvians, I could have ended up with the Germans or Russians, but 20 years later was proud to serve in the United States Army and take care of its wounded in Vietnam.

Meanwhile, back in the late summer of 1944 our desire to escape to Sweden remained strong. My father, having left his hospital in Aluksne, could, under the pretense of looking for jobs in western Latvia, explore escape routes to Sweden or one of its islands. Before long, he was able to find a way out, had made the appropriate contacts and had returned to Jurmala to get us organized. We got to the western shores of Latvia by train and horse-drawn carriages, stopping along the way to spend a night in Dzukste, my maternal grandfather's childhood home, and Talsi, my grandmother's childhood home. Grandmother's home, called "Renci," was impressive with its open spaces, rolling hills and the family cemetery on one of them. It was fun to spend some time with cousins, running through wheat fields, sleeping in a barn in Dzukste and, in Renci, stuffed like sardines in a single bed with several of the cousins. But then things turned serious. We found ourselves near Mazirbe in the middle of the night, huddled in a barn in the woods within a few short yards of the beach where we were supposed to board a boat to Sweden. It was dark, and it was silent except for the waves of the sea. It was scary. The Lord's Prayer helped. Father had left us to make final plans and we were alone with Mother. After what seemed to be a long time, he returned only to tell us we were going back to Jurmala. The whole episode was strange to say the least. We the children had been given little or no information about what lay ahead and now we were going back.

What happened was that, after leaving us in the barn, Father scouted the area, met the fishermen who were to take us across the sea to Sweden and assessed all the risks involved, which were significant. If caught on land or on sea by the Germans, you'd be looked upon as a deserter to be shot. If Russian ships saw you, they would simply fire a few cannon rounds into your boat and send you to the bottom of the sea. There were also stories of fishermen collecting the gold and silver they expected for their services only to throw you overboard once at sea and then return for the next group of refugees trying to escape the approaching Russians. Father deemed the fishermen less than trustworthy, and, at about the same time, he'd been alerted that a German patrol was in the area. With those two strikes against us, he made a decision to go back to Jurmala and instead attempt an escape to Germany.

The decision to abandon Sweden was made by Father based on the facts and the situation as he saw them. There were no discussions, no debates and no questions. In that barn in the woods, we were scared but there was no talk, no crying, and only total trust in Father's decisions supported by the Lord's Prayer. In the middle of the night on that remote seashore, his assessment of the situation was correct and his decision to get us to Germany worked out. By the way, I don't know how my father did it, but he found a farmer with a horse-drawn carriage to get us out of the forest. I'm sure the farmer was well paid, but he did get us to a railway station and on our way back to Jurmala.

As we look back at WWII, Germany, Germans, Hitler, racism, Communism, Stalin and Russia, it is impossible to make full sense of who we were and what was to become of us. A book written on the subject of Latvia caught between two giants might attempt to put it all in a logical, historical perspective, but as the summer of 1944 progressed, going to Germany - its western part – had become our only choice, with its vague promise of survival in American or British hands. One of my mother's good friends had married Professor Staudinger, a German physicist at the University of Freiburg in southwestern Germany. Professor Staudinger eventually received the Nobel Prize for his work on atomic particles, but in 1944 he was also willing to help our displaced family. In Freiburg, there was also Eierman, the teacher who, as an officer in the German Army, had lived with us in Aluksne before his disabling spine fracture in a car blown up by a landmine. By the fall of 1944, he was back in Freiburg and was also offering to help us. It is hard to imagine how my parents were able to communicate with the Staudingers and Eierman, but, in spite of bombardments of all the major German cities and trains, the mails and telegraphs continued to function. So, for us it was away from the sea and Sweden, back to Jurmala and off to Freiburg, Germany, if possible.

As Latvians within the German scheme of things, we were classified as "half citizens." We had passports and, with the proper authorizations, were free to move and travel in German-controlled territories as well as Germany itself. We had money and could buy railway tickets to any destination. By the late summer of 1944, the Russians had reached the Baltic Sea in Lithuania and East Prussia. Latvia had been cut off from the rest of Europe. Travel back and forth between Germany and Latvia could only be done by ship. The ships that brought fresh German troops and supplies to Latvian ports were then used to get wounded soldiers back to Germany and, with them, if there was left over space, refugees fleeing the Russian Communists. We were able to get passage on one of these ships and had also secured railway tickets from our port of landing in northeastern Germany (now Poland) to Freiburg in Germany's Southwest. It was a good plan and had the promise of success.

The weeks before our departure, in late September 1944, were chaotic and hard to imagine. The Russians were very close to Riga but, miraculously, their commanding officers had made a decision to rest and regroup the troops before launching a major attack on the city. That decision was a stroke of great fortune, and it essentially allowed us to escape. It could have gone the other way, but those are the fortunes or vagaries of war. In the right place at the right time, you live. A few paces or hours the wrong way, you die. Some friends and relatives were making plans to stay. Others were still hoping to go to Sweden, but after our adventures in the woods of western Latvia, Germany was the goal.

Grandmother was a strong, practical woman and head of a household since age 15 and the death of her mother. She'd been through WWI and was brought up with century-old tales of wars and how to survive them. Burying your china, silverware and other valuables was one of them and we carried it out without any fanfare. It was what you did and as you did it, you were hoping to be back. We also packed and were ready to leave home on a moment's notice. We each could carry one suitcase, but we were also allowed to ship some other things, including my father's bicycle, to Mr. Eierman in Freiburg. It is amazing to think that what we shipped arrived in Freiburg in spite of the chaos of war. Allied fighter planes by this time had total daytime control of the western part of Germany, yet our bags and the bicycle made it to Freiburg, a tribute to the amazing German sense of order and organization. Sadly, I was not allowed to bring, nor ship, my teddy bear. He had been my companion and security for the 10 years of my life and now in spite of all protestations had to be abandoned to an unknown fate it Jurmala. In packing, priority was given to food (canned and dried) and such hard currency as silverware and old coins that had value under any condition. Of lesser material value were photographs, but father would not make a move anywhere without his album of family photographs (which we still have 70 or more years later). We can put a dollar value on gold rubles, but old family pictures remain priceless.

Another tale of planning for survival and giving

one's children a sense of responsibility was a trip brother Janis and I were asked to make to get some pork meat canned. Grandmother was a born farmer who could not live without a garden, a cow, chickens and a large pig. In preparation for our flight from Latvia, the pig had been slaughtered and my brother and I were to bring the meat to a small cannery. It was packed in four small suitcases and we, at the age of 10 and 12, were to deliver it to the cannery. It involved a ride on a fully packed train with our suitcases full of raw meat beginning to leak bloody fluid. We accomplished our task and a week later we were dispatched to pick up the now-ready canned goods. It entailed more rides on very crowded trains. One of the trains did not have any room in the carriages and we had to ride on the bumpers between the carriages. Hard to imagine doing this at any age, but it probably gave us some resilience in later months and years.

Our grandmother and grandfather had left Riga by ship at the end of August and because their son, my godfather Janis Berzins, was one of the most decorated officers in the Latvian Legions, a partially disabled Waffen SS sergeant was ordered to accompany them and get them to a safe place in Germany. It turned out to be Berchtesgaden, very close to Hitler's retreat in the Alps of southern Germany.

Mother's brothers, Andris and Ansis, their wives, Ina and Antra, and all of their children also managed to get to western Germany and survive the war. There were others who reached Germany to be killed in air raids such as the firebombing of Dresden. Then there were those who were caught, by the Russians, in eastern Germany and deported to Siberia - one can only imagine their horror stories.

As to our own family, we left Riga during the first

days of October 1944. As arranged by Father, lifeboats picked us up near the Riga Castle and ferried us down the river Daugava, out to sea and to the steamship *General von Steuben*, a luxury liner before the war now moving soldiers and refugees. The Germans were obviously proud enough of this Prussian general to name one of their finest ships in his honor, but from the perspective of many years later I can take pride in him as a general in the American Continental Army during the Revolutionary War - a Prussian-American who fought for us with George Washington. We were assigned to cots on the promenade deck. The ship had been painted gray, the sky and the sea were gray, and the refugees were a mass of gray humanity. There was no joy on that cruise in 1944 and, even though we were accompanied by two destroyers, we went through some hours of absolute fear as Russian submarines had been noted in our proximity. It was the last trip the *von Steuben* was to make from Riga, which fell to the Russians on October 13, mere days after our departure. The *von Steuben* continued its rescue voyages from the far western coast of Latvia and Lithuania until February 1945, when it was sunk by a Russian sub off the coast of Lithuania. It perished with its crew, the wounded soldiers and all refugees aboard – the total number of the victims exceeded 5,000 and represents one of the greatest sea disasters in history. The Russians considered it a major naval victory and the submarine captain responsible was honored with the Gold Star of Hero of the Soviet Union. We and the other thousands who were aboard the *von Steuben* in October 1944 may have been "in peril on the seas" but did make it to dry land and the port of Gdansk.

As we came off the ship, we expected to go on our own to the nearest railroad station but were not allowed to do so. Without any explanation, we were forced onto a train for what turned out to be a three-day journey through Germany. Initially, we had some food of our own, and, during the first day of travels, we stopped at railway stations where German Red Cross ladies gave us soup and bread. But as our wanderings continued, there was no food and no water. Finally, our train arrived, in the middle of the night, at a concentration camp complete with high barbed wire fences and SS troopers ordering us to get off the train, shouting, "Ivan steig heraus!," meaning, "Filthy Russians, get off the train!" There were also Allied planes in the sky, strafing something in the surrounding area. It was a grim scene. "Get off the train!" was the order from the SS troopers, but Father had once more assessed the situation and had other orders for us. He had us fall behind, as if we were planning to be the last ones off that train, but instead of turning right to get off, he has us turn left and climb into a tool closet next to the toilet at the end of our carriage. Somehow, the six of us and our suitcases managed to fit on top of each other in that small space. No talk, no chatter, no noise - in fear for sure.

After a while, somebody came through the train, making sure it had been cleared. He stopped at our closet and pushed on the door, but since it did not move with our weight against it, he moved on. We stayed in that closet for as long as the train stood still in the camp. It seemed like hours, but then it started moving. We got out of our closet to find ourselves alone on the train that previously had carried at least 1,000 refugees. We searched the train for anything to eat and found some bread crusts, which we ate without hesitation. We were hungry. The train kept going, and eventually stopped at an empty railroad station. We got off and piled into its waiting room while father established our location and made plans for our next moves. We all spoke German, we had documents allowing us to leave Latvia to go to

Freiburg and we had money to pay for railway tickets, hotel rooms and food when available. It was now a matter of getting there. We bought our tickets and soon were on the next train south.

It was October of 1944. The Allied armies were in France, Belgium and Holland and during the day their airplanes controlled the skies over western Germany, and the trains moved only at night in full blackout conditions. It took us three nights and days to reach Freiburg. We spent one of those days in Cologne in a deep underground shelter while above us the city was being bombed, probably as part of an operation called "Hurricane." I remember the sound of the bombs, the trembling ground, the mass of huddling people and the occasional hysterical cries. The shelter was close to the historic Cologne Cathedral and when we emerged, we were glad to see that even though large sections of the town were rubble, the cathedral itself had been spared. The destruction wasn't much different from most of the other Germany cities, where rubble was the norm. A couple of years later, on a French School trip to neutral Switzerland, I remember thinking how different its towns looked with all of the buildings, shops and restaurants intact. It was in such sharp contrast to a walk my mother and I had to take a year after the war to visit relatives in a refugee camp outside Frankfurt. We went for miles and miles, from the Frankfurt railway station to the Hanau camp, through nothing but rubble, and the only thing that comes to mind to describe it are the pictures of Hiroshima after its atomic bombing or Haiti after one of its major earthquakes. The bombing of Cologne was a memorable event in our lives as we went on to think of war, survival and the future. In any case, we had survived and arrived in Freiburg where the Eierman family took us into their apartment while we arranged for other accommodations.

GERMANY

O nce in Freiburg, it did not take long for Father to be assigned as a physician to Polish factory workers in a town called Emmendingen, approximately 10 miles north of Freiburg, and again luck was on our side. In November, within a few days of our move to Emmendingen, Freiburg was carpet-bombed and the apartment building where we had stayed was destroyed. The Eiermans, who lived on the first floor, had been quick enough to get to the basement bomb shelter and survived, but all the families living in the upper floors of the building had been killed. As a result of this experience, and for the rest of the war, when in doubt it was down to the bomb shelter as quickly as possible. Thus, we spent many nights sleeping in the basement of our house in Emmendingn as bombers flew overhead to and from missions on towns and factories throughout Germany. During the last months of 1944, these major raids were only at night, but later they also went on during the day leaving impressive contrails in the sky. Once Western Allies had reached the Rhine River (around January of 1945) there were the long-distance bombers high in the sky and fighter planes below them, close to the ground, almost every day, and we spent as much time as possible out of the town, hiding in the woods and hills surrounding it. There were only a few minor bombings of Emmendingen itself, but a sudden attack from the skies was a constant threat.

As I reflect upon on our escape from Aluksne to Jurmala and the approaching Russians, the chaos, the unknown future, the aborted trip to Sweden, the trip by ship from Latvia to Germany, the Russian submarines, the train through Germany, the concentration camp, the hours in the tool closet, the bombing of Cologne - I think of fear, but I also remember a certain calm, with total faith in Father's decisions in one crisis after another. We were alive and there was always hope. Grandfather, Grandmother and Mother were also confidant the Lord would be with us and that our frequent prayers would be answered. They were, and they gave us much peace in the worst of times. There was also the excitement of seeing new places, of being at sea on a large ship that had been around the world with a crew who still had colored pamphlets of its tropical cruises, complete with pictures of beaches, palm trees, bikinis, exotic cities and wild animals – just like the advertisements I keep getting in the mail 75 years later. The mountains of the Black Forest were a new sight and impressive to our eyes that had not seen anything other than the low hills and flat fields of Latvia. What a thrill to be running up these mountains or taking a hike to a remote village. Learning to speak in a dialect of the local peasantry ("Allemanisch") was also fun. One day at a time. There were scary ones and good ones, but on the whole, at age 10, optimism prevailed.

The days in the woods above Emmendingen could be great fun. No different from any other boys at any other time, we played games, we fought with each other and looked for imaginary treasures. One day, shortly before the end of the war, I was kicking my way through some bushes that seemed like a good hiding place and sure enough there was a treasure – an 18th-century French cavalry pistol. Somebody must have hidden it to prevent it from falling into the hands of advancing allied troops.

There were no papers with it, there was no way to locate its owner and so the pistol became mine. It is still one of my prize possessions and a curious reminder of those days spent in the woods to avoid roaming fighter planes looking for targets of opportunity or bombers with plans to blow up the Emmendingen factory (and our house). One of the town's wine cellars was a shelter we frequently used when the air raid sirens sounded the alarm. It was a long shaft of a cavern, dug into the side of a mountain and it provided absolute safety for several hundred people. We spent many hours in that deep cellar while planes threatened the area. For moral support and comfort, I found myself cuddling and holding hands with a German girl of my age who had been moved out of the frequently bombed industrial cities in the Ruhr to the relative safety of our smaller town and its wine cellar. I am sure she survived the war. I hope she is doing well and has some good memories of those scary hours spent underground with little Kristaps.

IMPRESSIONS OF
OUR GERMAN LIFE

During the fall of 1944, there was still some rationed food in the stores, but as time went on, there was less and less of it, and during the last months of the war we survived on a diet of lentils. Occasionally, we would try to get some extra potatoes, bread or butter from peasants in the surrounding countryside. I remember one of these expeditions for some food in a village outside of town. Mother had given me a small silver spoon to trade for anything edible I could find, and I was approaching that village at a time when they were distilling their fermented cherry crop to produce kirschwasser spirits (literally "cherry water"), famous in that part of the world. War, fighter planes, bombers, and approaching enemy armies were not about to interfere with kirschwasser distillation. It was a dark, cloudy afternoon yet the entire area had the unmistakable aroma of cherries, the aroma of the same kirschwasser I may buy on my way home today and enjoy after dinner with a few memories of those dark days. The elderly German farmer/peasant I first contacted was very friendly, spoke with a heavy Allemanisch accent and insisted I share some of his kirschwasser. Those sips of his product were certainly my first experience with alcohol. A first class start! We sat in the kitchen in semi-darkness, sipping the kirschwasser and I was able to exchange my silver spoon for some eggs and vegetables. Lentils, however, were the fare of survival and some fun for us boys, age 8-12. ("Beans, beans, the magical fruit, the more you eat, the more you toot...") Lentils, lentils follow suit. My three brothers and I all slept in a very small room and even though the primary function of the lentils was to keep us alive, they were also musical and aromatic fun at night. The atmosphere in that room was anything but sweet cherries, and setting fire to one of my brother's emissions was a fine experiment in chemistry and physics. Luckily, the whole room did not explode. There might have been bombings, strafing, nights in air raid shelters and the unknown future, but boys will be boys and fun is fun. Fun and mischief that kept us "resilient," as Yale Psychiatry Professor Steve Southwick would one day write in his book on that subject. It was similar nonsense and craziness that kept us sane in the crazy world of the Vietnam War and the 3rd Surgical Hospital 20 years later.

We did not attend any German schools and we were made to read and study with our parents and grandfather at home. I missed formal schooling from the winter and early spring of 1944 to the fall of 1946. The spring term of 1944 in Latvia had been totally chaotic as we escaped from Aluksne to Jurmala and faced the ever-present threat of approaching Russians. The summer and fall of 1945 were equally confusing. There were no functioning schools in Emmendingen and our future was uncertain. There was the threat of being returned to the Soviet Union. That situation stabilized when father started working as a surgeon for the French Army and we were enrolled in one of their schools in Freiburg. It took a few months to learn the language but by the fall of 1946 we were back on a formal educational track.

When we arrived in Freiburg and then

Emmendingen in October 1944 the war was not going well for the Germans and most of the ones we knew did not seem to have great enthusiasm for Hitler and his Third Reich. The family living above us in Emmendingen was mourning their son who'd been "lost in action" on the Russian Front. There were no heroic pictures or flags of the Reich in their apartment, just the picture of a very young man in Wehrmacht uniform. Everybody was of course conscious of the destroyed cities and the constant threat from the allied bombers and fighters the air. We were all aware of how difficult it was for our Freiburg host Eierman family to deal with their 15-year-old son, who'd been inspired by Nazi propaganda, going to school during the day and manning, with enthusiasm, an anti-aircraft gun during the night. It was all too similar to what we had experienced in Latvia during the year when my parents had a difficult time dealing with me and the pictures of Lenin and Stalin that I had posted in my room.

There was only one functioning store in Emmendingen, run by some confirmed Nazis. Upon entering, customers had to give the arm-in-the-air salute. If you did not salute and shout "Heil Hitler," the storeowner made you leave the store and re-enter to perform as expected.

Christmas 1944. It is always in my thoughts as we celebrated the holidays in the Congregational Church on the Middlebury Green in Connecticut with its brightly decorated tree, candles in the windows, wreath on the church door, carols, children and pageantry. It is all light and joy. It is our Christmas. It is good, but in the midst of it, as we sing and celebrate the birth of Christ, 1944 keeps coming back. The walk through the blacked-out streets, the large stone church without any lights other than a few candles, the cold air, the darkness and the very subdued congregation singing softly in German many of the hymns we know in their English version. The memory of that dark church at the height of the war always adds meaning to the celebration of our faith in Middlebury and in peace.

Father worked as a physician to the Polish workers who had been brought to work in the Emmendingen factory. The German authorities who assigned him to that position did not think he was qualified to take care of Germans in spite of the fact that at the completion of his basic surgery training in Latvia, he was sent by his professor Paulis Stradins on a rotation through major surgical centers in Germany and had spent a year doing research on tissue cultures in Copenhagen. As time progressed, he became well known in town and the local Germans went to him for their care. The house we lived in was next to the factory and we were very conscious of it being a bombing target, but fortunately the allied officers in charge of bombing southwestern Germany had better choices on their books. The town was hit by the occasional bomb and strafed by fighter planes, but it was not wiped out like Freiburg, Frankfurt, Dresden and most of the other major German cities. The bombs that were dropped on Emmendingen were of a random, harassment variety. We can speculate about why we and the factory next door were not bombed. There are no real reasons. We were lucky. We survived in spite of our proximity to that major target. We took common sense precautions by sleeping in the basement bomb shelter, the wine shaft or hiding in the woods, but as is the case in war at all times, luck also plays a big part.

Our own shelter was a room in the cellar reinforced with extra wooden beams and sandbags. Similar shelters throughout the land had saved many lives and it did give a sense of security as there were bombers in the air almost every night - American bombers on their way to and from major targets further east of us. As these bombers passed over us, they came under fire from anti-aircraft units and chased by fighter planes (as long as the Germans had them). At night it was quite a spectacle as search lights tried to fix bombers in their crosshairs with artillery fire coming up from below. You never knew when one of the bombers would be hit, drop its bombs or come crashing down upon us. At first, these bombers were in the air only at night, but by the early spring of 1945, as the Germans were running out of fighter planes, they were also flying during the day. The daytime spectacle was different from the nighttime fireworks. On a clear day, the contrails of the bombers high above us were a remarkable sight covering the sky from one side of the horizon to the other. In the early spring of 1945, they also seemed to be flying higher. I believe it was the time America was introducing a new version of a bomber that could fly higher with a greater bomb load. You could also hear them and, as with my memories of Christmas, the sight today of contrails left by intercontinental aircraft in and out of New York bring back those high-flying bombers. They were a constant presence, and when peace came in May of 1945, it was very strange to have clear skies and silence - no murmur of high-flying planes, no air raid sirens, no anti-aircraft artillery fire. Just deafening silence.

There are other memories such as the very impressive Tiger Panzer tanks in the park next to the

Emmendingen Catholic Church. They were probably on their way to engage Allied troops advancing through eastern France, moving only at night and spending their daylight hours under the cover of trees. They were indeed an impressive sight, but I remember being puzzled by their crews and how quiet or sad they seemed. They knew their fate, I guess.

A demolished American Jeep with its large white star, left for no good reason on the side of a road outside of town. I imagine it was there to make us somehow feel better about the bombers and fighter planes that were harassing us.

The puzzle of an "English" woman married to a dentist in town was interesting. She actually was Irish, and it was only years later that I learned about the Irish/ English conflicts and finally understood how she could be pro Germany.

A woman who spent time with us in our apartment was dressed and spoke like all other Germans, but always had a yellow star on her chest – a Jew. Our parents did not have a problem being friends with her at that time, but that may not have endeared us with the local Nazis. It is sad to think about her fate, but I hope she survived the war to live in peace for the rest of a long life. I think she was in an important administrative position at the factory and was sheltered by the Germans who counted on her work.

A column of French and African prisoners of war

in tattered, unfamiliar uniforms being marched through town. Why? From where and to where? We saw them but what were we to think about them, having nearly been consigned to a concentration camp ourselves?

The schools of Emmendingen may not have been operational, but one of our neighbors had an extensive library, and I remember reading avidly a variety of his books, among them John Fennimore Cooper's *Leatherstocking Tales* - in German ("Laederstrumpf"). The erotic tales in Bocaccio's *Decameron* were also there. They were of even greater interest to me and remain memorable to this day. I suppose this reading made up for some of my missed schoolwork and years later were revisited in a Comparative Literature course at Yale.

On hilltop, not too far from Emmendingen, there were several ruins of medieval castles and a chateau of a later era. Exploring these sites was fun and it did bring to life a lot of history. There was also an insane asylum, and its director was the father of three or four daughters. He was a quiet, cultured man. I find it hard to imagine him implementing Hitler's policies and euthanasia of the mentally deficient. His daughters were all musicians, and one of the cultural highlights of the dark winter of 1944-45 were evenings at their house with chamber music performed by these young ladies. One of them became my piano teacher. Under her very strict tutelage, I was soon able to play some Mozart and Beethoven, but, alas, it was a technical exercise performed without natural talent, and the day I was excused from her lessons, at age 13, was a happy one.

Finally, the war was racing to a close. On the Western Front, the German troops were surrendering to the Allies as quickly as possible, while in the East, they continued to resist advancing Russians and their fearsome reputation for rape, torture and plunder for every foot of land gained. By the end of April of 1945, it was obvious there was not going to be much resistance to the Allies in Emmendingen. There were no German troops left in town and the locals did not seem to have any interest in putting up a fight. The French Army had crossed the Rhine River north of us and was moving south to occupy the southwestern corner of Germany. Even though they were not encountering resistance, they delivered an artillery barrage prior to marching into town. We were in our basement bomb shelter, huddled in its darkness, relieved that the artillery shells were not exploding directly on top of us. Suddenly, the barrage stopped and there was absolute silence. It was silent, but we did not dare move. We waited and then after what seemed to be hours, we heard the cadence of footsteps on the street above us - no shouts, no shots, no sound other than footsteps. Father's curiosity could not stand it. He left us in the basement shelter and went upstairs. We sat there motionless and then we heard a rifle shot. We didn't know what to expect, but, much to our relief, father returned alive (curiosity had not killed the cat). The French had arrived and were cautiously moving down the street. When Father suddenly pushed aside the window shutter to see what was going on, he'd been greeted with that rifle shot. It hit the house a couple of feet from the window; the bullet hole remained for the rest of our stay in Germany. A few days later came May 8, the day of German capitulation. How strange it was – silence, no howling air raid sirens, no fighter planes, no bombers, no artillery fire. There was room for joy, but I don't remember celebrations. The future remained unknown, but the war was over and it was a beautiful spring day. It was all a change for the better, to be sure, but far from the end of the road for us.

POST-WAR

The French had arrived. To my young eyes, most of them looked like the Germans that they had just conquered, but it was interesting to see the Moroccan and Senegalese who were with them. Amazingly enough, the Senegalese were on horseback wearing long robes and turbans. They were pitch black and a sight to remember. Before this, I had seen only one African, he with a circus passing through Latvia before the war. The post-war already was the beginning of a new world, with new people, new ideas and different cultures.

It was also a new world of hope and freedom, but it was not well defined, and for several months confusion reigned, often suddenly and without warning or cause. Father was arrested and taken to a camp for high-ranking Nazis. Somebody had sent an anonymous note to the French authorities denouncing him as a Nazi war criminal. It was probably one of the Polish workers at the Emmendingen factory, but the exact origin of this note remains unknown. Father had never belonged to a political party. Even in Latvia, before the war, he had stayed out of anything related to politics, such as President Ulmanis' dictatorship or its opposition in the mid 1930s, and certainly had no ties to the Nazis. His release was arranged very rapidly by another family friend, General Abraham, who was on General DeGaulle's staff. As a young officer at the French embassy in Riga, he had met and married one of mother's good friends. Mother was able to reach her, and the General Abraham immediately went to the camp where father was held, vouched for him and had him released. In a matter of a few more weeks, he was hired by the French Army to work as a surgeon in a military hospital they had established in the old insane asylum outside of town. That switch from suspected Nazi to a working surgeon in the French Army was huge and brought many changes to our lives.

We went from very meager rations to a full French military diet, which included a daily liter of wine for every member of the family, no matter his or her age. We, the four boys, were sent to pick up the food and the buckets of wine that went with it. We had more than enough for ourselves and were able to feed some of our neighbors with our generous rations. Life was much better, but the future of the world and our family remained unknown.

The Western Allies seemed to be on a course of restoring democracy in their "zones of influence," with material aid for the reconstruction of the destroyed cities and societies of Europe and Asia. The Russians and the Chinese had other plans. Spreading Communism through the world was their goal - from Europe to China, Korea, and Southeast Asia. As part of his plan for world control, Stalin was demanding the repatriation of all people who had escaped him to the West. They (we) were considered by him to be enemies of Communism. In Stalin's mind, we belonged back in his hands to be executed or sent to Siberia. As Latvians, we were quite familiar with the Russian process of dealing with anybody of an ideology different than Bolshevism. His demands were a major threat we could not ignore. A large left-leaning segment of the Western Allies seemed to favor this repatriation to the Communist world. We had to do anything in our power to protect ourselves. The German Mayor of Emmendingen had been father's patient and was willing to help by certifying us as German citizens. Fortunately, we did not have to go that route. Saner minds prevailed and we were allowed to stay in the West. With a few exceptions, the Latvians who had been apprehended in the eastern part of Germany ended up in Siberia and many of them were hanged or shot. The Yale chaplain, well-meaning, left-leaning Bill Coffin, was in the American army in charge of some Russians who had fought with the Germans, and he had arranged for their repatriation. In later life, he apparently had some regrets about it, as he had witnessed the hanging of these men as soon as they were in Communist hands.

For many reasons, Father felt strongly about getting out of Germany and Europe. The United States, Canada and Australia were options, presumably beyond Stalin's reach. France was a brief consideration. The French Army was eager to keep Father in their ranks and give us citizenship, but that was not a good choice for us. Father's next assignment would have been away from the family and into the combat zones of the French colonial wars in Indochina and North Africa. Father was also extremely concerned about the large Communist percentage of the French population who he thought could easily put the entire country at the disposal of their ideological leaders in Moscow. Father's instinct for survival could be seen in the fate of his French superior officer and surgeon at the hospital in Emmengingen who survived duty in Indochina but on his next assignment, in Tunisia, was killed by a hand grenade as he was leaving his hospital. In any event, a few Latvians stayed in West Germany, but the majority of us ended up in the United States, Canada or Australia. There were a few who went to South America, among them mother's sister, Irene and her husband, Harry Ebersteins, who was a very gifted portraitist. He had trained in Latvia but had also spent time in Belgium where he had done a portrait of their Queen. They chose Venezuela because of its climate and the hope to be painting portraits of the generals then in charge of the government. Those plans disintegrated as the Junta was deposed, but they loved Venezuela and stayed there. Harry taught painting and produced some beautiful tableaux of Venezuelan wildlife. Irene, who had studied music (primarily voice) in Latvia and Milan, also had a career as a teacher, organist in several Caracas churches and the director of the Venezuelan National Choir.

Gradually, the chaos of the war and its aftermath seemed to be resolving on the larger scale as well as in our individual lives. We were enjoying relatively normal days spent swimming in the community swimming pool, hiking in the Black Forest and bicycling to such interesting destinations as the Kaiserstuhl, an old volcanic mountain near the Rhine River some 10 miles northwest of Emmendingen. The Kaiserstuhl area is said to be the warmest spot in all of Germany and is also known for its excellent wines ("Kaiserstuhlers"). The vineyards are spectacular, and nearby there are many orchards with cherries in the late spring, plums of all varieties a little later and apples in the fall. We were too young for the wines, but the pounds of cherries, plums and apples were always a feast.

Two summers before our emigration, around my 14th birthday, I also had a very unusual trip to some distant relatives Mother had located in the southernmost corner of the Black Forest, not far from Lake Constance. She thought it might be fun for me to visit them, and I am certain it was yet another part of her plan to teach us self-sufficiency, similar to our pork-canning trip in Latvia and the visit to the kirschwasser village to trade that silver spoon for food. I was to spend a week with these relatives. To get to their home from Emmendingen I'd have to go south to Basel, and, once there, change trains to go east in the direction of Constance. Basel is a Swiss city, south of the Rhine River at its bend to the north, but its railroad station was in German territory. German, French and Swiss border guards were in charge, and entrance into Switzerland was limited to the very few with appropriate passports and special visas. You could change trains in Basel, as in any other German railroad station, but you could not leave it to go into town. I got to Basel, changed trains and reached my destination without any problems. It was a good week in the mountains with a couple of boys of my age and its high point was a badger hunt. They had a dachshund who was as friendly a pet and companion as any of its million cousins we all know, until he showed his true self as the badger ("dachs") hunter or hound ("hund") he was. We were playing around in the fields and woods and that friendly little dog was with us when we discovered a badger hole. His excitement was immediate and in a second, he was down that hole, where, deep underground, we could hear growling, barking and squealing which stopped as the badger vanished through an escape tunnel some 20 or 30 yards away. Years later, in Vietnam, as I was hearing stories of Vietcong underground tunnels and the fighting inside of them, the badger hunt would always come to mind.

The week had been fun, but now it was a Sunday and I was to take the trains, via Basel, back home to Emmendingen. What follows is very strange. My brothers still don't believe it, but it is absolutely true.

When time came to leave, I got on the train back to Basel, empty except for a French border guard officer, his wife and their children of approximately my age. It was not unusual for the train to be empty, since the German people were still restricted from unlimited travel and we were in a remote corner of the land. I exchanged a few words with this family, and they thought I was French. The border guard was planning to take his family for an afternoon in Swiss Basel and did not need any special permits to do so. The railroad station in Basel was also empty, and I decided to stick with the French family by following them without saying a word. In addition to being fluent in the language, I was also dressed as any other French boy, complete with a typical beret on the top of my head. We passed the German guards, who would not dare stop a French officer. We then came to the office of the French guards who waved us by after our "father" had exchanged a few words with them. The Swiss, who were in the next office of the exit corridor, also let us pass without any questions and we found ourselves on the steps leading from the station to the street below. I cannot imagine what the French family was thinking, but they did not say a word as they let me tag along into Switzerland. It was absolutely amazing, and I had not seen anything like it since Latvia in 1939. All the buildings were intact. There were no bullet marks on any of the walls. There were stores displaying their wares in large, undamaged windows. Little coffee shops were open and selling candies and chocolate. It was all beyond imagination. It was also a beautiful summer day with happy, well dressed people taking their Sunday walks, and I was amidst them like any other kid wandering the streets. But my train back into Germany was waiting and I was due to board it in about half an hour. What to do? There was no choice; the time had come to go back to the wide stairs leading into the station. I was the only one around, went up the stairs and walked into the corridor I had left an hour or so earlier. The Swiss guards were in the midst of a loud conversation in their office and the French were playing cards. I saw no reason to disturb them and walked past their offices unnoticed. The Germans spotting a "French" boy who they thought had been vetted by the Swiss and French, did not say anything and I made it to my train with time to spare. My ticket to Emmendingen was in order, was properly punched by the German conductor and I was home in approximately two hours. My brothers thought it was all a made-up story, and it really was like a fairy tale. For about an hour, I was away from the remnants of war, in neutral Switzerland, in a world remote from anything we had experienced during the previous eight years. Mother believed me and gave me an "A+" in independent action and survivorship. But an hour in Switzerland was but a short surreal experience. We had to think of true survival and how to get out of Germany and Europe. The threat of Communism was present. It wasn't a dinner-table political discussion, it was reality - separation of family, deportation, execution.

While awaiting our ultimate move, we remained in the apartment next to the factory we had had since our arrival in Emmendingen. Mother, with her teacher's training, also saw an opportunity for her children to learn French and immerse themselves in French culture. Thus, in January 1946 we were enrolled in a French high school in Freiburg. The "College Turenne" was for the children of the French military and civil servants who were now governing the French Zone of Germany. I imagine Father's position and performance as a surgeon in one of their military hospitals had made our matriculation possible, on the assumption we would be seeking refuge in France and we, the children, needed a French education. We may not have spoken a single word of French in January of 1946, but by the spring of that year, we were doing fairly well with the language and, by 1947, were able to keep up with all schoolwork. We also assumed French manners, customs and dress, and the last year at the College Turenne, I was even elected President of my class.

We had come from being Latvians, Soviets, humans semi-acceptable to the Nazis, nonentities in the mass of refugees in western Germany and were now French schoolboys in a lycee called College Turenne. It was a new world and we were in it.

When we first started at the "College," it was a boarding school. Classes were held in a German high school building that had survived the bombings of 1944. The dormitories were two luxury hotels a city block from the main railroad station. The boys were in one of the hotels, the girls in the other. The hotel was still run by its old staff of waiters, porters, cook and maids. We were the spoiled children of a victorious army and were to be waited on. Our beds were made, and if we put our shoes in the hallway before going to bed, they were polished during the night. Our meals were prepared by the kitchen staff and served to us by waiters and waitresses. The meals were in line with the best of French cuisine. We were also given a glass of diluted white wine with lunch and dinner. At first, that seemed like culture shock, but it did not take long to get used to it. We had come a long way from rummaging for bread crusts on the empty train leaving a concentration camp some 16 months earlier.

The following year our hotel dormitory arrangements disappeared, and we were now boarded in an old rehabilitation hospital. We went from luxury hotel rooms and service to six in a room with cafeteria-style meals. We made our own beds and our shoes were no longer polished. We did, however, continue with the wine at lunch and dinner. (One of the memories of that year of 1947 in the hospital dormitory is the marriage of Queen Elizabeth, a historic memory as we continue to follow her reign 70 years later.) At the end of our second year in school, even those hospital-type arrangements were terminated, and brother Janis and I became commuters, sleeping at home in Emmendingen and taking the train to school in Freiburg. Brothers Andrejs and Ludis remained in a French Elementary and Middle School in Emmendingen.

Education at the College Turenne was strict and productive. Indeed, I have happy memories of many of my teachers in Latvia, Germany and America, and one of them, Madame Schaeffer, who taught English in Freiburg, was the best and can take full credit for the ability I had to read, write and speak English upon arrival in America. It was English with a combination of French and British accents. It would be amusing to most Brooklynites, but it worked.

Daily life in those years after the end of World War II was good, but, again, on the level of world politics, there was reason for concern. Stalin was stabilizing his stronghold on all of Eastern Europe with the exception of Greece where, with Western help, Communist expansion was stopped. The wars in Indochina and North Africa were not going well for the French. China, under the leadership of Mao, was turning into a Communist empire of a billion or more souls (minus the 50 million or more he killed or let die of starvation). South Korea was about to be invaded by Communist North Korea. More than ever, our sights were set on America.

COMING TO AMERICA

America made sense but getting there was not a simple matter. The U.S. government had agreed to take a specific number of what it termed Displaced Persons, and the number of those from the three Baltic countries (Estonia, Latvia, Lithuania) was in the range of 200,000. All of them had to be sponsored by somebody or a private organization such as a church. The government had to be assured that all the refugees would be housed and fed without being a burden to the State. There were no food stamps, no cash in hand, no other subsidies by taxpayers. Transportation to the states would be provided but once there, you were on your own and on your sponsor. There was also a very thorough process of investigation designed to eliminate former Nazis and criminals from entering the country. To contain the potential spread of disease and tuberculosis, everyone had to undergo a physical examination complete with chest x-ray. The whole process took several years, and, finally, in the fall of 1949, we were deemed fit to enter the United States.

So it took us more than four years from the end of the war in the spring of 1945 to our departure from Germany in the fall of 1949 to complete the process of escape from war-torn Europe and the escalating threat of Russian Communism, manifested by the Berlin blockade, the testing of atom bombs and the fermentation of revolution in all corners of the world. Our sponsor in

America was Reverend Richard Zarins, the minister of the Latvian Lutheran Church in New York City. The Reverend Zarins was an old family friend. Our families had close ties dating back at least four generations. He had also been one of my grandfather's students and one of my mother's classmates. He and his family were willing to take us into their home in Brooklyn until Mother and Father had found jobs and were able to provide us with food and shelter. Brooklyn and the Zarins were to be our destination.

Our trans-Atlantic transport by a World War II troop ship was arranged by the U.S. government. Packing was not a major problem since you could take only what you could carry. We went by train from Emmendingen to an old army camp for final processing, then to the North Sea port of Bremerhaven and, on October 1, 1949, we were taken to the docks to board the American troop transport ship *General C.H. Muir*. Onboard, the men and boys were separated from the women and girls. The sleeping quarters were four layers of cots, tight enough so that when in the cot, you only had a couple of inches between your nose and the person above you. It was anything but fun and we spent as much time as possible on the open decks.

Capable of carrying 3,823 troops, the *Muir* had been used extensively during the war and was now carrying men, women and children to the New World. The ship left the Bremerhaven dock in the late afternoon and headed out of the sheltered harbor into the North Sea. While we were in the Bremerhaven Bay, the waters were relatively calm, and dinner was served. Among other items, we could have as many hotdogs and oranges as we could eat. Many of the refugees had been on limited rations for years and could not resist the temptation of having one or more of the hotdogs and several oranges. It was a feast and a celebration that came to a rocking end as soon as we emerged from the calm bay into the North Sea known for its storms, high waves and rock 'n' rolling ships. The physiological effect was immediate and dramatic. With the exception of those of us lucky enough to have old sea-faring genes, seasickness swept through the refugees aboard. The palpable joy and sense of relief to be on the way to a new life in America were now replaced with regurgitation of those delicious hotdogs, tasty mustard and irresistible fresh oranges. The stairs, the decks, the railings were covered – mustard yellow with bits of light hotdog bites and oranges.

That first night on the North Sea and passage into the British Channel was the beginning of close to two weeks at sea. None of it was smooth sailing. The North Atlantic was stormy all the way. Mother was seasick the entire time, and in our family only brother Andrejs and I never became ill. The waves were gigantic and towered over the ship. There was a library aboard and we did spend some time there, but as silly teenagers, we also played some sillier games. There were always some of the passengers on the verge of throwing up, hanging onto the railing, anxiously staring at the ocean. We would occasionally help them to do so by running up next to them and pretending to be seasick with the appropriate noises and a handful of orange peels released into the ocean. The effect was immediate and took care of any of their doubts about avoiding yet another cataclysm. Not exactly nice behavior.

We arrived in New York the day before Columbus Day, October 11, 1949. Our ship carried close to 2,000 refugees of many nationalities. Among the Latvians on board were the Padegs brothers, Andris and Juris, who became our very good friends. Their father had been deported to Siberia, but the mother, a dentist, had escaped to Germany with the two boys and had made the decision to go to America. Andris was in his early 20s and Juris must have been 18. Once in New York, we continued to socialize, dance in a Latvian folklore group, sing together in the church choir, and go to the same parties. Andris eventually married our cousin, Mara Berzins, had an outstanding career with IBM as one of their early computer engineers and ended up as one of their Senior Fellows. Juris married Gita, bright, attractive and my dance partner. Juris was the first Latvian refugee taken in by Yale and became a very successful New York lawyer. He was a year ahead of me at Yale College in the class of 1954 and graduated from Yale Law School in 1957. We arrived together in New York on that morning of October 11. The seas had settled, and the first sign of being close to land was a red lightship and buoys to mark our passage between Long Island and Staten Island in sight of lower Manhattan and the Statue of Liberty. The excitement of it is hard to describe, but I am fortunate to have a photograph of that moment taken by brother Janis. I am standing on some stairs above the crowd of other refugees at the bow of the ship. The skyscrapers, as they were in 1949, are in sight. I could not be happier in my used suit that had been sent to the refugees in Europe by some well-meaning church group in America. It had been taken in at the waist, but seemed to fit, and it kept me warm on the North Atlantic. I had no idea of what lay ahead, but certain it had to be better than the previous 10 years going back to the Molotov-Ribbentrop agreement. We passed by the Statue of Liberty, the symbol of a new life, a free life, a life of work and promise imagined by the millions of future Americans who had passed it since its dedication in 1886. We passed Ellis Island, the other icon of entry into the New World. We did not stop there since it had been closed down a few months earlier. Instead, we landed on a West 22nd Street dock.

Framed by the 1949 Manhattan skyline and photographed by brother Juris, I arrive in America as a refugee with eyes fixed squarely on the future.

It was a momentous day, its details and emotions hard to describe. We had arrived in America and had set foot on a dock in New York. The scene was chaotic as we claimed our luggage and lined up to pass through Immigration. We had all been screened, examined, processed, had documents to prove it and big paper tags attached to our coats, identifying us and facilitating the entry process for the clerks and officers in charge, but it still took most of the day. By the time we came out of the Pier 22 gate and were met by Mrs. Zarins, it was already dark. We had been watching the Westside Highway during the day, and in our wildest dreams of a few days earlier could not have imagined that nonstop flow of cars. As we came out onto the street in the evening, the spectacle was even more impressive. The lights of the city and the speeding cars with blazing headlights were dazzling. Having lived for years in full blackout or minimal lighting, to us Manhattan and its traffic seemed unreal. We were stunned but we had made it, and now it was a matter of taking our first steps in this New World. Led by Mrs. Zarins, the journey began with a subway ride to Brooklyn and the Latvian Lutheran Parish house on 2nd Street, only a block from Prospect Park. Our quarters were in the basement of a typical brownstone featured in so many pictures of old Brooklyn and New York. It was cramped but would be our home while Father and Mother found jobs and an apartment of our own.

The next day was Columbus Day and we ventured out to Prospect Park to see, for the first time in our lives, people play baseball. It was a major change from a Sunday scene in a German park where kicking a soccer ball would have been the norm. We also met the Zarins' children, two boys and a girl. The boys, Bertram and Kristaps, eventually went into Medicine. Bertram became an orthopaedic surgeon with a spectacular career at Harvard as one of the first experts in arthroscopic surgery and world-renowned specialist in sports injuries. The younger brother, Kristaps, also had a world-class career as a vascular surgeon at Chicago and Stanford Universities. Even though they were a few years younger, they guided our first steps in this new world of Brooklyn, Prospect Park and baseball.

During the days after our arrival in Brooklyn, and without any hesitation, Mother took on the education of her children as her absolute first task. She was an educator, the daughter of an educator, and we did not have a day to waste. I was marched off to the closest school which was the Manual Training High School. The high schools in New York were superb. The Manual

Training High School devoted much attention to "shop," the use of tools and the preparation for a variety of jobs, but, at the same time, its academic program was amazing. It had a Classics department where, under the direction of Mr. Greene, you were taught Greek, Latin, Ancient History and Classical Literature. I was interviewed and tested. The courses I had taken at College Turenne were assessed, and, at the end of several hours, the decision was made that I belonged in the 12th grade and would, upon the satisfactory completion of all the standard courses, plus an extra one or two in summer school, get my high school diploma on about my 16th birthday, in August 1950. It was a consensus that the English I had acquired under Madame Schaefer was good enough to do the work. Less than 48 hours after stepping off the boat, I was an American high school senior. What followed in the afternoon of that day was even more amazing and is the ultimate American story.

The French Club was having a meeting and the teachers who had been examining me felt I should go to it. So, up we went from the Principal's Office to one of the upper floors of the building, where the club was meeting. I was introduced to the group, consisting of some 30 girls and a few boys. I was asked to say a few words, and, before I knew what was happening, the club had decided to make me their President. Kristaps, Christofle, Christophe, Christopher Keggi with accented English - not a problem. I was an American among other Americans of multiple former nationalities and religions. A different name but no more different than the names of the other boys and girls in Brooklyn: English, Irish, Scottish, Polish, German, Jewish, French, Swedish, Italian, Spanish. That second day in country I was accepted as an American like the rest and it has been the same ever since. I was somewhat amazed by the girls at the meeting. By comparison to the relatively quiet, self-effacing Latvian, German and French girls I knew, this was a much louder lot. They all talked, laughed, moved, looked at you - it was almost like a scene out of "Saturday Night Fever," but I was not ready to be Johnny Travolta. Even though I was happy to have had that unexpected reception, I did not know what to do. I was scared and embarrassed. It was the ultimate American experience, but I did not know how to deal with it and never went back to the club.

Those first weeks at the Manual Training High School were fabulous. The teachers seemed to go out of their way to help me. Mr. Greene of the Classics Section and Mrs. Boyle, the English teacher, suggested extra books to read about America. One of them was the story of Davey Crockett, the western frontier and the Alamo. We were fully accepted by the teachers and students, encouraged to learn and move forward in our new land. It was sad when we had to move to a different part of Brooklyn and switch to the Bushwick High School, but we could not stay with the Zarins forever. Father had found a job as a glorified orderly or surgical assistant at the Lutheran Hospital on the Upper West Side of Manhattan and had started his studies to take the New York State Medical Licensure exams. Mother went to work as a chambermaid at the Hotel St. George in Brooklyn. It was time to get out of the Zarins' basement and live on our own. This meant a small apartment on Bushwick Avenue in a section of Brooklyn that was deteriorating, but at one time that had been home to a large community of German immigrants. We were across the street from their Protestant church where, on Sunday mornings, in addition to the regular service in English, they still had one in German for their elderly parishioners. We were on the second floor of a building owned by an old German naturopath who practiced his trade on the first floor. We had four tiny rooms aligned like train carriages with windows in the end ones only, one looking out to Bushwick Avenue, the other into a small courtyard. There was a toilet on our floor but to bathe or shower, you had to go downstairs and use one of the tubs the naturopath had for his patients. There was no refrigerator, only an old fashioned "icebox" with a block of ice delivered once or twice a week by the proverbial iceman. The milkman, in similar manner, left bottles of cold milk at the door of the building. It was old fashioned and primitive, but we could afford the rent and it was home. We stayed there for two years until father passed the required examinations (at age 47 in a new language!) to get his New York State License and started his medical practice in Manhattan on West 72nd Street and Riverside Drive.

During that first year in Brooklyn I also had to work to make a few dollars. Since mother was already a chambermaid at the Hotel Saint George, I went there, pretended to be 18 and got a job as an usher. It consisted of working on Saturdays at Jewish weddings, handing out yarmulke skull caps to the arriving guests, opening the main door of the room as soon as I heard the "good luck glass" being smashed and helping the father of the bride in any way possible with the hope of getting a 50-cent tip at the end of the afternoon. My mother also arranged for me to give French lessons to her middle-aged housekeeping supervisor, in her apartment close to the hotel. I would get there by subway, taking my job with total seriousness, but it was a very uncomfortable experience for 15-year-old Kristaps since his student presented herself for the lessons in very loose peignoirs - a situation that would now probably be classified as "sexual harassment." As was the case with the Manual Training French Club, I did not know how to deal with it and quickly gave up my budding career as a teacher of French, sex object or "boy toy."

The Bushwick High School was different than Manual Training. The teachers were less interested in their students and one of them even suggested I be sent to a special school for foreigners. As it turned out, I was able to surprise him with award-winning scores in several subjects on the New York State Regency Examinations and win the French Embassy Medal for comprehensive knowledge of French and French culture. By the spring of 1950, I was lacking only one or two courses for graduation from high school and was planning on completing them in summer school. Bushwick did not have a summer school and I had to take those final courses at the Thomas Jefferson High School. I was to graduate shortly before my 16th birthday and the time had come to think about colleges. In Brooklyn, without having had exposure to any of the major universities, the choices seemed to be Brooklyn College or the City College of New York. We had, however, heard of a man who, without any apparent selfish motivation, was helping Estonian and Latvian students make their way into select American universities. He is one of a few individuals who have had a truly huge impact on my entire life.

William Sudduth worked for American Express and had served in the Army during WWII. After the war, while still in Germany, he had become familiar with Estonian and Latvian refugee students and was now spending his free time, without any compensation or recognition, helping some of them to get into the best American universities. With his help, Andris and Juris Padegs, our shipmates on the *General Muir*, had been accepted by Dartmouth and Yale. There was nothing to be lost by calling him. I was very lucky to get an appointment and to meet him in his apartment in Manhattan after his workday with American Express. I went alone by subway from our Bushwick home. My visit was amazingly short, and I didn't know what to make of it. Within a minute, after establishing I was only 15, he made it very clear I was too young to go to college and should consider a post-graduate year in a private prep school. He was willing to help, and over the course of a few days I was invited to visit the Brunswick School in Greenwich, Connecticut, was accepted and given a scholarship. Since Brunswick was not a boarding school, I would have to be "taken in" by a local family, and the school was able to arrange it with the Nye family. Thus, instead of going to one of the New York City colleges, I was off to the Brunswick School for another year of secondary education and then a university in the fall of 1951.

Mr. Sudduth did not need to do it but found himself in a position to help and did so for so many of us. He represented the best of men and an example for me to follow. I thought of him frequently, many years later, as I worked as teacher of surgery and was able to help more than 200 foreign fellows.

My father was a stern fellow and proud of his Nordic, Estonian and Viking heritage (he pronounced it with an accent, "We-king"). The expression of emotions was not in his repertoire, but the day of my departure for Greenwich was different. There were no tears or endless words, but I truly felt his love for me and all of us. He insisted on taking the subway from Bushwick to Grand Central Terminal with me. He further insisted on carrying my small bag and standing on the platform as the train left. The old Viking was going soft on us. He had allowed and encouraged us to do a lot on our own at the earliest of ages. He had gotten us through all the horrors of the war without a whimper or complaint. We knew he loved us and the album of family photos that never left his hand was probably the greatest expression of that emotion but coming with me to Grand Central and carrying my suitcase is a vivid memory of his love. He was an inspiration and I loved him in the same "We-king" way.

Mr. and Mrs. Nye could not have been nicer. Their son had left for college and I am certain it was Mrs. Nye's idea to harbor young Kristaps. It was very nice yet uncomfortable in many ways. I had no other choice and accepted it, but the life in Greenwich with the Nyes, my scholarships and other forms of assistance have left me with a strong feeling it of "better to give than to receive." I am sure the Nye family was happy to help me, but I am equally sure they were happy to see me switched to the Lovejoy family on Round Hill. With the Lovejoys, I was "earning" some of my keep by helping their blind son at home and at Brunswick, where he was a classmate. It was a good relationship, but it ended when I chose Yale instead of Wesleyan. The Lovejoys were hoping I would go with their son to Wesleyan, but I felt happier with the idea of working my way through Yale on my own terms. There was much to be said for independence then, and it has been part of my life course. Living with the Nyes and Lovejoys was a great experience. It was an education on families, America, American manners and American customs ranging from daily showers to sit down dinners.

The Brunswick School was the right place at the right time. There were only 13 of us in the senior class and all of us were given close attention by the teachers and the headmaster, Alfred E. Everitt. Everybody tried to familiarize me with American customs and ways. Football was an example of the process. Even though I had never been exposed to football, I was encouraged to go out for the team. As an absolute novice, I was assigned to play defensive guard with the simple instruction to "get down on your knees and don't let anybody through." We won, we lost, and I was proud of having earned my varsity "B."

I did well in most of the courses, especially mathematics and chemistry. I don't remember my exact ranking. I made honors but not the top.

Very early in the academic year, Union College came to Brunswick to present their institution as a potential destination to our class. I met with the person doing the interviews and shortly thereafter received a letter from Union offering me admission and a full scholarship. It seemed fabulous and an offer I could not refuse but decided to first seek Headmaster Everitt's advice. With the letter in hand, I went to see him. It was quite a surprise for me to hear he wanted me to ignore the offer by saying with very strong conviction, "You are going to Yale!" I had heard of Yale, but what little I knew was very vague. Mr. Everitt, however, was very clear that Yale was where I belonged. Like Mr. Sudduth, he was going to help even though the easiest path would have been to send me off to Union. A few weeks later, he had made arrangements to take me to the Admissions Office at Yale. It is a drive I remember as if it had happened yesterday. Mr. Everitt picked me up in his 1930s Buick. He was the driver and Mrs. Everitt sat in the passenger seat. I was in the back. We left Greenwich and headed north on the Merritt Parkway. There was very little conversation as we went, but, as he had turned off the parkway and we were approaching New Haven, there was a view of the city and he was proud to point out the towers of Yale. The hill on Derby Avenue is still there, but the trees are now much taller and there is no view of New Haven. I think of Mr. Everitt and that old introduction to Yale and every time I approach New Haven.

We drove into town and parked on College Street in front of Phelps Gate, the entrance to the Old Campus. The Admissions Office was next to the gate. Mr. Everitt went in while Mrs. Everitt and I sat in the waiting room.

In due course, I was brought into the office to have a conversation with the lady who seemed to be in charge and was told I would hear from them by April. There was nothing else I was supposed to do but wait. Mr. Everitt was encouraging, and even though there were alternatives I should have been exploring, I decided to wait for Yale. The letter of acceptance and scholarship came in early April and allowed me to start thinking about summer plans and jobs to pay for books, clothing and some of the other expenses not covered by my tuition scholarship. I do not remember the name of the lady who interviewed me, but the dean responsible for the admission of "unusual" students and young Ford Scholars was Arthur Howe, who many years later referred to me as one of "his boys."

I finished the year at Brunswick with my best marks in the sciences and thought I would major in Chemistry at Yale. That was not going to be the case, but at Brunswick I had the reputation of being a "scientist" and "cosmopolitan" in view of my language skills. I did not make the highest honor rolls but was good enough to get the Yale acceptance and scholarship letter. I had learned a lot in the year at Brunswick and the learning went well beyond the academic. As the weeks progressed, I became integrated into the social scene and the lives of my classmates. In the beginning, I was going back to New York City for Latvian activities such as the church choir, the folk dancing group, the long subway rides to pick up a date near Coney Island to bring her to a party in the Bronx, then back to Coney Island and eventually home to Brooklyn. During the second half of the year, I was more involved in the Greenwich life and also intrigued by a very attractive young lady from Old Greenwich. Most of my classmates were old enough to be driving cars, and I had mastered that skill on an old Model A Ford in the Lovejoys' back yard. I was learning about American girls, school dances and limits of necking (above the neck or the waist) on the way home from the dances. It was a continuation of that first day as a complete American at the Manual Training High School in Brooklyn.

By the end of the school year, my combination of British and French accents was gone, and I was off to Yale in the fall. I also had to make plans for the summer, hoping to make it interesting and productive of some cash. I also felt ready to see more of America. Mother's brothers Andris and Ansis and their families had settled in Colorado. Our grandparents were also with them - more specifically with Ansis in their rented home in Colorado Springs. Ansis and Antra, his wife, had four children. Their quarters were crowded, but when contacted, they assured me I could have the living room couch for the summer. They were equally encouraging about a job. They knew a builder in the midst of some major projects who would probably be willing to put me to work. That was exciting news but there was a problem. I did not have any money to get out to Colorado. I had to find immediate work in Brooklyn to earn enough dollars to buy a bus ticket to Colorado Springs. Scanning the employment section of the *Brooklyn Eagle*, I was lucky enough to find a job as an usher at the Loewe's Poli Movie Theater just a few blocks from the Hotel St. George where I had worked a year earlier. It was 1951 and movies and movie theaters were still a weekly event in many lives. You could hear the news on the radio and read it in the newspapers, but if you wanted to see it, you went to the movie theater where, before the main feature, you had the weekly newsreel. At most of the theaters, you had ushers who led you to your seat, and at the Loew's Poli, in the heart of central Brooklyn, they were a "spiffy" lot in fancy red, gold-braided uniforms, military bearing and polite manners. I felt fortunate to get the job but did not tell the manager of my hopes of soon getting to Colorado. After two weeks on the job, I had enough money for a bus ticket and went to resign, but before letting me go the manager wanted to tell me I was making a mistake. In his opinion, I was destined for a great career in the Loew's Poli organization, and in a matter of months I would probably be the manager of one of their theaters. It sounded interesting and I was pleased to have had done a good job as an usher but was determined to go West. He seemed disappointed but wished me luck.

The trip to Colorado by bus took two days and nights from New York. There were no interstate highways, so it was slow going, but fascinating as we passed through towns both large and small, crossed mountains and plains and met a variety of fellow passengers. The Greyhound bus did not have any air-conditioning or ventilation system other than its windows. There were two buses, caravan style, on the same route and if you were in the second bus, the exhaust fumes from the bus in front were overwhelming. It was still long before emission controls and there was nothing you could do about it. Even today, when I'm stuck behind a school bus with fume problems, I think of that bus ride with the smelly bus in front. At almost every stop, I sent postcards to the family back in Brooklyn. I still have those cards written by that 16-year-old, in Latvian, describing his impressions along the way. It was interesting to be in New Jersey, Pennsylvania, Ohio, Indiana, Missouri, Kansas and Colorado. It was a trip I could not have imagined just a year earlier. Once in Colorado Springs, after a night on the living room couch, Uncle Ansis introduced me to the builder who was to have a job for me. We talked, and it became obvious he had doubts about my ability to do heavy labor. I was probably 6 feet, 1 inch tall and could not have weighed more than 180 pounds. It was a disappointment, but he said he could use me for some weekend work in his cabin in the mountains near Cripple Creek. So, the following Saturday I was brought up to this cabin where he was planning an additional porch. The cabin was approximately 50 yards from the main road where a large pile of gravel had been dumped by a truck that could not reach the cabin itself. My assignment for the day was to move that load of gravel from the main road to a spot near the cabin. I was given a shovel and a wheelbarrow and left alone. It was a major effort, but I finished well ahead of the builder's return. He seemed amazed that not only had I done the job but had done it with time to spare. That effort convinced him I was qualified to be a laborer at the site where he was building the school for disabled and blind children along with occasional lesser jobs digging ditches up in the mountains. My hourly wage was to be the minimum 55 cents an hour. I could not have been happier since it would allow me to pay for my food while with the Berzins relatives and save enough to buy such essentials as a suit, shirts, pants and shoes, not to mention a ticket back to New York. It would also leave me a little pocket money for the beginning of my freshman year at Yale.

My start at the regular construction job was delayed by several days because within a day of having had moved that test pile of gravel up in the mountains, I developed a high fever and was very sick for several days. It was some type of tick-born Rocky Mountain fever. I recovered without any ill effects, but it was a miserable experience and not a very pleasant start to the summer. The job involved moving wheelbarrows full of cement, hauling bricks, digging ditches and doing whatever else was required. There were two other college students and an older man who were doing the same type of work. It was fun, educational and interesting to be with them.

Each morning, Grandmother sent me off to work with a lunch pail packed with an apple, a big sandwich and some milk. At about noon, we had half an hour to rest and eat lunch. Typically, we sat in the shade of a tree, talked and ate the food we had brought. The old laborer would join us, but his eating habits were different. He would go to his car and pull out a bottle of whiskey - no apples, no sandwiches, and no milk, just whiskey - and join us in the shade to sip his liquid lunch. It was an education to witness it. Occasionally, I would also work on weekends but had enough free time to enjoy the mountains, the rock formations in the Garden of the Gods and Pike's Peak. I was fascinated by Cripple Creek, a historic old mining village, easily imagined as it might have been 60 or 70 years earlier, complete with gun fights, houses of ill repute, stagecoaches and gun-toting marshals trying to maintain law and order. The local Latvian community was close-knit, with most having been in the United States for only a year or two. They organized excursions into the mountains and had a very active church. On one of these church picnics, I was resting from having climbed rocks and played in a mountain stream. My head was in the lap of one of the girls in the group and as she was looking at my hair she suddenly exclaimed, "You have gray hairs!" and pulled them out for all to see. I had just turned 17, and, from there on, their numbers increased in regular fashion until they were all I had. Each week I also spent a few hours reading the Bible for confirmation in the Latvian Lutheran Church by my grandfather Ludis Berzins at the end of the summer. (By the time my grandfather died at the age of 95, he had baptized, confirmed and married all family members for three generations. I was baptized in 1934, confirmed in 1951 and eventually married by him to Julia Quarles in 1957.)

That summer went by fast. It had been a good one with many new experiences and heavy work. It was also good to have been with my grandparents and my mother's brother's family. My grandparents were amazing. Grandmother, who was 71 at the time, was taking care of the entire household while her son Ansis and daughter-in-law Antra worked. Grandfather helped with some of the household tasks but also spent time writing and getting ready for the next church service and the sermon he would have to deliver. They were very close, both emotionally and physically. It was good to see the love they continued to share in their advanced years, having survived two World Wars, emigration to the States and the loss of two sons. Grandmother was totally functional until my grandfather's death 13 years later, but then she died within months of his departure. It was also a new experience to be with Ansis and Antra and their children. They were being brought up in a very liberal manner significantly different from the more disciplined life I had experienced as a child. Ansis was an accomplished artist who was hired by the nearby Air Force Academy to be in charge of educational illustrations. Antra was the daughter of a famous Latvian poet with many of her father's artistic qualities.

At the end of the summer, I had saved enough money to buy a bus ticket back East, along with a dark blue, double-breasted suit, another jacket, a couple of shirts and a simple, medium-sized suitcase large enough to hold all these earthly belongings. I have an excellent memory of my bus trip to Colorado, but I have no recall of my return trip to New York. I imagine it has something to do with the very intense focus on getting to Yale and starting a new life. I left Colorado in late August and, after a few days with parents and brothers in Brooklyn,

I packed my suitcase, took the subway from Bushwick Avenue in Brooklyn to Grand Central Terminal in Manhattan and boarded the train to New Haven. There, I walked from the train station to the Phelps gate of the Old Campus. I had everything I needed in my small suitcase, so carrying it as I walked from the railroad station to Phelps Gate was not an issue. It was much more complex for one of my roommates from the wealthy suburbs of Detroit. He, too, as with all students from anywhere in the states, had arrived by train, but he had to worry about his big steamer trunks that needed special transport from the station to our room in Durfee Hall on the Old Campus.

YALE COLLEGE

The first week at Yale was a very busy one. Class schedules had to be arranged. Our two-bedroom suite had to be furnished. The scholarship and bursary matters had to be settled. Books, pre-owned, if possible, had to be bought. Future athletic activities had to be considered. We were given a variety of intellectual performance tests and had to pass a physical fitness test (25 pushups, 50 sit-ups, etc.), had to demonstrate our ability to swim 50 yards and were photographed in the nude to make sure we did not have defective posture requiring special exercise classes - all remnants of the late 19th-century ideal of educated minds in healthy bodies ('mens sana in corpore sano"). If you failed at swimming, fitness or posture, you had to go to special classes at Payne Whitney Gymnasium until you met the Yale standard.

I was placed in the highest level of French Literature class, above average math, basic English and biology. I was upset the educators in charge had not considered me good enough for the advanced chemistry course and complained about it. I was urged to follow the advice of these academic advisors, but I insisted on being placed in the mid-level class. Having thought of myself as very able in chemistry based on my New York Regency examinations and grades at the Brunswick School, it came as a major shock to find myself surrounded by students from all over the country who were head and shoulders above my knowledge of the subject. Within a couple of weeks and a few quizzes, I was very happy not to be in the advanced course. I passed swimming and posture, but in spite of being in extremely good shape from a summer of hard construction work, I could not do 50 sit-ups at the time of testing. I had to come back a few days later by which time I was able to do them and did not need to go to any special fitness classes. For reasons that were not clear to me, the swimming team was trying to recruit me, but having fenced at our French school in Germany, I went out for fencing.

I also had to have a bursary job to pay for my room and board and felt extremely fortunate to miss working as a dishwasher in one of the dining rooms (which was a standard spot for freshman scholarship students). Erich Auerbach, a world-renowned professor of Comparative Literature, was looking for a bursary student to help him with work related to his major book called *Mimesis*. It would involve bibliography work in the library and typing out materials he was writing by hand. He was very pleased with my knowledge of languages and my ability to decipher his handwriting in German, French and English. I was fluent in French and German, knew some Latin and was able to decipher basic Italian and Spanish If I was able to do what he needed in a few hours, he did not think I had to worry about the 14 hours per week that we, as scholarship bursary students, were supposed to spend on our jobs. That gave me some time I may not have had with any of the other jobs. Those extra hours were more than welcome in my schedule, which included two courses with afternoon labs on "Science Hill," three other courses and fencing practice. The days were full and, much to the amusement of my roommates, I would go to bed shortly after dinner since I was convinced trying to study in a tired frame of body and mind was not effective. To bed at eight and up at four for some productive work with the rested mind more receptive to the academic has been my way of life. Except for activities centered on the fencing team, I had no social life. I did not have any dates, there was no thought of rushing a fraternity nor driving to Vassar or Smith to meet girls. There was neither time nor funds for such "frivolities."

I did, however, maintain ties with the New York Latvians. I remained with the folk dancing group and became a member of the student fraternity Lettonia (Latvia in Latin) as soon as it organized its activities in America and accepted new members. I enjoyed socializing with its female counterparts such as the Dzintras, my mother's University of Latvia sorority. Lettonia was an extremely important part of our lives. It had been founded in 1870 at Dorpat University (the "Heidelberg of the North") in Estonia. It was the first all-Latvian fraternity and one of the very early nationalistic organizations of any kind in the Czar's Russian empire. One of its founders had been my maternal grandmother's uncle, while my maternal grandfather (Ludis Berzins) had joined it in 1890. My grandmother's brother was a member as well, as were my father and all of my mother's brothers during Latvia's independence years between the two world wars. My brothers and I were thus fourth-generation members. Everybody tried hard to preserve Lettonia's traditions, code of honor, rituals and songs. Formal dances in tails and white ties were organized and all of us were expected to do the Viennese waltz, the majestic Polonaise and the tango. The foxtrot was a given and the occasional polka allowed. Bowing and kissing the ladies' hands was also part of the routine. It is amazing how hard this group of poor, recent immigrants worked to continue with their pre-war customs. With a few rare exceptions, my social life, such as it was during the first two years at Yale, was in New York. My dates for any of the formal Latvian functions were arranged by mother, who was very eager to have us in permanent relationships, possibly leading to marriage, with Latvians girls, primary from her sorority. As time went on, I had the occasional date in New Haven – with the sister of a roommate and a girl from Woodbridge who seemed determined to have a Yale relationship, even with a recent immigrant/scholarship student. Embarrassing as it was, there were also a couple of town girls ("townies") who made it a point of being at all of my fencing meets, sitting in the front row and then sending me letters – "fans" – almost as scary as the "bobbysoxers" that first day at the Manual Training High School.

The Yale fencing captain sports his "Y" while seated on the Senior Fence.

The fencing team and its activities such as trips to Harvard, Princeton, Columbia and the New York Athletic Club were probably the most fun for me. At the Athletic Club in New York, we had team dinners with menus picked out by Papa Grasson, our emeritus senior coach. As a Frenchman from Belgium, he felt we should be exposed to Continental culture and French cuisine. It was with the fencing team I had my first glimpses of Boston. It was fun and, more often than not, we were beating the Harvards.

Fencing became a major part of my life and it gave me a sense of belonging. At the French lycee, we had fencing lessons in gym classes. It was a sport, but it was also considered a traditional skill required of officers and gentlemen. The College Turenne, named after one of the most famous French marshals, was a pseudo-military institution under the jurisdiction of the French army. The principal of the school wore a uniform and almost all the students were children of military families. As a military school, it offered the services of a fencing master who was still an active member of the French army in Freiburg. He represented centuries-old traditions. Fencing was also in line with old Lettonia customs. Fencing, with possible dueling for honor's sake, was an integral part of the German fraternities. A "friendly" duel leaving you with scars on your face or shoulders was one of the initiation rituals. It was honor, pride, conquest of fear – the ultimate badge of a true gentleman. As children, we had heard about it from Father, uncles and Grandfather. If you were a student of theology at these old universities, as was the case with grandfather Ludis Berzins, you could excuse yourself from that aspect of the regimen and concentrate on the literary and spiritual, but almost everybody else was involved. Of course, swordplay was quite different from fencing, the sport, but it was close enough to attract me to the home of the Yale fencing team on the 7th floor of Payne Whitney Gymnasium. It was there that I spent four happy years of companionship, training, competing, experiencing the joy of winning and the agony of defeat. The greater lessons of life were all there – friendship, teamwork, discipline, leadership. Amusement, too. Freshman year, I was mentioned in *The New York Times* in a small article on the last page of its sport section, as having won my matches against Columbia. True glory, even if my name was spelled as "Frisfrops Kagi." There were no superstars on our team, but in three out of the four years we were Big Three (Yale, Harvard, Princeton) champions. The year of my captaincy, we only had one dual-meet loss, to Columbia, which I blamed on my poor performance due to a strep throat. In spite of it, we had a better record than any Yale fencing team for some 15 years before us and 15 years after us. I was very proud of our team. We had worked hard, kept fit, had disciplined training and functioned as a group. Individually, I came close to winning the Easterns, which in 1955 was considered a national championship. Tied for first place, I lost in a fence-off ending up in third place. It was a disappointment, but probably a blessing. Had I won, I may have considered trying for the 1956 Olympics in Australia, which would have meant joining the Army and not going to medical school. One of my Princeton opponents of my approximate skills elected the Olympic route. He joined the army, was assigned to minimal clerical duties in New York and spent most of his time training at the Athletic Club and fencing in all the tournaments required to make the Olympics squad. He was successful and represented the United States in Australia only to be badly beaten by the Europeans.

Thus, in the spring of 1955, I called an end to my fencing career, although not my interest in the sport. Fencing is as antique as wrestling and was one of the original modern Olympics events, but at Yale in the 1950s it was still considered a minor sport and frequently ridiculed as comparable to effete tip-toe dancing by those who had never experienced its physical demands, concentration, millisecond reflexes and intense eye-to-eye contact. As the captain of the team in my senior year, I was assigned to the Yale Athletic Committee to review the designation of "major" or "minor" sports. Rowing, baseball, football, basketball and track had been the major sports for many decades. Those who played them received a "major Y" to put on their chest – all other sports were only worthy of a small "minor Y." You could get a major "Y" by earning three minor ones, by winning a national championship or being captain of a team. It did not seem right, and the work of our committee led to the elimination of the major/minor classifications of varsity intercollegiate sports.

Incidentally, one of the members on this committee was our 1955 classmate Dick Raskind, the captain of the tennis team. I had known Dick from some pre-med classes we shared and our common residence in Saybrook College. He was the ultimate bright, masculine, physically fit Yale athlete and champion tennis player. Ten years later, it was a surprise to hear he had elected to change his gender and become Renee Richards. I first encountered him as a woman while running the New York Marathon. As I was running north on 3rd Avenue, all of a sudden, among the spectators standing on the sidewalk, there was Dick Raskind dressed as a woman. We exchanged a few words and I continued to call him Dick - he didn't seem to mind. He was now living his earliest childhood dream of waking up in the morning, reborn a girl. It has been a cultural experience to meet with him at various Class of 1955 events and to learn many years later that he, in retrospect, would not go through his sex change again. Renee has had a very successful career as an ophthalmologist in New York and his life story has been documented in many books and journals.

The effete image that some of our classmates had of fencing was somewhat troubling. In the world and language of political correctness, inclusion and diversity, I would have to describe myself as a victim subjected to untold discomfort and anxiety, destined to psychological turmoil and failure in life. Somehow, we survived without demonstrations or edicts and apologies issued by the president of the University. With a love of sports and a wish to be an American, I also went out for intermural tackle football and played for Saybrook against the other residential colleges at Yale. We also played Harvard's Adams House at the end of the season – the Friday afternoon before "The Game" on Saturday. The Adams House game was always followed by a reception in the master's quarters, in coat and tie, with sherry, tea and finger sandwiches. It was a genteel, civilized setting after an afternoon on the muddy, cold athletic fields of Yale or Harvard. For fear of major injuries, my mother and the fencing coach were not in favor of my decision to play football, but I managed to do so for two seasons with only a relatively minor back injury. I played tackle on offense and end on defense. It was good fun and I enjoyed the experience of this American, truly masculine sport. "He ain't played a down of football in his life" - a Louisiana pejorative phrase explained to me by our New Orleans son-in-law Howard, does not apply to me.

I also enjoyed going up to the Payne Whitney boxing floor, one above fencing. Boxing as an official intercollegiate sport had been discontinued at Yale in the 1930s, but punching bags and Mosey King, the old coach, were still on hand. Mosey was a fixture at the gym; decades earlier he had been a lightweight national champion. He was a little "punchy," but he loved to be with students and teach them how to work out with his bags. His days started and ended at the gym. He lived in a simple room in the eastern part of New Haven and jogged to and from the gym in a white sweater and khaki pants. It was always the same outfit, be it fall, winter or spring. You could always see him on Elm Street on his way to the gym in the morning and then back home at night. His sweater and pants were always the same and most of us had the impression they were the only pieces of clothing that poor Mosey owned. If not working the bags with the occasional student, he was handing out towels at the locker room entrance. His life ended on a dark winter night as he was starting to jog home. Crossing the street, hit by a car, he was dead on the spot. He had lived alone and did not seem to have any relatives or friends. Everybody felt sorry for "poor old Mosey," yet when they found his safety deposit box, it revealed stocks worth half-a-million dollars, which he'd bought many years earlier upon the advice of some of his boxing students. It took time, but eventually one of his distant cousins was located to become the recipient of Mosey's fortune. We all loved Mosey. His life and love were Yale. He is a good memory.

On the floor below fencing was wrestling, where, during the spring trimester, the coach gave judo classes. The coach, one of the O'Donnell brothers who were involved with Yale sports as coaches or trainers, had taught hand-to-hand combat during WWII. At the height of the Cold War in the 1950s, all of us were likely to be drafted or spend voluntary time in the military services. None of us was interested in being in a hand-to-hand combat situation, yet all of us had thought about it, had seen graphic war movies and knew veterans who had lived to tell their stories. Spending a few weeks in those judo classes was interesting, but for me did not lead to a great desire for a black belt or some other mark of high performance in that sport. O'Donnell, like Mosey, was one of the interesting characters around the gym and he did manage to teach us a few of the judo basics.

Squash was an extra, introduced to me by Jules Cohen, a member of our fencing team, who was also an accomplished racquets player. As an undergraduate, I did not play much of it, but once in medical school, it would become my major athletic activity. There were squash courts at the medical school, and I played in there several times a week.

SPORTS FOR LIFE

S ince I am on the topic of sports, I might as well interrupt my chronological flow with an account of my athletic activities after the days of the Yale fencing, intramural football, squash and some judo were done – and how sports have remained a critical part of my, and my family's, lives.

At the 3rd Surgical Hospital, Mobile, Army ("MASH"), there were days and nights of intense surgical activity, but when the troops were not in the field we could expect relative peace. "Sloth" was the word for the hours we spent in the horizontal in the shade of our tents with the warm (no ice available) gin and tonics we started on at four in the afternoon. The "dinner" at the mess tent ("slop on a tin tray") was followed by another nap while waiting for the temperature to drop down to tolerable double-digit levels. It was then, usually around nine, off to play poker at the 173rd Airborne Brigade "officers' club" tent and Bloody Marys into the night.

After a few weeks of that lifestyle, my uniform and belts seemed to be shrinking. Something had to be done. Thanks to a very lucky night of winnings, I cut out the poker and the Bloody Mary calories. That helped with the weight gain, but there had to be more physical activity. Without gyms, fitness centers or swimming pools, running was the only choice. Thus, several of us started running around the inner perimeter of the 173rd home camp just before dark, when it was a little cooler than at the height of the day. We had to be very careful since there were armed guard posts along the way and after dark the orders to shoot at anything suspicious were strict and enforced.

So, when back in New Haven, after it had become clear that there would be no time for leisurely academic afternoon squash games, running once again seemed to be the logical choice to keep the flab at bay and maintain fitness sufficient enough to stand long hours in the operating room. Unlike in Vietnam, the run had to be in the morning before any other activity. The process was also easier if you had companion of similar determination, and I was fortunate to have a neighbor who had agreed to run in rain, sunshine or freezing snow. Tom Cook was my man, and the two of us were regulars at six o'clock in the morning around Westville and the Yale Bowl. We were a bizarre sight, since jogging and running were rare activities in those days. Two miles was our approximate distance and seemed sufficient to keep us in some sort of shape. It also established my lifelong habit of exercise in the morning, so much easier to maintain than the choice between exercise or a drink before dinner in the late afternoon. After leaving New Haven and settling in Middlebury, I continued the early morning run routine, but increased the distance to a minimum of three miles at least five times a week. After a year or two of these solitary runs, I was talked into running in a 10K race on a very hilly course in Waterbury. Having completed this race, the next step was longer distances. By this point in time, the 1970s, running had become more popular, and several of us in the Waterbury area started to think marathons. The fitness craze was on, and we were no longer jogging, we were now runners.

I was one of the early members of the National Jogging Association and they were having a medical meeting in Hawaii in December of 1979, at the time of the Honolulu Marathon. A couple months ahead of it, I decided if I wanted to subject myself to the increased training regime, Hawaii in December would be a good goal to have. I started running six miles five times a week and increased the weekend distance to 10 miles on either Saturday or Sunday. Two weeks before the race, I forced myself into a 15- to 18-mile run and then eased off to the "usual" 6- to 10-mile runs in preparation for the race itself. With an active surgical practice and a busy family, there was no time for lengthier preparations. The idea was to be able to run 20 miles without too much strain and then "tough it out" the last six miles of the race. That was the plan and that is how it went in Hawaii. I was happy to finish in about 4 hours and had enough energy left to enjoy the rest of the Honolulu medical meeting and activities. There is an emotional high with the finish of a marathon and it is easy to make a decision to run again for the thrill of it. My second one was two months later in Las Vegas, then Boston in April. The Las Vegas one was unique, with very unusual respiratory muscle pain at the end of the high-altitude run. It was strange to have neck and chest pain from the extra work of getting enough thin air into your blood, heart, lungs and muscles. Boston was unique with its amazingly severe quadriceps cramps for the last six miles. Each run fed the need for more. So, in the fall of that year there was the New York Marathon followed by the Marine Corps in Washington one a week later. Back to back 26-mile runs was the challenge. I completed both of them and the family was there to cheer me on in New York. Caroline and Julie watched me come down the Queensborough Bridge into Manhattan and were amazed at how well I seemed to be doing at that halfway point of the race. They were at the finish in Central Park, too, and described me then as "exhausted." Father was also there, awaiting me with a special cocktail of his own devising – a mix of honey and vodka. He felt I would need it and I did enjoy it. The Marine Corps Marathon a week later was the real workout. I ran it wearing my NY Marathon t-shirt from the week before and had to agree with the many spectators who spotted it and identified me as insane. I must admit that, at the end of that run, as I was recuperating in a hot tub, I thought it was the end of my long-distance running. But daughter Katie was a student in Boston and, as the winter went on, I made the decision to give the Boston Marathon another shot. Having had a very positive experience with some muscle-cramp-relieving wine offered to me by spectators the year before, I asked Katie to meet me at the 22-mile mark with a bottle of sweet German wine ("Spaetauslese"), which I drank to the finish without experiencing the quadriceps cramps of the previous year. It was my best Marathon time ever, at 3 hours and 42 minutes.

Knee pains are the most common affliction of runners, but I became more and more aware of hip discomfort, and when, during the summer after that second Boston marathon, I was introduced to rowing, it seemed like a good way to stay fit without the pounding of the hips.

Daughter Mara was home from Northfield Mount Herman, where she had started rowing and seemed to be showing great potential in the sport. She had been a superb swimmer, but with Olympics in mind, she felt her chances of getting there were better as a rower. Adolescence, hormones and energy to burn had to be dealt with, and an hour of hard, early-morning rowing would be good. I was able to arrange for her to row out of the Yale Boathouse on the Housatonic River in Derby while she was at home for the summer. I took her there and met Norm Thetford and Baxter Walsh, who convinced me I should be joining them in rowing for fun, fitness and participation in the rapidly expanding world of competitive veterans' sports. For Mara it was the beginning of her road to World Championships and the Olympics. For me it was the beginning of some 15 years of sport, friendship and competition in America, Canada, Europe and the Soviet Union. Rowing is a total body sport and requires strength of the upper extremities, back and lower extremity muscle groups with absolute conditioning of the heart and lungs. It also required the acquisition of oar and water handling skills, teamwork and willingness to go beyond the highest levels of mental and physical performance. Finishing a competitive hard row has many similarities to the completion of a 26-mile marathon. It is the satisfaction of "giving it your all" and the euphoria of being able to do it.

We rowed in the morning before work. Being in a boat on the water by 5:45 meant getting up at 5:00, driving to the Yale Boathouse over the empty country roads at speeds well above the limits, rowing hard for 45-60 minutes and, after a quick shower, being back on the road to work, in my case, the Waterbury Hospital operating room by 7:30. After our row on days without scheduled surgery, I enjoyed breakfast with the others, solving the problems of the world, exchanging jokes and discussing the potential evils of the eggs and bacon we seemed to be consuming in significant quantities. In the course of a couple of years at the Yale Boathouse, we grew from a foursome to several eights, pairs and single scullers. We entered multiple regattas and won medals in the United States and Canada. It was also fun to go to Europe and row in Scotland, England, Holland, Sweden,

Germany, Yugoslavia and Austria. In 1989, before its collapse, we also organized the first veterans' regatta between the Soviet Union and the United States. It was held in Latvia, where I had started an Orthopaedic Education Program, and the Communist government, in the spirit of "glasnost" and change, was willing to support the event. The "Soviet" rowers were Estonians, Latvians and Lithuanians. Our American crew was primarily from the New Haven Rowing Club, Yale and Harvard. We rowed hard and celebrated with gusto. There was no shortage of beer, champagne, brandy and vodka – it was a historic event.

In the United States, I was able to organize a Yale veterans' row against Harvard in conjunction with the traditional regatta on the Thames River in New London. It was fun but would have been greater fun if our Yale boat had not been beaten by a huge margin. Another unique race was a row around Manhattan in a four-with-cox. We started at the Columbia Boathouse north of the George Washington Bridge, rowed down the Hudson River where we waited for absolutely slack tide since the shifting tidewaters of the Atlantic Ocean, the East River and the Hudson River currents can cause unpredictable surges strong enough to break a boat of any type, not to mention a flimsy racing shell. After waiting for the appropriate moment on the Hudson near Battery Park, in sight of the Statue of Liberty and Ellis Island, the spot I had passed in in 1949 on the refugee ship *General Muir*, we started the race north, up the East River, under the Brooklyn, Manhattan and Queensborough bridges, to the Harlem River and back to the Columbia Boathouse. We were the only veterans crew in the race, and our average age was a good 30 years ahead of the college youngsters. Our savvy coxswain, Jimmy Segaloff, with his 30-year advantage in experience, wisdom and navigating skills, got us well ahead of the "kids" by some clever short cuts along the banks of the East River. We entered the Harlem River many boat lengths ahead of the competition, but no matter how hard our aging bodies tried and no matter how hard Jimmy tried to get us to row harder, one of the younger college boats just kept creeping up on us. With less than 100 yards from the Columbia Boathouse finish, they passed to leave us in second place. The race was some four hours of rowing, we were more than happy to have finished the course and we had beaten all but one of the competitive boats – a sense of satisfaction reminiscent of that first marathon on Hawaii.

Rowing was rewarding in many ways and it was ultimate for fitness, companionship, competition and travel fun. But as the years passed, our club and its membership changed. We were asked to leave the Yale Boathouse and build our own. My life was also changing, with greater commitments to international orthopaedic education, the Keggi Orthopaedic Foundation and family. I was operating and lecturing throughout the former Soviet Union and the Baltics. Every year, our foundation was sponsoring 10 or more foreign Orthopaedic Fellows to spend time at Waterbury Hospital and Yale. I wanted to spend time with them, and they expected to be with me in the operating room and our various Waterbury/ Yale Orthopaedic conferences. Teaching became a major obligation. As a family, we had also grown with a vacation house and golf club membership in Scottsdale, Arizona. There were by now sons-in-law and grandchildren. Golf had always been there during marathons and rowing, but with the aging muscles and joints, it made more and more sense as the sport for an aging body. The Country Club of Waterbury was superb, but the fairways, mountains, sunshine and sunsets of Arizona at the Desert Mountain Club were also a major draw away from the rowing.

Eventually, it seemed like an easy decision – more golf, more family and no more early-morning runs to the river.

Until my engagement and marriage to Julie, I was only vaguely aware of golf, but since her family had been players for at least three generations in America and Julie had been among the best, it was clear I should try it. I did, and it became an immediate attraction and "addiction" for the rest of my life.

Golf is a four-letter word, a disease, "a good walk spoiled," and volumes have been written about it. The jokes abound. It was invented by a bunch of drunken Scots with a shot of whiskey to be drunk on every one of the 18 tees, but those of us who play sober or with a little drink or two, love it in any form or shape. As opposed to daughter Caroline, wife Julie, and grandsons Christopher and Alexander, I never had a golfer's swing but was able to muscle the ball long distances with enthusiasm and joy. As time has passed, that aspect of the game is gone, but the balls go down the middle and the chipping and putting remain satisfactory. Even though walking and carrying a golf bag for 36 holes took some endurance, I never thought of it as a true sport with the cardiovascular demands or running or rowing. With age, that too underwent change and playing out of a cart with a red flag that allows you closer access to the tees and greens, now seemed like a satisfactory stimulus of all systems – mind included, keeping track of scores, bets, etc. Back to back marathons and rows around Manhattan became ancient history along with the 300-yard drives, but there was the companionship of fellow golfers, the competition, the dollars lost or won, the drinks after the game and the hope it will last a little longer. It has been fun to play, it has been fun to watch world-class golf by daughter Caroline, 15 club championships by wife Julie and the way the grandchildren are now hitting the ball.

Swimming has always been with us. As children, we were taken to the beach by my mother and grandfather. In Latvia, they had single-sex and mixed (co-ed) swimming hours. Nudity was the rule during the single-sex hours, and as boys we were allowed with the woman up to a certain age. It must have been the age of four, since I still have memories of all that "femininity." In Aluksne, we swam in the lake and I don't think we wore bathing suits until the age of 6 or 8 - a photograph of father with the four of us naked boys attests to it. The photograph is a minor embarrassment I would prefer not to have publicized, but the lady editors of any previous story of my life have always insisted on having it displayed. Sexual harassment by some very fine ladies, for sure . . . Ah well! In Emmendingen, Germany, there was a swimming pool where we swam almost every day during the summer months. It was never a major sport, but in later years in Grand Cayman my confidence in being able to swim below and above water made snorkeling and scuba diving enjoyable. With age, it has also become a way of keeping muscles, heart and lungs in functional condition without the weight-bearing abuse of running. The swimming pools of Arizona and Middlebury have been of great help to me in staying in relatively livable shape. Recent exercising supported by a noodle in the Naugatuck YMCA pool has become a major sport for this former marathoner and rower.

Starting with fencing, a positive part of my life at Yale, sports have been a daily must above and beyond the physical work of standing in the operating room, fixing fractures, replacing joints, or fusing spines. I like to think it has allowed me to function better and to deal with some of the more stressful aspects of life. Fencing, playing squash, running, rowing, golf and some swimming have been good to me. In Latvia, splashing around in the cold waters of the Gulf of Riga until September 14, my grandfather's birthday, was a part of his life, along with a brisk daily walk, which he took until the day of his sudden death at age 96. I often think of his personal routine and on his insistence on some form of physical activity in his life and in the lives of his students at the boarding school he founded in Czarist Latvia in 1905 and the schools he directed during Latvia's independence. He lived, he worked, he wrote and remained active in body, mind and spirit his entire life. He was and continues to be an example to follow. A man of God at peace with the world. God, I'm sure, was with him, but his daily walks also helped.

REFLECTIONS ON UNDERGRADUATE DAYS

F encing and all the other athletic activities cleared the mind of major concerns as I struggled with pre-medical courses at Yale and through life for years afterwards. Those pre-medical courses were tough. I made it through, but that struggle made it clear I would not be a chemist or basic scientist. As I was coming to that conclusion, I became more and more aware of the literature I was reading in French, the courses on the history of art, religion and music that I was taking, and the general education I was getting above and beyond the sciences that were preparing me for medicine. I was obviously determined to complete those pre-medical courses and was fortunate to do so. Many potentially superb physicians and surgeons fail organic chemistry and abandon medicine. In retrospect, it might have been better to spread these pre-medical courses such as biology, chemistry, organic chemistry, physics and mathematics over a period of four years, but in the end it all worked out and, in my case, made the junior and senior years at Yale more enjoyable. My brother, Andrejs, was less fortunate, and the pre-medical load he placed upon himself as a freshman at Dartmouth was disastrous. Better advice, better planning, would have kept him from having to leave Dartmouth and abandon the hope of becoming a doctor. He would have been a good one, but that first year and unfortunate planning did him in.

Toward the end of my freshman year, I, too, was concerned about my grades in these pre-medical courses and worried about losing my scholarship. The Korean War was going on in full force and the Marine Corps was advertising a platoon leader course for college undergraduates. It guaranteed payment of college expenses in return for two years of active military duty upon graduation. Active military duty started at the level of a second lieutenant combat platoon leader in Korea. It was said the life expectancy of a platoon leader in that situation was a few minutes at best. I am very proud of the heroic men who served our country as platoon leaders but was happy I did not have to become a marine in order to finish college. I later thought about it, especially in Vietnam, in the relative safety of the hospital, and had mixed sensation of having avoided full combat military duty by becoming a doctor. We were in a combat zone with the occasional close firefights and mortar attacks near our tents, but every wounded man arriving at the hospital was a reminder of my own good fortune mixed with a sense of absolute respect to the true military service we were witnessing. We worked hard, we were away from home, we saved lives and limbs, we were giving our 13 years of education to a worthy cause, we were exposed to danger, but there was also the question of, "Should I have been a Marine? What kind of Marine would I have been? Would I have measured up to the wounded I was seeing?" I also thought and think about my godfather, who was one of the most decorated men in the Latvian German units fighting in Russia, the risks he had taken, the courage and leadership under fire he had shown. Many thoughts, with many mixed emotions - but in the end, I feel good about having had the opportunity to serve in a combat zone, as a surgeon to the wounded of the 173rd Airborne Brigade, 1st and 21st Infantry Divisions and Special Forces. If called, I would go back again, but in the summer of 1966, after 10 months up front, it was good to be going home to wife Julie and the children, to be at Yale, teach orthopaedic surgery and the lessons learned from war wound care.

Survivor thoughts can intrude at any time. The luck involved in it, destiny, fate, God's will. Why me? Why us? Saved to live, for what? All of these thoughts come to mind with Vietnam, but they apply to so many of the other events in my life during WWII. A few minutes or days one way or the other would have changed it all. The German invasion of Russia with its "liberation" of Latvia in 1941 saved us from deportation to Siberia or execution by a few days. The Russian tank attack during the summer of 1944 was stopped just a few miles away. Father's last-minute decision, in the middle of the night, in a barn in the woods, not to attempt escape to Sweden, was courageous and lucky. The Russians delaying their advance on Riga by a few days in October of 1944 allowed us to be on one of the last ships to leave Riga for Germany - lucky again. Father's decision to hide on the train as we arrived in the German concentration camp was risky, but successful and lucky. Surviving the bombings of Cologne and Freiburg - the list is long. Surviving, moving on – resilience, as studied by Steve Southwick, son of my mentor, Wayne Southwick can be complicated and works in many ways.

In any event, having reached the conclusion, fairly early in the fall of my freshman year, that I would not be a chemistry major, the decision to do French Literature was easy. I was qualified for the advanced courses based on my years in French high school and would complete the major requirements by taking only one of these courses each year. This left me with the opportunity to take a variety of other liberal arts courses offered by

Yale. It was fun to read the works of all the "greats" of French Literature: Racine, Moliere, Montaigne, Rousseau, Flaubert, Hugo, Camus, Sartre, and to have them interpreted by very scholarly professors. Their lectures may well have been better preparation in psychology and psychiatry than the formal courses in these subjects I'd later take in medical school. I had time for a series of other courses that were truly of the liberal tradition. I could not be happier about that, since they have had a major impact on my life and the interpretation of history, the world and politics. They were superb courses such as the history of religion, given by the dean of the Divinity School, history of art by Vincent Scully and the history of music by junior professor whose name I do not remember but who has made it fun to enjoy music ranging from Gregorian chants to jazz. A semester studying *The Divine Comedy* with Professor Bergen was interesting, but not as inspiring as I would have hoped it would be, based on the enthusiasm expressed for it by Professor Erich Auerbach (for whom I worked as a bursary student).

These undergraduate courses in history, literature and art led me with enthusiasm into the history of medicine with Professors Thomas Forbes and John Fulton at the Yale Medical School and its world-class library established by Harvey Cushing. It was absolute joy to spend as much time as I desired among centuries old books and medical illustrations in the "cellars" of the library. In those days, those of us who were involved in the study of the history of medicine were allowed into these cellars without any supervision or white gloves. We could see, read and feel the works of Gersdorff, Pare, Larray and more. Ten years later, after my tour in Vietnam, it was fun to revisit some of these old friends while writing about war wounds and their management. These war surgeons of centuries past, their thinking, their emotions were so similar to some of those I had experienced and gave me a sense of continuity with their work on the wounded young men of centuries long gone by.

On this point, I am a surgeon and cannot call myself a true historian, but I do believe we should all be exposed to the thinking of our predecessors, many of whom had brilliant ideas that continue to have applications today. The "minimally invasive" muscle sparing, muscle splitting approach to the proximal femur as performed in 1826 in Philadelphia by John Barton is but one of many historical examples. Dr. Barton's description of inserting his finger into his incision, splitting muscles with his finger and feeling the femur is what I was doing 150 years later while working out the anterior approach to total hip replacements. History matters, and in the courses of my teaching career, I've insisted my conferences with students or residents start with a reading from a text of orthopaedic history. It may sound like church with the reading of the old testament, but I hope it will have made these young men and women better persons with a better perspective on the past, their own lives, the performance of surgery and, of course, the future teaching of surgery.

Back briefly to my undergraduate days. As I've indicated, being elected captain of the 1955 fencing team in the spring of 1954 was a major moment in my life and I took it as a serious responsibility. I was convinced that as a team we could do better than we had done in the past. Thus, in the fall, when we reconvened, we started a daily program of stretching, muscle strengthening and general fitness such as running up the stairs of the Payne Whitney gymnasium - something that would have sounded very foreign to previous teams. We concentrated on the basics of the sport and the selection of those who would compete in our matches was based on performance against other members of the team. That kind of objectivity had not always been the case in the previous three years I had been with the team. It worked, and we had a season that would not be equaled until the 1970s, when Henry Haratunian, of Armenia and the Soviet Union, became the coach. Our team picture and the official captain's photograph on the Yale fence, with major "Y" on our chests are reminders of our work, our achievements and the good times we had. We gave it our best "for God, for Country and for Yale," as we said it in the days before political correctness.

The senior society, Scroll and Key was a major part of my life during that senior year (1954-1955) and continues today, more than 60 years later, as I get ready to go to lunch with two of my classmates from our group. At the end of my junior year, I knew I was being considered for election by at least one senior society, "Manuscript," but it was an absolute surprise to be tapped by Scroll and Key. It was a spring evening and I was in my Saybrook College room, listening to a Bach Brandenburg Concerto while waiting for the knock on the door at the exact hour of eight. When the moment came, there were two seniors standing outside who then proceeded to tap me on the shoulder - "Manuscript! Do you accept?"; "Scroll and Key! Do you accept?" My "I do" to Scroll and Key was followed by a handshake and a small white envelope with a card in Latin directing me to report to a specific spot at a specific hour. The rest should remain a secret, but there is nothing secret about the 14 other members of our class who then became the best of friends for life. That spring evening in 1954 was far, far beyond any expectation, thought, plan or hope of five years earlier as my refugee boat sailed to America.

INTO MEDICINE

What to do after Yale College was a major question. All of us had to consider military service; indeed, unless you were deferred for medical reasons, it was inevitable. The Cold War was at its peak and we were all registered for the draft as soon as we turned 18. At least a third of our class was in ROTC, ready to be commissioned into the Army, Navy or Air Force upon graduation. In our Scroll and Key group of 15, eight were in ROTC and went on active duty within weeks of graduation, two were deferred for medical reasons, two of us went to medical school to later serve in the military upon completion of specialty training, two of our brightest were drafted and served as enlisted men for two years. Only one went through a year at Oxford and three years in law school without being called. In my own case, it was clear that medical school would delay military service, but it was also clear that as a physician, I could be drafted up to the age of 45 and should volunteer for service at a time of my choosing rather than be drafted out of a residency program or practice a few years later.

But did I really want to go into medicine? Did I really want to spend four more years in school followed by the demanding work of an intern and resident for another five years after that? There was also the cost. The alternatives were immediate military service followed by a career in international banking based on my knowledge of French and German, Latvian, and some understanding of Italian and Spanish. This was intriguing, as I was becoming acquainted with some very successful financial types lately of Scroll and Key, the income they were generating and the lives they were leading. Comparative Literature was a choice, but that contemplative life did not seem to be for on- the-move young Kristaps. I was the most familiar with medicine and my father's work in surgery. I was also aware of how happy, fulfilled and satisfied he was with his life, and, in the fall of 1954, I applied to medical school. I loved Yale, and its medical school was unique. It had no daily quizzes, weekly hour tests or written homework. As a mature and responsible college graduate, you were expected to know the required knowledge to be a physician and the only examinations you had to pass were the national boards at the end of the second and fourth years. You could also start "specializing." If your interest was in basic research, you were not pushed to spend extra hours in the operating room and could devote yourself to more time in your laboratory. Those of us interested in surgery could minimize our time in a pharmacology lab in order to see more surgical procedures.

So, it made some sense for me to apply to the Yale School of Medicine and hope to be accepted in spite of my less-than-brilliant grades in chemistry, physics and biology. Having submitted the required paperwork, I was encouraged when I was asked to appear for an interview, the first step in the acceptance process. My interviews were with Dorothy Horstman, one of the great virologists of the era, and Tom Forbes, a professor of Anatomy with a passion for the history of medicine. I don't remember the details of those interviews, but a few days later I received a letter of acceptance and was asked for a deposit of $120, a significant sum in 1954. My father was able to send me the money and I could proceed with the rest of my senior year knowing I had an assured spot in the Yale School of Medicine, Class of 1959. It was a relief, and I felt lucky as I watched some of my classmates struggle with their applications to a variety of other medical schools. That $120 Father sent me was the first significant financial contribution by my parents to my Yale education. They were in no position to help, and I was pleased not be a burden on the lives they were starting in America and the help my brothers may have needed. I was and remain grateful to Yale for the scholarship and the bursary job I had with Professor Auerbach. I was also happy to be able to work during the summers and other vacations to have enough money for essential and some incidental expenses.

These jobs, by my own choosing, had been, with a few rare exceptions, outdoors and of a physical nature, such as construction work in Colorado, sheeting houses or landscaping on Long Island. My most exciting job came during a Christmas vacation when, at the age of 19, I was hired as a messenger for a garment shop on the West Side of Manhattan specializing in ladies' fancy underwear. My job was to deliver the bras and panties to stores throughout Manhattan and frequently required waiting for the packages to be prepared in the same room the models were using to try on the wares. It also paid well.

But medical school was going to be different and would not allow a lot of time for outside work. Even though I received some support from the school, the majority of the cost was covered by a very generous grant from the Kingsley Trust Association (Scroll and Key). The Army, which I joined as a second lieutenant in the Medical Service Corps, also helped. As a member of the active reserve, I attended weekly drills and was paid a full day's pay for the three hours spent in uniform, listening to talks about army rules and regulations, learning to salute, etc. During the summer, I spent two weeks on active duty, learning how to clean and fire a rifle (M-1) or .45 automatic pistol, live in a tent and learn more about the ways Army life. In 1957, it was two weeks at Fort Devens in Massachusetts and in 1958, two frigid weeks at Camp Drum in upstate New York. The dollars earned helped, and, having had the basic exposure to the Army, I did not need to go for basic training when, at the completion of my orthopaedic residency at Yale, I started active duty at the Beaumont General Hospital in El Paso, Texas. My father had also established himself in private practice in New York and was able to provide some help with the final school expenses. The net of it was graduation from the Yale School of Medicine in the spring of 1959 with only a minor student loan debt.

However, my main source of support during this period, in so many ways, came from Julie. We'd married after my second year in med school and she worked as a reference librarian in the New Haven Public Library. She, with some help from her father, was providing for our life in a third-floor apartment on Winthrop Avenue. Julie and I had met during the summer after my first year of medical school, when I was told about a "work" opportunity by a fellow member of Scroll and Key. It was the job of tour leader with UCLA Professor Kneller on a bus trip through Europe. Professor Kneller's tour was spectacular, but the majority of his travelers were girls and he needed more boys. The boys paid less but he also needed some male tour leaders who were given the trip for free. I qualified with my knowledge of foreign languages and a strong back you need to help with the loading and unloading of the bus at all the stops through Europe. The tour started in London at the Changing of the Queen's Guard in front of Buckingham Palace.

There were three Smith college graduates on the tour: Julie Quarles, Jane MacKenzie and Patsy Goodwin. Before getting to London, they had already been in Paris, where they'd met Jan Deutsch, one of my Scroll and Key friends who was spending two years in England and Europe on a Clare Fellowship (the best you could hope for as a Yale undergraduate). In the course of the Guard's ceremony, Julie approached me with a letter from Jan, which was brief but destined to be the beginning of a lifelong relationship. "Kris, this is to introduce Julie Quarles. You will be traveling with her for two months. She is big enough for you. Have fun! Jan." It was almost love of Julie at first sight. She was close to six feet tall ("big enough"), attractive, smart and well educated at Emma Willard School and Smith College. She was also familiar with several of my Yale classmates, and it did not take very long for us to establish a strong relationship.

We traveled on a bus from London north through England to Carlisle, where we took a ship to Bergen in Norway. From there, it was on to Demark, Germany, Switzerland, Austria, Yugoslavia, Italy and then France. Memorable sights, museums and cities with much history. Copenhagen with the Tivoli Gardens; Hamburg with its "son et lumiere" performance of Vivaldi's *Four Seasons*; Freiburg, the Alps (Jungfrau) in Switzerland; Vienna, which had just been freed of the Russians; Venice and the world- class Royal Danieli Hotel; the celebration of my 22nd birthday in Florence; Rome in all its imperial glory; southern France and the end of the tour in Paris – and of course most notably the evolution of a relationship with Julie that, by the time we reached Switzerland, was destined for a life beyond our summer on the bus. After our farewells in Paris, Julie went on to Finland and Russia before coming home to her parents, who had just moved from Wisconsin to Greenwich. I sailed back on the *United*

States and had enough change in my pocket to take the subway to my father's office and family apartment on West 72nd Street.

It had been a sad parting in Paris. Having shared an amazing summer with Julie, I was suddenly alone, facing a grim second year of pharmacology, pathology and other basic sciences at the medical school. On the ship that brought me back to America was a crowd of students ready to party. I remember it as five days of time in the bunk or staring out to sea. The few days in New York with my family and our Latvian friends were also blank until Julie's return and the beginning of a new life for both of us. We met in New York, at her parents' in Greenwich, or at Yale, where I was earning my room and board as a freshman counselor in Bingham Hall on the Old Campus.

Very early in the relationship, I brought Julie to my parents. They had been hoping I'd find a Latvian bride, but were very happy with her, her manners, her mind, her education and her family. I was presented to Julie's parents, who seemed pleased and welcoming. At Yale, we spent time with my college and senior society friends. Julie also had some friends from Smith who were in the New Haven area. We were busy with medical studies, work with my Bingham Hall freshmen and, for several months, Julie was occupied as a saleslady in a shop in Stamford. Things moved quickly for us. By Christmas 1956 we were making marriage plans. Our formal engagement came in April and our wedding day was July 27, 1957.

After meeting during a whirlwind grand tour of Europe, things moved quickly for Julie Quarles and me. We were married the next summer.

I should mention here a couple of stop-gap jobs I took during the summer after graduation from Yale College that were major influences as I made my final choice of medicine as a career. I was a companion that summer to boys in two different families. The first was an old New York and Harvard family who lived in Manhattan but had a house on Long Island for the summer and needed someone to help with their two sons and their heavy schedule of tennis, beach, sailing and golf. The family could not have been nicer, and it was fun to be with the boys. The father owned an old family brokerage house on Wall Street and, along with his wife, was involved in a number of charitable activities, owned racehorses and was very active in the New York Racing Association. I had the interesting experience of spending an afternoon with them in their private box at the Saratoga racetrack, but, above all, I learned that the high life was not as exciting as it first appeared. On a typical day, after a leisurely breakfast, the father was picked up in a limo to be driven into Wall Street and was back in the afternoon in time to get ready for the social functions. In general, he seemed tired and bored. When I asked him about what he did at work, he replied, "Sign checks." I was glad to have had exposure to the ways at the top of the financial and social world, but to me it had little appeal as a life of choice.

My second companion job that summer came during the month of August with two boys who were spending time with their father, recently divorced and re-married. He was very busy and was not going to have much time to spend with the boys in view of his high-flying real estate operations between New York, Philadelphia and Washington. I was to be their companion. He had rented, in New Jersey, a spectacular hilltop home, complete with swimming pool, and my job was to keep the two boys occupied. While on Long Island, I'd commuted to and from my parents' apartment in Manhattan, but in New Jersey I stayed at the house there. Most of my "working days" consisted of sitting at the poolside, sipping gin and tonics with the father's new second wife and watching the boys swim and play. The father would, usually, be back in the evening to have cocktails and dinner but did not seem to have much time for the boys.

We did however become good friends and would later meet from time to time in New York. Julie and I even had two special vacations with them. The first was the week after Christmas in Pinehurst, North Carolina, in the midst of my second year of medical school. By that time, Julie and I were about to be engaged and she was part of the trip. It was also the beginning of my golfing career. Julie, who was an excellent golfer, was eager to play the world-famous Pinehurst #2 course. I decided to join her on the assumption I could learn how to play the game by spending an hour at a driving range the day before the game. We got to the course as scheduled, but there was a frost delay with several foursomes waiting to play. When it was our turn to go, I assessed the situation and decided, since I was a beginner, I would play from the forward ladies' tees. As I approached them club in hand, there was an audible groan from the players waiting behind us. That groan was even louder after I whiffed the ball a few times. Even our caddy could not resist a laugh. Quitting, however, was not on my agenda, and I completed the full 18 holes running from one missed shot to the next. We did not delay anybody, the caddy laughed all the way and poor Julie stayed the course for better or for worse.

The second get-together with the family came the following summer, when Julie and I were invited to join them to sail from New London to Cape Cod. They had rented a 56-foot sailboat from a close friend and we were to join them along with an I.M. Pei, who was on his way to becoming one of the world's greatest architects. We went to New London and bought groceries and fruit, but the largest purchase was at the liquor store. Our friend proclaimed himself to be an expert sailor, but Julie, who had done a lot of sailing on inland lakes around Wisconsin started doubting that as soon as we left the docks of New London. Her doubts were confirmed within a few hours as we ran aground on a sandbar near Fishers Island. I was able to dive overboard and push us off, but it was the beginning of a series of adventures. After the "visit" to Fishers, the decision was made to reach Point Judith that night. The seas were calm, the stars and moon were out, there was only a slight breeze and we were ready to go. It was going to be a simple matter of following numbered buoys through the channel between Fishers

Island and the Connecticut/Rhode Island coast. All was well until I discovered we were not finding the right numbers on the buoys and were in the midst of rocks. I was in the bow of the yacht and was able to push away from the rocks, get us to some identifiable buoys and a clear course. It was done, we had been lucky, and my next job was to fix a stiff drink for our captain at the wheel. We did reach Point Judith, anchored, had a couple more drinks and slept.

The next day, as we were trying to get under way, our lines and sails became tangled and I, as the crew, was sent up the mast to straighten out the wind-blown mess. The sight of it attracted a coastguard helicopter which hovered above us, watched and offered to help. We were able to resolve the situation on our own and set sail to Cape Cod. The course was going to take us out of the sight of land and, much to my surprise, I was assigned to do the navigating. My army reserve courses on map reading apparently qualified me for the job and I was able to get us to where we were hoping to go. Had we been in a race to Bermuda we might have missed the island and been on the way to Africa, but we made it into the bay and harbor of Woods Hole where we encountered the New York Yacht Club and its fleet of boats, there to watch the yachts *Columbia, Weatherly, Easterner* and *Vim* in their trial races to qualify for the defense of The America's Cup. Our progress through the harbor and past these multimillion-dollar yachts was an adventure highlighted by being pushed away by one sailboat after another. There were some very anxious moments, but no harm was done and the party at the end of the day was a good one. The next day, we sailed out to see the cup contestants. That was another adventure as we were straying off course and had to be redirected to avoid catastrophic interference with the race, but it was a beautiful day on the Atlantic.

The trip had been with anxious moments, but it is a great memory. As was the case with my experience on Long Island, I felt fortunate to have been with this family in New Jersey, North Carolina and the high seas, but high-flying real estate was not for me. I was happier than ever to be in medical school at Yale.

MEDICAL SCHOOL

From the very beginning, medicine, to me, had always been synonymous with surgery. Medicine was surgery as practiced by my father, Janis. He had always made a point of saying that as a surgeon, you were a physician but also had the additional physical skills to treat patients by surgical intervention, which in so many illnesses, not to mention injuries, might be the only solution.

My Class of 1959 was the first to be able to move into the new Harkness dormitory, with its single, square rooms designed by Richard Kimball, the father of one of my Scroll and Key classmates. The dormitory was a symbol to the commitment to medical education the Yale Corporation had made a few years earlier. There had been some discussion of shutting down the school or turning it into a pure research institute, but the idea to go with a world-class medical school persisted and the university was now putting money into new buildings, new research facilities and new arrangements with the New Haven and Grace hospitals. For me, there was not much joy in facing the hurdle of the first two years of basic sciences, biochemistry, pharmacology, physiology and pathology, but it was knowledge to be acquired in preparation for the encounter with real patients, diseases and injuries during the last two years of school. The magnitude of the task struck home on the first day of school, when the reading of the simplest of medical textbooks required a dictionary to interpret all the new words. Anatomy and the dissection of our cadaver added some palpable reality. The history of medicine was also fascinating, and I was privileged to be exposed to it in Professor Tom Forbes seminar and on the student editorial board of the *Yale Journal of the History of Medicine and Allied Sciences* chaired by John Fulton, the famous neurophysiologist, who in his advanced years enjoyed entertaining us with stories that may or may not have been related to medicine. Some of them were erotic and risqué, causing embarrassment to Miss Thompson and Miss Stanton, old-fashioned Smith College graduates who were the functioning heart of the library. They sat with us at the editorial board meetings with their heads bowed as Professor Fulton related some of his earthier and sexual experiences while doing research in the South Pacific. They did seem "uncomfortable," but had led very productive lives assisting the doctors in their work.

Dr. Gardner, the Professor of Anatomy, was a very deliberate teacher and could assess our knowledge of the tissues we were dissecting in a matter of seconds. We were not reprimanded, but in the spring of the first year, the last few weeks of anatomy, I was deserving of a few words of advice. I was getting ready to go to Europe, was helping with the selection of new members of Scroll and Key and had not gotten excited about studying the bones and tendons of the foot which we had finally reached in our head-to-toes dissection. This was very obvious to Dr. Gardner as he passed by our table and his comments contained foresight: "Dr. Keggi, you are big and strong and will probably be an orthopaedic surgeon. You must study these bones, joints, nerves and tendons." I had not been exposed to orthopaedic surgery as we know it, but Dr. Gardner knew what he was talking about, and having taught thousands of students he was good about assessing us. It was in line with what Paul Beeson, the Professor of Internal Medicine, would tell me two years later: "Dr. Keggi, you did well on our service, but you must go into surgery." I guess they recognized a future surgeon when they saw one and I took it as a compliment. Another six years later, I operated on Dr. Beeson's knee and we both had a laugh about his earlier comments. He inscribed his classic textbook, "To Kris Keggi, sharp-eyed surgeon." We both knew that biochemistry, liver function and the Krebs Cycle were not my strong suit and I was better with work requiring "sharp eyes," decision making, stamina and all other known and unknown attributes of good surgeons, above and beyond grades in an organic chemistry lab.

I did, however, need to know the "numbers" well enough to pass the national boards at the end of our second year. I passed, and that was all I needed to move forward into real medicine and surgery. Our grades were not announced, but when we received them from the examiners, the names of the top 10 in the entire country were included in the envelope. Amazingly enough, my best friend, drinking and poker-playing buddy, David Skinner, was number one in the land. We all knew him to have an outstanding mind and memory, but to be the best in the land did come as a surprise. We remained friends until his premature demise. Our wives were friends. Their first daughter, Linda, is my goddaughter and it was fun to follow Dave's career through his Harvard, Mass General surgery residency, two years of research in the Air Force, a professorship at Johns Hopkins, the chairmanship of the surgery department at the University of Chicago and finally the presidency of the New York Presbyterian Hospital as it merged with the New York Hospital. One of the greatest.

Dave and his wife Ellie and Herb Kaufman and his

wife Nancy were our best medical school friends during this period. Herb, who had done his undergraduate work at Princeton, went into gastroenterology, inspired by one of our great teachers, Howard Spiro, and settled into a very successful private practice outside of New York City in Westchester County. Our closest friends outside of medicine were the Siphrons, Gurneys and Offners. Joe Siphron was one of my Scroll and Key classmates and was at the Yale Law School. Upon graduation, he and his wife M.J. settled in Manhattan, where Joe rapidly became a partner in one of the major law firms on Wall Street. We were to remain in close contact with him in New York, and in Connecticut, at their weekend home on Long Island and our house in Grand Cayman. His son John is my godson. It was sad to see Joe, who had kept himself in superb physical and mental shape, die of lung cancer, probably caused by smoking in his earlier years. A.R. ("Pete") Gurney, the brother of Steve Gurney, another Scroll and Key classmate, attended the Yale School of Drama and, upon graduation, taught English Literature at MIT. His passion, however, was writing plays, and he rapidly became one of the greatest playwrights of our era, with works dealing primarily with the vanishing ways of the old WASP establishment. *The Dining Room*, *Love Letters* and *The Cocktail Hour* were among his best. He died suddenly during the spring of 2017. Mel Offner and his wife, Rosemary, who was one of Julie's Smith College friends, were the third couple we socialized with. Mel was an accomplished sculptor and Professor of Art at Smith. Many years later, we had a great time with them when they came to visit us in Grand Cayman. That trip and snorkeling with up-close exposure to living fish led him to do some sculptures of these underwater creatures. The maquette of one of these works is one of our proudest art possessions. There were others, too, so our social life was not lacking. Our apartment on Winthrop Avenue was within walking distance of the Yale Bowl and was a venue for many football game-related parties. The last two years in medical school were good years and it wasn't all studies and work.

Some of the courses and clerkships were easier than others and in line with the "Yale system." We spent more time and effort on the subjects we were interested in. It was useful to spend two weeks on dermatology, but I did not volunteer for special assignments such as the study of an unusual rash discovered at the West Haven Veterans Hospital. It was the opposite with my surgical clerkships. In order to learn as much as possible about surgery, I would stay late at night, come in on free weekends and do reading above and beyond the course requirements. Dr. Richard Selzer was a senior assistant resident on my first surgical rotation and taught me the very basics of surgery, starting with how to scrub my hands before operations. Even though he became a well-known author of such books as *Mortal Lessons*, he was not too talkative on my first day in the operating room. As I was scrubbing my hands, all he said was, "Just remember, each finger has four sides. Make sure you get them all." It must have been a bad day for him, and he did eventually become more talkative. I was fortunate to spend time with him since he was a good teacher with a dry sense of humor, somewhat cynical, but fun to be with. It was also good to have him as a friend after he'd given up the active practice of surgery in favor or writing in the basement of the Beinecke Rare Book Library.

Doctors Lindskog, Hayes and Glenn, the three major professors of surgery, were inspiring, each in his own way.

Dr. Gustaf Lindskog, the chairman of the surgery department, was one of the pioneers in surgery of the lungs and chemotherapy of tumors. His stern and calm demeanor was similar to my father's. They probably had the same Swedish/Baltic DNA. Many felt uncomfortable in his presence, but as a father figure he inspired confidence and you knew exactly where you stood with him. If you were up to speed with the work in his seminar, he knew it, and if not, it was probably the end of your hopes for a surgical career. At surgical group rounds on Saturday mornings he walked in at exactly 8:00 a.m. and would sit in the front row, in the last seat on the right, next to the entrance door to the Farnam auditorium. As a student, intern or resident you were expected to arrive in a clean and starched white coat - before 8:00. Coming in late was unacceptable. If Dr. Lindskog was seated, you would not dare come in, but if you did, you'd be greeted with his steady blue-eyed gaze, marking you for life as disorganized, unreliable, and unsuited for surgery. Happily, I did not "screw up" and was the beneficiary, along with David Skinner, of one of his top two letters of recommendation, a ticket to any of the major surgical internships and residencies after medical school. It was truly meaningful to receive from him, many years later, the occasional hand-written note of encouragement or remarks about a mutual friend or patient. My feelings in his regard were Hippocratic to say the least - "to hold him who has taught me this art as equal to my parent." The interview with him at the end of my surgical clerkship was also different, and most of it was spent discussing the recently published, somewhat scandalous French book *Bonjour Tristesse* by the 18-year-old Francoise Sagan. I was lucky to have read it, but his bringing it up was a total surprise, something I might have expected from one of the professors of psychology, gastroenterology, dermatology or ophthalmology. But there it was with "Gus," - the stern, the remote. He was and remains a major figure in my life and my surgical career. Many years later, I felt fortunate to be able to honor him by giving some funds to the Yale Medical School Library for a small reading room in his name.

Mark Hayes was a professor of general or abdominal surgery. He complemented Lindskog. There was nothing stern or remote about Dr. Hayes. He was a friendly, talkative, "nice guy." He was the one who found the jobs for the residents who'd been eliminated in the pyramidal teaching program which started with 14 interns and five years later finished with only one chief resident. Those cut along the way, without any commentary by Dr. Lindskog, went to Dr. Hayes for future plans and he would always be able to counsel them, be sympathetic, understanding and above all get them superb jobs at other institutions. I had many conversations with him, and upon my return from Vietnam he sponsored me for fellowship in the American College of Surgeons before I completed my specialty boards in orthopaedics.

William Glenn was the professor of cardiovascular surgery. He was a major contributor to the evolution of cardiac surgery in the 1950s. There was nothing flamboyant about William Wallace Lumpkin Glenn ("Willy Lump Lump Glenn," as we called him, imitating cardiac sounds he might have been describing). He tended to be quiet, his operative style was slow, but he was highly respected for his work and for the research he was promoting. He had been a pioneer in several areas of early heart surgery and his cardiac membrane oxygenator was unique. He also tried to convince me that I should become a cardiac surgeon, and I considered it very seriously. He wanted me as a medical student on the first official open-heart operation, with his membrane oxygenator, at Yale. With the dean's permission, I was allowed to leave my pediatric clerkship for a week and go back to cardiac surgery for that historic operation. I was number 17 on the team, in charge of lights and cameras. It was also my job to do a complete medical student workup of the patient with a four-page handwritten note in the chart. The operation went well, and Dr. Glenn performed it efficiently and in good time. The patient did well, and it was the beginning of a new era in Yale cardiac surgery. Even though I did not go into cardiac surgery, I continued to have a close student/mentor relationship with Dr. Glenn for the rest of his life and felt very honored when he chose me to replace his wife's hip at Waterbury Hospital. It was yet another Hippocratic moment.

My most profound exposure to general surgery, gynecology, urology and cancer care came with my thesis work with John McLean Morris, Princeton man and general surgeon, who had trained at Harvard and had served in WWII as a surgeon. Even though he was a general surgeon, he was on the Yale faculty as a professor of gynecology in charge of cancer surgery. The radical operations he was performing had much appeal and were reminiscent of some of the stories of major abdominal operations performed by my father. The pelvic exenterations he was performing for advanced cancers were dramatic and covered the fields of gynecology, intestinal and urological surgery. At the time of my study of these patients, new radiological advances were also being made. "Movies" of angiograms, barium enemas and intravenous pyelograms were being developed. One of our studies concerned the effectiveness of the Mathisen Nipple urethral implantation, which in theory was supposed to prevent reflux of colonic contents into the kidney. Our study showed the Mathisen to be ineffective, which turned out to be the subject of my first presentation at a national surgical conference, the 1959 Congress of the American College of Surgeons in Atlantic City. I did it, but it was a terrifying experience to be excused from my duties as surgical intern at Roosevelt Hospital long enough to drive to Atlantic City and give a talk to the more than 1,000 surgeons, professors and Fellows of the College of Surgeons facing me in the darkness of the auditorium. I am sure it was edifying in the long run, but I was happy to be going back to New York as soon as I was finished. It had been a great experience to work with Dr. Morris and to be exposed to the ultimate in intestinal, urological and gynecological surgery, but at the end of it, I came to the conclusion I did not want to be a general surgeon, urologist or gynecological cancer specialist. Neurosurgery was never of interest, thus my final specialty choices were cardiac or orthopaedic surgery. The question was settled once and for all upon Dr. Wayne O. Southwick's arrival at Yale in the fall of 1958.

Dr. Southwick, the new Chief of the Orthopaedic Section in Doctor Lindskog's Department of Surgery, took our class by storm. He was only 10 years older than most of us, full of life, enthusiastic about teaching in the rapidly expanding field of orthopaedic surgery. He was different from the other professors we had encountered. He seemed to enjoy being with us in the hospital and at Pepe's Pizzeria, which in 1958 was only a block away, behind the Yale School of Nursing dormitory. He had many stories to tell about the pioneering work he had seen in orthopaedics while doing innovative spine surgery with Dr. Robinson at Johns Hopkins. He also told us tales of his service as a surgeon with the Marines during the Korean War. He encouraged all of us to think on our own. Residents on his service were given freedom to do different operations through different approaches and to be prepared to do the operation with or without total supervision by an attending senior surgeon. It all seemed in the best of the Yale system traditions with historic themes from Johns Hopkins, Halsted and Cushing. "YOYO" - You're On Your Own" was the word.

Think outside of the box. "You can do it, Kris" was the refrain.

Having lived through a war, heard about war surgery since childhood and studied its history with Drs. Forbes and Fulton in the Yale Medical Historical Library, I was excited by Dr. Southwick's images and teaching of the basic management of war wounds. All of us knew we would probably spend some time in the military and could be in a war zone, taking care of casualties. Six years later in Vietnam, his teachings on "saving life and limb" were the foundation of my work in and later my own efforts to pass it on to the next generations of surgeons through local, national and international lectures and publications. Debridement, immobilization of the extremity and delayed closure of the debrided wounds had all been passed down to me by Dr. Southwick. Orthopaedics was also emerging from what had been a specialty dealing with deformities to be treated with casts and braces in crippled children to a vast field of spine surgery, reconstruction of the joints and new methods of operative fracture fixation. It was a specialty that was dealing with the musculoskeletal system from the head to the toes, with men and women, children and the old. As general surgeons were isolating themselves to abdominal surgery, they no longer were trained nor interested in fracture surgery. In the 1960s, there were still a few old general surgeons and family practitioners in smaller hospitals who were taking care of fractures, but they were a rarity. By 1970, all work on bones, joints, muscles and ligaments had passed on to the hands of orthopaedic surgeons.

Reconstructive surgery, osteotomies, the decompression of spinal cords and spine fusions were exciting, but there was also great satisfaction in taking care of major fractures. The patient arrived in the hospital near death, in severe pain, with a deformed leg and an X-ray showing a broken femoral shaft. After the appropriate life-saving measures and the nailing of the fracture, the pain was gone, the leg was normal looking, X-rays showed the bone to be fixed and the patient was ready to go home. The whole process was visible, palpable, dramatic, and most of the patients did well. It was a positive experience for both the patient and surgeon. It was the way for me to go, and Dr. Southwick was the ultimate enthusiastic mentor to make orthopedic surgery, from the meticulous dissection of the cervical spine to the fixation of major fractures, my lifetime choice. It was the right choice without regrets. It was Dr. Southwick's enthusiasm and encouragement ("You can do it, Kris.") that won the day, proving Dr. Gardner in anatomy had been correct in assuming my future would be in orthopedic surgery. In those early years of the specialty there were no power tools and some physical strength and endurance was required. The acetabulums, the femoral shafts, all had to be reamed by hand. The osteotomies were done with handheld drills, chisels and a mallet. The application of a body cast was a workout. Thank you, Dr. Gardner, and, above all, thank you, Dr. Southwick for pointing me in the right direction.

As we talk about height and size, all of us on the larger side of those statistics had to deal with Dr. Averill Liebow, professor of pathology, great teacher, a world-class authority on pulmonology pathology, an amazing mind and a "character" of the first order. He had the ability to remember every student by last and first name and had studied their general background. He was also of short stature – 5 feet, 6 inches at the most - and he made a point of saying his height was that of the "normal" male. The rest of us who were taller could draw our own conclusions if we wanted to, but as far as he was concerned, 6 feet, 3 inches was very abnormal. We all knew about his views, and in the first lectures with him, those of us in the "abnormal" category would try to hide in the back rows of the auditorium, but to no avail. Within the first few minutes of the lecture, I was targeted: "Dr. Kristaps Keggi, yes, you, in the back row, stand up!" After a few words on the height of the normal male, Kristaps would then undergo a barrage of questions. That was one way to learn pathology and it was anything but a comfortable experience. Whenever in his vicinity, be it in class or anywhere in the medical school, I tried hard not to stand next to him. If the situation as unavoidable, I tried to bend my knees and squat to make sure that *he* did not feel uncomfortable. In one of the small seminars on microscopic pathology, I made the error of asking Dr. Liebow for help in identifying a strange cell, assuming he would look into the microscope from his lesser height, without sitting down in front of it - big mistake. "Stand up, Dr. Keggi," he commanded, and as I stood and he sat he looked up and before answering any questions, made his point again: "The trouble with you, Kristaps Keggi, is that you are too damn big!" So much for political correctness, but somehow we loved and respected him. All of us who had him as a teacher are better physicians because of him, having learned how to deal with "discomfort" and then move on. He was also very interested in the history of medicine. During the rest of my years in school and residency, before his departure for San Diego, he no longer picked on me, and I remember many very friendly moments with him. I learned much more than pathology from Professor Averill Liebow.

There are many memories of those four years in medical school, but some stand out. My first repair of a laceration in the emergency room is one of them. The patient was a middle-aged male with a cut on his arm.

It was a clean wound and not too deep. It required a few sutures to approximate the subcutaneous fat and no more than 10 nylon ones to bring together the skin edges. I had been on the emergency room rotation for a few days and had watched several laceration repairs and the resident in charge of the emergency room thought I was ready to do the work on my own. I was offered the opportunity to perform. I was left alone with the patient and advised to call for help if I thought such was needed. An hour later, it was done – the skin prep, the draping, the local anesthesia, the subcutaneous sutures, the skin closure and dressing. My patient watched it all and came to the conclusion that "this must have been your first operation." He had been a "patient patient" and at the end of it he gave me a dollar bill for my efforts. He inscribed it, wishing me luck and a successful career. I carried that dollar bill in my wallet for years, but when wallets were replaced by money clips, the bill was delegated to old documents and papers. As inscribed by that patient in the spring of 1958, that dollar stood by me during many of my future operations.

There was also one of the longest, if not the longest, case performed on the Yale cardiovascular surgical service. It was before the introduction of Dr. Glenn's membrane oxygenator and the first open heart case. The chief residents, with guidance from Dr. Bill Bloomer, a relatively young assistant professor, undertook the repair of a large aortic aneurysm. A human cadaver donor graft of the proximal aorta with all its vessels was somehow available. It was to be sutured into place, bypassing the aneurysm. The operation started on a Friday morning and was successfully completed by noon on Saturday. It was a football weekend, and in the course of this marathon operation I brought in Steve Gurney, one of my Scroll and Key classmates, to see the action. He was able to handle it and was impressed by the sight of the patient's heart and lungs totally exposed by the incision and the chest wall dissection required to do the work. All was well until about the 10th postoperative day when the patient died suddenly while having a tracheal aspiration by his private-duty nurse who was getting ready for a duty shift. That was in the days when there were no specialized intensive care units with physicians and other experienced personnel to deal with major medical crises. The anesthesiologist on this longest case was Arto Abrahamian, who had been my mentor during my two weeks on anesthesia. Arto eventually left New Haven and came up to Waterbury Hospital, where he remained on staff for at least 25 years. Arto had emigrated from Armenia and was a great Harvard-trained anesthesiologist. He was fun and a good man. In addition to his superb medical skills, he was also known for his humor of the very "earthy" kind. Being of a Renaissance/Rabelaisian inclination, I enjoyed them and still remember many of them. They were good ones but must be extremely careful about telling them in our days of absolute correctness. It has taken some courage to even mention them in this text. It is a confession, and I hope, you who read this, will not be offended by the inappropriate, occasional laughs I have had over the years. Forgive me.

A few more memorable thoughts come to mind as I think about medical school, and my clerkship on internal medicine is one of them. It was my first rotation of the third year, and it started at the West Haven Veterans Hospital. One of the great sights from the upper floors of the hospital was the construction of the interstate highway below (I-95). It was to open sometime later in the year. It was a part of the major interstate highway system brought into being by President Eisenhower and

Connecticut's Senator Prescott Bush, the father of our first Bush president. It was the beginning of a new era of travel in the United States. The fall of 1957 was also the beginning of a new era in space. The Russians, much to the surprise of the entire world, launched "Sputnik," the first satellite. As we were trying to learn medicine at the Veterans Hospital, we could tune into our radios to hear Sputnik's beep – beep – beep as it circled the Earth. As our politicians tuned into this Communist achievement, the space race was on and 12 years later we had an American on the moon. As with the interstate highway system, it is now impossible to imagine life without satellites, space stations and plans to go to Mars.

It was all very exciting, but we were there to learn medicine and Tom Amatruda was there to make sure we did. Tom was to finish his career as the Director of Medicine at Waterbury Hospital, where we were good friends, but at the VA in 1957, he was a demanding, no-nonsense assistant professor. Every detail of a patient's illness was reviewed in terms of basic physiology, biochemistry, pharmacology and pathology. If I know or ever knew any biochemistry, it was due to Amatruda. As students, we would not dare present a case to him without having reviewed it at the most basic level. The time on his service was tough, even uncomfortable, but very constructive. There were no shortcuts such as we took in the biochemistry lab where we would combine ourselves in teams of 12 to do the experiments supposed to be done in groups of three - one of us would do the math and another mix the chemicals, etc. (I was perfectly happy being the "dishwasher" of the pipettes, beakers and all other equipment.) But, now, we were dealing with live patients and Amatruda made sure we knew that biochemistry was not an exotic, incomprehensible experiment, but the science essential in the treatment of many medical diseases. I got the message, but for the rest of my surgical career felt fortunate I could stop a sudden hemorrhage in a deep wound without having to remember such basic biochemistry as the Krebs Cycle.

Most of us male students were looking forward to obstetrics and gynecology clerkship. We had lived with women all of our lives and knew they were different, but now we were going to get all the facts and answers to all the questions we may have had about them. We were familiar with the basics. God had taken one of Adam's ribs to create Eve (obviously stem cells). Eve scheming with the snake, harassed Adam into biting the apple, causing their expulsion from paradise and all of our subsequent human imperfection. We had learned about women in literature and we had girls as friends and girlfriends. We had dissected the female pelvis in anatomy, but this was going to be different - and it was, starting with the first pelvic exam. ("Doctor, you are going to do what? You are so . . . young!" or, "You are so good looking, you cannot do this to me!") There were, of course, the sad cancer patients that I studied with Dr. Morris, but even though I was very interested in their tumors and the surgery they were having, I could not imagine myself as a gynecologist. Obstetrics was exciting, with its true miracle of birth, the baby's first cry, the meaning of life and love – it was all there. The sudden surgical emergencies to save the lives of both mother and child seemed challenging and exciting, but not exciting enough to deal with the rest, which included the pros and cons of abortions. On a lighter note, even the sudden gush of amniotic fluid, the shoes sloshing full of it, if you did not get out of the way fast enough was not fun. Ob-Gyn was an important chapter in our education, but not a life I wanted to pursue.

Men and women, women and men. There are things we do equally well, or poorly, as the case may be, but there are differences above and beyond the obvious physical ones that on occasion are hard to comprehend. What do you do as a surgeon when one of your best female colleagues starts crying in the middle of a case discussion, conference or even a major operation? I have chosen to wait for the crisis and tears to subside, move on and look at the positive, but wonder about it on a biological, philosophical and practical level. We are frequently told to think of our "feminine side" and are "toxic males" if we do not show it. There is no question about intellect and surgical skills, and some women have been the best of our residents. I also take pride of encouraging the first (as far as I know) female graduate of the Yale School of Medicine, Mary Williams (Clark), Class of 1967, to become an orthopaedic surgeon. Unfortunately, we missed her for our residency program, but a few years later I was privileged to be on the Admissions Committee that accepted African-American Claudia Thomas as our first female resident. Mary and Claudia and most of their feminine successors have been superb (the same "superb" ratio as our male residents), but they *are* different - so as they say in France, "Vive la difference!"

Speaking of which, in our second and third year of medical school we learned about the feminine hormonal cycles. Let's just say that the teaching back in 1957 was different. It would probably be considered offensive and inaccurate today. The first introductory lecture on the subject by Dr. John McL. Morris started with the statement that women, like female monkeys, are not supposed to have menstruations nor hormone induced emotional fluctuation. They were meant to be copulating at all times, and any ovum produced would be immediately fertilized by a sperm deposited there by these regular and continuous sexual encounters. It would be interesting to hear a debate on this subject between some of our professors from the past and those from the present generation. As students, we listened, we read, we talked to our patients, we learned how to examine them, but most of us have come to the conclusion that women are our absolute equals, but different and occasionally incomprehensible. They are our grandmothers, mothers, our wives and our daughters. They nurtured and taught us. They were in charge of our families, and many of them also achieved success in the sciences, literature and art.

Among the women in my own family, my grandmother as a young woman at the end of the 19th century was a writer and did not think she had time for a husband until she fell in love with Grandfather Ludwigs Berzins at the age of 25 and went on to have a family of six children. Since her own mother's death when she was 15, she had also been running the Smidhen family farm and estate. Grandfather may have been a famous writer, folklorist, national leader, teacher and theologian, but she was in charge of the family and life as they knew it, including good times, some very bad ones, two world wars, flights from Latvia and finally life in a foreign country at the age of 70. She was bright, loving and practical. She loved all of us and we loved her, but she could also be tough. I think of her every night and every morning when the words she taught me, while I stayed with her, always come to mind. In the morning it is, "Wash the sleep out of your eyes and go," at night, "Now wash your hands and go to bed."

Mother Ruta was on her way to a doctorate in education when she married, and, even though her career was interrupted by four sons, war and resettlement in the United States, she continued to write, edit a scholarly journal dealing with Latvian education and produce a major book on her father's life and works.

Aunt Irene was an accomplished artist and singer who had studied opera in Milan. She continued as a teacher of voice and organist in Caracas. She was the director of the Venezuelan National Choir until her late eighties. Her paintings and watercolors were also of very high artistic quality.

Aunt Ina, wife of mother's brother Andris, was a physician who settled in Colorado in her forties, passed all the appropriate examinations and practiced medicine the rest of her life.

Our daughters have been world class athletes with successful careers. I have encouraged them to pursue their goals as they have seen them. I love them and I respect them.

There had never been any question in my mind about feminine "inferiority;" we are the same but different. If anything, the opposite may be true as you think about the biological task and responsibility of bearing and nurturing children with all of its implications. As men we often do not think about the complexities of carrying and bringing a child into life. As men, without those biological complexities, we march through a simpler adolescence and life. Endless books have been written on the subject and as we deal with it on a daily basis, we must appreciate it.

In my years as a student and surgeon, I have encountered many superb women of great achievements. Dorothy Horstmann, a famous Yale professor who made her way through a male world in the 1940s and 1950s to become one of the greatest virologists of her era, interviewed me for admission to the Yale Medical School. I still think of it as one of the high points of my life. It was also wonderful to have her as a friend as my life at Yale and in surgery proceeded on a path she had predicted. From our first encounter, she thought I would be a good surgeon and I am happy to have lived up to her expectations. I also had the pleasure of meeting Barbara Stimpson, a Vassar graduate with Yale and Scroll and Key family connections, who was the first woman to become a fracture surgeon on the Columbia University staff and enlisted in the British Army at the beginning of WWII because the American Medical Corps did not accept women. She served with distinction as a surgeon in North Africa, Italy and England. She is unique and has not received the recognition she deserves among women in orthopaedics. Her uncle, Henry Stimpson, Secretary of War under Roosevelt, was much embarrassed when she came to visit him in her British Major's uniform. It was interesting to hear her stories, told in the gruff old voice of a habitual smoker. She was a great woman who had been brought up by her father, a Congregational Minister with four daughters, who encouraged them not to be intimidated by jobs or careers thought to be for men only. Definitely a pioneer in her field.

There have been many women in our program and on my service. There has never been any question about their competence. It has been good to work with them and to teach them. I will continue to encourage my granddaughters to be physicians and surgeons if that is their choice. Both of them would be very good ones. Times have changed and half the graduating medical doctors are now women. Many are or will be leaders in the field, practice superb medicine or surgery and do research at the highest of levels.

SURGICAL TRAINING

At the end of three years of medical school, it was time to start thinking about the next step. Decisions about specialty training and internships had to be made. It was absolutely clear in my mind I was headed into a surgical career and its beginning would have to be the best possible internship in a city or part of the country that would be best suited for Julie and me. Even though I was encouraged to apply to the Harvard programs, I could not imagine myself in the Boston/Harvard environment. I considered such hospitals as Cook County in Chicago and Charity in New Orleans, both with the reputation of allowing even their interns to perform major operations, but settled on Roosevelt Hospital in New York. Michael Hume, one of our younger professors of surgery at Yale, had trained there and was extremely enthusiastic about it. The hospital had been founded in 1842 by surgeons and it had been a training ground for some of the great names in American surgery – Sims, McBurney, Halstead and Cushing, among others. It was a hospital that was still run by superb surgeons with patients such as the Duke of Windsor coming there for their operations. Half of the hospital was for the care of these private patients and the other was devoted to the indigent, non-paying patients. Interns and residents would scrub with the best of New York surgeons, watch their work and then, under the supervision of senior residents, try to perform at their level. The "esprit de corps" seemed great.

Roosevelt's trauma center was located on the West Side of Manhattan, near the docks and Time Square. That rough part of town had much appeal to those of us interested in maximizing our surgical skill by taking care of major accidents and gunshot wounds. Julie had some doubts about being in Manhattan, but accepted it and had one-and-a-half good years working as a reference librarian in a large advertising company and enjoying the best of the city's museums, ballets and shows. July 1, 1959 would be the start of two great years of general surgical training.

At Yale, we were finished with medical schoolwork at the end of May and decided not to attend graduation in favor of a three-week motor trip to the west. Julie's brother, Joe, was getting married in Colorado Springs, which was our primary destination, but we drove as far west as Yellowstone National Park and Mount Rushmore, where, under the gaze of Presidents Washington, Jefferson, Teddy Roosevelt and Lincoln, we had our first buffalo meat hamburgers. We covered a lot of Indian territory, visited friends in Iowa and Julie's grandmother in Milwaukee. It was a great trip, a good way to finish formal schooling and start life in surgery. On that trip, it was also strange to be addressed, for the first time in life, as Doctor Keggi and on written documents to add M.D. to my signatures and name.

We got back east in time to move into our Manhattan penthouse before the start of the internship. It was probably one of the smallest penthouses in town, but a penthouse all the same. From its terrace between two apartment buildings, it even had a narrow view of the Hudson River. The bedroom was big enough to hold one king-size mattress. It was wall to wall "mattressing." The kitchenette and living room were adequate and we were excited about the prospect of spending time on the terrace until it became clear, in a matter of minutes, that it was not going to be the case because of the huge flakes of soot coming down from all the surrounding apartment house chimneys. With the exception of the soot, it was a perfect spot. The penthouse was on West End Avenue, just south of West 72nd Street, and was arranged for us by the superintendent of the building who was a Latvian and one of my father's patients. My father's office and the family apartment were around the corner on West 72nd Street, so I was familiar with the area. It was within walking distance of Roosevelt Hospital and a short bus or subway ride to work for Julie.

The two years at Roosevelt Hospital passed quickly. The surgical training was excellent and in line with its long history of surgical education. There was little or no basic research. Your promotion to a higher status in the residency was based on your clinical and surgical skills. I felt highly rewarded when, at the end of my internship year, I was asked to take over a rotation normally handled by a second-year resident. It was the emergency room rotation, where, as a member of the surgical staff, even a junior one, you were responsible for everything that went on in that department while you were on duty. In moments of crisis or major emergencies, you as the surgeon issued orders while all others, including more senior internists or pediatricians, followed them. If your actions were correct, you had the full support of the chiefs of surgery who were the chiefs of the hospital. You were in charge and treated, if you felt qualified, any patient who arrived in the emergency room, be it on foot, police car or ambulance. More senior residents were always available in consultation, but you were encouraged to deal with as many problems as possible without bothering others. If you could set the minor fractures, suture lacerations, deal with ankle sprains and locked knees, you did so, and then sent the patient to the appropriate clinics in follow-up. If a patient came in with a major injury, such as a traumatic amputation after being run over by a subway train, you started the life-saving work while awaiting further help from more senior residents. It was amazing work for me to be doing at the age of 25.

Another dramatic part of the rotation were the calls for on-site medical assistance by the police in cases of major trauma, accidents, shootings and obstetrical emergencies such as the delivery of babies in a car or on a dirty rug in a decrepit apartment. Being called to the scene of a shooting was a good introduction to my future Vietnam scene, while dealing with an elevator full of people caught between floors at the height of a heat wave had all the overtones of a truck full of illegal immigrants dying in the heat of a Texas July. At that time, anyone found dead on the street or anywhere else had to be pronounced dead by a physician before being moved to the Bellevue Hospital city morgue. I'd be taken by a police ambulance to wherever the dead body had been found. I was on that duty roster during the spring of 1960 when the waters in the Hudson River were warming and the bodies of those who had fallen or had been dumped during the winter were decaying and starting to float to the surface. These "floaters" were brought ashore to the West Side docks to await the official pronouncement of their demise by one of us from the hospital. The official record required the documentation of a complete examination, with notes all on heart sounds, respirations, pulses and pupils. The floaters did not need any of that since you could smell death as soon as you were deposited at the entrance to the dock. I was also once called to the most fashionable duplex apartment on 5th Avenue to pronounce its aged owner – attired in an elegant suit, white shirt and stylish tie - dead in his easy chair with a spilled drink next to his lifeless hand dangling over the side of the chair. At the other end of the social spectrum was a dead woman in a flophouse hotel, just west of Time Square. You could imagine her 50 years earlier as an attractive young singer or dancer coming to New York to seek a brilliant life on the stage, but ending it in solitude and poverty, discovered only after her neighbors hadn't seen her for a week or more and had become aware of an unusual smell coming from her room. Life and death in New York.

As interns, we were observed and gradually allowed to do some real surgery. It started with making skin incisions for operations to be performed by a more senior resident. That might not seem like a major task, but I remember the sensation of sliding a scalpel across the skin for the first time, scared about going too deep, slipping, making the cut too long or plunging into the abdominal cavity. Typically, these first cuts would be tentative, to be repeated two or three times before getting through the skin and encountering blood. Most of us learned fast, but there are those who, many years later, still make incisions as if they were first year interns. I have had the experience of trying to teach some of our "academically" best and "numbers smart" residents in their third year of training how to make a skin incision, how to feel the thickness of the skin with the knife by finally putting my hand over theirs to guide it into an uncertain surgical future, with frustrations, stress, early heart attacks and premature retirement. At Roosevelt, most of us progressed quickly and were doing inguinal hernia repairs and appendectomies early in our first year of surgery. I was allowed to do my first appendectomy on one of my off-duty nights. It was a memorable evening after a wineless dinner with Julie in a nearby restaurant.

My very first "operation," was a D&C (uterine dilatation and curettage) on the gynecology service. It was my first rotation in the summer of 1959. The chief resident, whom I had observed on some previous D&Cs, felt I was ready to do one on my own. The patient was an 18-year-old who claimed to have missed two menstrual periods and was now having spontaneous vaginal bleeding. The most likely source of the "spontaneous" bleeding was one of the abortionists in the area or the hotel across the street, who would have started the bleeding with the proverbial coat hanger and then sent the patient to the hospital to have the procedure completed in the safer environment of an operating room by an trained surgeon (me!) employing sterile instruments, good anesthesia and, if necessary, blood transfusions. We took my patient to the operating room where I dilated the cervix, inserted the proper curettes and scraped out some non-specific bloody tissue. At the end of my curettage, the chief resident made a few passes at the uterus with a curette of his own and concluded we had done our job. The patient went home the same day, and all seemed well until she returned a few days later and wanted to show me something. Wrapped in some handkerchiefs was a small human being no more than 2 inches long, complete with a head, a face, arms and legs. It was both sad and educational. We had obviously taken part in the termination of the life of that small being and it brought to mind all the moral, religious, philosophical and legal issues of abortion. I think of this 18-year-old single girl and her child every time these matters are discussed. My conclusion, then and now, is that abortion is the pregnant woman's choice. It was her right to have the abortion, but I am glad to have had a career in hip replacements.

From a purely surgical training experience, it was a

lesson learned. We seemingly had done everything right but had failed. For the rest of my surgical life, with every operation I have undertaken, I have been aware of potential failure and trying hard to avoid it. Post-operative hematoma, infection or dislocation was always a possibility, a reality to be recognized and handled as well as possible. With every operation there always had to be an exit strategy in case of major disaster. I thought of it as I scrubbed my hands in preparation for every incision, then put it in the back of the mind to do the primary job as smoothly as possible. I enjoyed conversation and even some jokes during operations, but liked to scrub by myself, without distracting chit-chat while thinking about the operation about to be performed and all its alternatives. That first operation was also a lesson in dealing with complications, then moving on to do it better. Steve Southwick has written about it – "resiliency" is the word that probably best applies to it, living with victory and defeat on a regular basis. Not surprisingly, some of our greatest surgeons have been athletes in their formative years - Halsted with Yale football and Cushing with Yale baseball are but two of the most memorable surgeon-athletes. I am sure Harvard and Princeton can come up with some names, too, but in these "Memoires" we have to give Yale the historic role it deserves.

It was all a superb learning experience. It was also fun assisting the outstanding surgeons on staff at Roosevelt. Max Chamberlain (University of Colorado football), one of the leaders in American pulmonary surgery, was an enthusiastic, skilled performer. His operations were in major contrast to the ones I had seen at Yale. He would do three thoracotomies in the time it took to do one in New Haven. He led a fast life and loved his work, and even went so far as to call himself "Lucky Max." He loved to teach us male residents but had much greater enthusiasm for the student nurses. When I was the second or third assistant on one of his cardiac cases, it was the young nurse who got all the attention and whose finger he guided into the patient's heart to feel the constricted mitral valve. He died as he had lived, crashing his sports car on Cape Cod. All those who knew him thought it an appropriate demise of a fast life in the fast lane.

Assisting as a second or third assistant to the world-class hand surgeon, William Littler, was also an experience to remember. If lucky, you were allowed to cut the sutures meticulously placed by him and tied by his first assistant. They all had to be cut the exact same length, and if you could not do it right you did not do it at all. I was somewhat tempted by life as a hand surgeon, but that temptation was quick to pass. The work I did with Dr. Littler and later in New Haven with Dr. Robert Chase was good enough to give me confidence in doing some major hand reconstruction with lepers in Vietnam and some lesser work on the clinic patients back at Yale and Waterbury Hospital. Dr. Littler also enjoyed being with us and would frequently come to our "liver rounds" on the top floor of the hospital on Friday afternoons.

Many others of superb surgical judgment and skills come to mind. Howard Patterson, one of the chiefs of the hospital who had been the commanding officer of the Roosevelt Hospital Unit with General Patton in North Africa and Italy, was great but did not have the showmanship of "Lucky Max" Chamberlain. He was from North Carolina and always addressed you as "boy," as in, "Do you hear me, boy?"

William Cassebaum was a general surgeon who specialized in the treatment of fractures. He was liked by all of us for his somewhat cynical view of the world, great honesty and vast experience with fractures and war wounds while in Africa and Italy. He was influential in my choice of orthopaedic surgery as a career. His commentaries on war wounds were also instructive, and I remembered them a few years later in War Zone D and in the Central Highlands of Vietnam.

Fred Thompson was one of the orthopaedic surgeons on the Roosevelt staff. He is known primarily for his hip prosthesis, and I had occasion to scrub with him on one of these procedures. The other was a hamstring tendon transfer which he completed with a drill I was sent to get from the trunk of his car halfway through the operation. It was sterilized and used with success, drilling a hole in the patient's femur, identical to whatever hole it had been drilling in Dr. Thompson's basement the previous day. The hip prosthesis he used was inserted through an anterior, muscle sparing approach, and I gave him full credit when talking about my work with that approach in total hip replacement surgery.

For two years, Roosevelt Hospital was a phenomenal experience, but once I had made the decision to become an orthopaedic surgeon, it was time to move on. The process had to start with an appointment with the chief, Howard Patterson. I knew it was going to be a hard encounter, since it had been made clear to me that I had been selected to continue general surgery training and practice at Roosevelt. I delayed the meeting for as long as possible, but finally had to face Dr. Patterson, not only chief of the hospital, but commanding officer of an Army hospital in WWII, past president of the American College of Surgeons and a staunch, Southern gentleman.

"Dr. Patterson, sir! After much thought and deliberation, I have decided to pursue a career in orthopaedics and would like your advice and recommendations."

"What do you want to do that for, boy?" - but after 20 minutes of trying to talk me out of my decision, he gave in. "Okay, boy, if that's what you really want to do, I want you to go to Special Surgery."

As he said that, he picked up his phone and called Tommy Thompson, who had been his tent mate in the war and was now the chief at the Hospital for Special Surgery.

"Tommy! I got this boy here who for reasons I don't understand wants to be an orthopaedic surgeon. Okay. take care!" Then, to me: "Boy, Tommy wants to see you now. Get into a cab and get your ass across town to meet with him."

"Thank you, sir!"

Twenty minutes later, I was sitting in Dr. Thompson's office. The interview was short, and I was told I could come into his residency program. There were, however, two caveats. First, I would not be able to start in July, and while waiting to start in January I would work in the lab on a research program. And second, at the end of three years of residency, if selected, I'd have to stay for another year as a "super chief resident." I had been accepted in a matter of minutes and it was a major opportunity in one of the very best programs in the land, but I had to say no. It would have meant that instead of finishing the three years of required training in the spring of 1964, I might be at Special Surgery until 1966. That seemed like a long time, and there were other opportunities. Our first child, Catherine, had just been born and life in Manhattan seemed difficult. Three years might have been tolerable, but five was impossible.

Dr. Patterson could not understand and was disappointed. I gave due consideration to offers from the Columbia Presbyterian program with Dr. Stinchfield and the Harvard Mass General Hospital, where I had the pleasure of meeting Dr. Barr, the innovator of herniated disc excisions. But, in March 1961, I decided to return to Yale and Dr. Southwick. Yale held the promise of intensive clinical work, research if desired and innovative surgery with much encouragement from Dr. Southwick. I was to be the first Yale graduate in his program. We also had the opportunity to move into a beautiful gardener's cottage on Killam's Point in Branford, where Julie could enjoy her passion for gardening in sight of Long Island Sound. It was an ideal spot for all of us - me, Julie, our new-born Catherine and Mara, who was to arrive at the Yale-New Haven Hospital a year later. It was all good, but there was turmoil at Yale, and for a few weeks our future seemed uncertain.

Shortly after my decision to return to Yale, Dr. Southwick was admitted to the hospital with a cardiac arrhythmia and many of my friends in New York, including Dr. Patterson, were commenting on it. They all thought I was making a very wrong decision about training at Yale, since Dr. Southwick would stop working or be dead in a matter of months. But my contacts in New Haven did not think it was a major issue and we (Julie and I) decided to stay the course. They were right. Dr. Southwick remained in active practice for another 40 years and died in 2016 at the age of 91. I was the first Yale Medical School graduate to join his program and have never regretted the decision to be one of his residents. It was always flattering to hear him comment and write about how lucky he was to have me back as a leader of his program.

At about the same time as Dr. Southwick's cardiac arrhythmia, there was also a scandal involving one of the Yale residents and some Yale-New Haven Hospital nurses, but it, too, was not significant enough to change our minds about returning to Connecticut, with its life on Killam's Point and a fixed three years of residency including an eight-month rotation at the Newington Children's Hospital, with its superb statewide attending staff and residents not only from Yale, Hartford and Dartmouth (their main affiliations) but also other programs throughout the United States.

Thus, on July 1, 1961, in spite of some of the controversies, we were back in Connecticut and Yale. The decision to leave New York was also reinforced by my last rotation at Roosevelt. Our first daughter, Catherine, had been born in February, and after making the decision to leave New York, we moved in with Julie's parents in Greenwich and I commuted to work by car. The early morning ride into the city was less than an hour, but in the late afternoon, on the way back to Greenwich, it would take at least an hour in bumper-to-bumper traffic to go from West 57th Street to the George Washington Bridge. The whole trip could be two hours. I did it for three months and it was the end of our life in the Big City.

My first rotation at Yale was at the West Haven Veterans Administration Hospital. Ben Bradburn, who had completed his surgical internship and a year of residency at Yale, two years of active duty in the Navy (some of it during our first Mideast crisis, with the Marines in Lebanon) and a year of orthopaedics with Dr. Southwick, was my "chief." It was fun working with him and it is fun to be with him many years later. He is a wonderful man with a great sense of humor. His primary interest then and in later life was hand surgery.

He spent as much time as possible with Dr. Robert Chase, who was rapidly becoming an academic hand surgeon of great stature and a few years later moved to California as the chairman of the surgery department at Stanford University. As a result of Ben's devotion to hand surgery, I was allowed to handle the "big stuff" - the hips, femurs, knees and spines. Doctor Southwick was the attending surgeon, but in his inimitable way, once he had established some faith in a resident's ability to operate, his presence in the operating room was neither guaranteed nor expected. We learned this early in our training, and, if "comfortable," accepted it with all of its responsibilities. It meant that the night before a major operation, you may or may not have seen before, you spent hours and hours reading about it in every textbook on hand. It also meant a review of the related anatomy, from skin to fascia, muscles, nerves and blood vessels to be encountered in the course of the operation the following morning. Dr. Southwick would tell us to get started and that he would be there, but that was a promise we could not count on and we had to be prepared to do it all on our own. In those days, all of us had considerably more operative experience than some of the later generations of residents with their regulated working hours. We were on call every other night and could be up without sleep for 24 hours or more. It could be demanding, but it meant greater hands-on surgical experience.

My first major case was an example of the Yale-Southwick system at its best, or worst, but probably unacceptable by any of our standards 60 years later.

The patient, Ben Butler, a relatively young African-American male, was admitted to our service with an advanced synovial sarcoma of the hip and his treatment was to be a hemipelvectomy. Ben Bradburn decided I should be the surgeon of record. Thus, in the middle of July 1961, at the age of 26, just two years and six weeks after getting out of medical school, I was to do a hemipelvectomy as my first major orthopaedic operation. Dr. Southwick was going to help but, as expected, Ben and I were on our own. I remember the night before the operation and the hours spent after baby Catherine had been put to bed, studying for the next day in the operating room. Everything went well without neurosurgeons, urologists, vascular and general surgeons looking over our shoulders. The patient did well and lived for several years after our work. It was the beginning of my orthopedic surgical life.

Dr. Ulrich Weil joined Dr. Southwick on the full-time faculty shortly thereafter and was a teacher of the highest order. His father had been the professor of orthopaedics in Breslau and Heidelberg, Germany. Ulrich had completed orthopedic residencies in Germany and at St. Raphael's Hospital in New Haven. His European education, interest in the history of orthopedics and knowledge of pediatric deformities was an asset for all of us trying to make sense of the various forms of dwarfism, for example. Ulrich's approach to teaching actual surgery was also unique. As opposed to Dr. Southwick, he would be there for the major operations we were performing but very, very rarely would he scrub in on our cases. His advice on what to do came from the "sidelines." It was reassuring to have him there, but we were the ones making the incisions, splitting the muscles, handling the drills and using the mallet. All of us respected and liked him. With my knowledge of German, we had a special bond and I was privileged, a few years later, to go with him to Baden Baden, Germany, one of the world's historic resorts in the Black Forest, to present a paper on club feet to one of the German orthopaedic societies and later published an article in the German orthopaedic literature on cervical vertebral body excisions. The resident who worked with me on the cervical spine paper was John Barrasso who, 20 years later, became a U.S. Senator from Wyoming. It was also through Ulrich that I was able to spend some time with Professor Endler, one of the "greats" in German orthopaedics. That visit to Vienna and to Professor Endler's country home in the Burgenland led to meetings with other Viennese surgeons. The Burgenland, land of the castles built to protect Christian Europe from the Muslim East, was the backdrop to a wonderful weekend of lengthy discussions on orthopaedics and history, in German, with one of the great surgeons of the day.

Back in Connecticut, another unusual story concerned a patient at the Veterans Hospital who had only one vertebral artery which would get occluded by an osteophyte whenever he extended his arthritic neck, causing him to faint. Angiography was getting sophisticated, and I was able to demonstrate his abnormality in precise detail and had come to the conclusion we should do an anterior decompression of the artery, excision of the offending osteophytes and an intervertebral body fusion pioneered by Doctor Southwick and his mentor at Johns Hopkins, Doctor Robinson. As far as we knew, this had never been done before, but having researched every conceivable study on vertebral artery surgery in the Yale Medical Library (no computerized searches in those days), I felt our plan to help this patient was sound, and it met with Dr. Southwick's approval. We scheduled the operation. Dr. Southwick said he would be there, and he did arrive after we had completed the decompression of the vertebral artery and were getting ready to put the bone graft in the prepared intervertebral space. In retrospect, it all sounds a little crazy to be decompressing a patient's only vertebral artery while still in training, without any precedent in the medical literature, but it made sense, we did it, it worked and we had saved the patient from sudden death or a major brainstem stroke. It also led me and some medical students into further studies on the vertebral arteries and the blood supply of the cervical spine.

Dr. Southwick's insistence on operating with minimal instruments was also of help in all my future operations. As residents, we were expected to do our work with a set of instruments identical to the ones he had used with the Marines in the Korean War. If he had been able to do major wound debridements in the midst of war and chaos with only a few simple instruments, we could do civilian fractures without an endless number of fancy retractors, hooks, levers, clamps and, more recently, three-dimensional reconstructions of the fracture images, computerized navigation and robots. That philosophy also had its benefits later as I worked in the tents of the 3rd Surgical Hospital in Vietnam and even later as I performed extensive procedures throughout the Soviet Union without the luxuries of our operating rooms in Waterbury and New Haven. I am certain it would have been a frightening if not an impossible task without that early "Wayne-O" training. Wayne O. Southwick was an extraordinary man. He was an inspiring teacher and great surgeon who loved to work with us. The operations we performed, with or without him, went well and I cannot recall any disasters - we had to know what we were supposed to do. He had his faults, but we loved and respected him. It was an era of rapid growth of surgery and surgical specialties. He created Yale Orthopedics, and Gary Freidlaender, one of his residents, then went on to establish a university department that produced some of the best teachers, research and clinical care in the world. Under their leadership we have produced more chairs of university orthopaedic departments than any other program in the land. Doctors Southwick and Friedlaender were also very supportive of my work in spine and joint surgery at Waterbury Hospital, as well as my resident training, work with foreign fellows and educational activities from Latvia on the Baltic Sea, through Moscow to Vladivostok on the Pacific Ocean.

Doctor Southwick was also a talented sculptor, with one of his major sculptures, featuring a couple of our orthopaedic residents playing basketball, displayed on Cedar Street across from the entrance of the Brady auditorium, where we meet for lectures and Grand Rounds every Friday. Some of his other works can also be seen in our clinics and office in New Haven. I was very honored to be given, by Doctor Southwick himself, one of his bronze statues called "Gabriella Blowing Her Horn." It is one of our family's proudest possessions and, since 2008, has been in daughter Mara's garden overlooking the lives of her twin sons, daughter and the friendliest of dogs.

We also learned to pass on as much knowledge and as many skills as possible to the residents and students behind us. It may be oversimplified, but there was validity to the dictum of "See one, do one, teach one." Ben Bradburn, my senior in the residency, was a believer in this approach to teaching surgery and I was its beneficiary. Ben also lived next to us on Killam's Point in Branford and we spent eight months commuting from there to Newington Children's Hospital (still known in those years as the Newington Hospital for Crippled Children). Above and beyond his intellectual, teaching and surgical gifts, he had a great sense of humor which made for many good times as we traveled every conceivable back road between Branford and Newington in Ben's sporty MG, which had a tendency to break down unexpectedly but was always brought back to full life and function by his mechanical skills.

The eight months at Newington were not as demanding as the work in New Haven. We were on call approximately once per week and when there, the evenings and weekends were leisurely. Even though the television images were rather primitive, it was football on weekends and in the course of that rotation, I became a fan of the New York Giants, their quarterback Y. A. Tittle and linebacker Sam Huff. I had to give up the Giants a couple of years later, since you could not live in El Paso, Texas, without being a Dallas Cowboy football and cheerleader fan.

The fourth year of residency was also notable for daughter Mara's arrival in October. It always was and is good to be with the family. Good to be with Mara, her older sister Katie and mother Julie who, busy as she was with the kids, still enjoyed her Killam's Point garden, her early crocuses, daffodils, lilies, and the rest of the horticulture she had learned at Smith College. Like any family with two infants, the scene was chaotic at times, but easier than life would have been in a New York city apartment. Caroline, the youngest of our daughters, missed Killam's Point but became the first Texan in our family when she arrived in 1965.

At the end of the Newington rotation, I returned to New Haven as chief resident. It was my fifth year of residency and the third in orthopedics. During these years, we learned a lot of surgery while expressing great enthusiasm for the Southwick program and helping with the recruitment of new, superb residents, among them, Augustus White, the first African-American to be admitted into any Yale residency program. His academic career at Yale and Harvard was spectacular and his contributions to orthopaedics and musculoskeletal research incalculable.

In all, that fifth year of residency was superb. We were exposed to every major orthopedic operation, from the upper cervical spine down to bunions and hammertoes. With Dr. Southwick's expertise and leadership in spine and hip surgery, we had maximum exposure in these two fields. It is thus that I first thought of myself primarily as a spine surgeon, at least until 1983, when my total joint practice had become so active I could no longer do both and elected to give up the spine. By then I thought of myself as best suited to hip surgery. I had made some contributions in the field of cervical spine surgery, though, and many years later I still miss some of its challenges, but hip surgery was the right choice.

I was commissioned as a Second Lieutenant in United States Army Reserve Medical Service Corps after my second year of medical school and had been in the active reserve in New Haven with weekly training and summer camps while in my third and fourth year of medical school. During my residency years, I joined what was known as a Berry Plan and was on inactive reserve status. The Berry Plan was conceived by Dr. Frank Berry, a Yale graduate who had served in the Medical Corps during WWII. The plan aimed for the efficient military disposition and use of physicians. As a doctor, you could be drafted up to the age of 45 and, of course, out of your residency. It was not unusual for somebody who had spent three years in training in surgery to be drafted to end up as a general medical officer in a venereal disease clinic somewhere in the middle of nowhere. By volunteering for the Berry Plan, you were deferred for the duration of your training, but at the end of it, you were to go on active duty for two years with the Army, Navy or Air Force in your specialty. In this manner, the physicians in training were safe from being drafted and knew they would be doing their active duty as specialists in their field. The two years of military duty in your medical specialty were a wonderful transition from training/residency to active practice and gave you a chance to think about the future, life and where you, and how, you would spend it.

As "Berry Planners," we were encouraged to contact the military and express our preferences for the location of our service. My friends in the Army and my reserve unit encouraged me to be as proactive as possible, go to Washington in person and talk to the officers in charge of the active-duty assignments. Julie and I, having spent most of our lives in the northeast, thought it might be fun to be out west in Arizona or southern California. At Dr. Southwick's urging, I was still considering an academic career, and it seemed likely that after the two years of active duty, we would probably be back in an eastern university (Yale!). In order to serve in Japan or Europe, you had to volunteer for an extra year of active duty. By staying in the United States or being assigned to Korea, you only had to do two years. I chose the two years in America. That final year of residency was also a time of worldwide unrest and continued Communist expansion. The Korean War had been concluded without a final peace treaty. The fighting had stopped at the 30th parallel where further discussions about the fate of the two divided countries were to be held and are still held more than 60 years later. In Europe, the Communists were solidifying their position in Germany and eastern Europe. In Russia, they were developing nuclear weapons and ballistic missiles. China was in the midst of its "culture revolution," which meant the elimination of any possible resistance to Communist rule. Just south of China, there was Vietnam, the former French colony, which after the French defeat at Dien Bien Phu in 1954, had been "temporarily" divided, with the Communists in charge of the north and the south to become a democratic republic. The Communists, under the leadership of Ho Chi Minh, were, with support from Russia and China, now moving into the south. By 1964, the war was still in the hands of the South Vietnamese army with assistance from American military advisors and Special Forces units, but it did not seem to be going well. The war and how to deal with it was a topic of great debate in the United States and abroad. The presidential election of 1964 was the epicenter of the debate. Goldwater, the conservative Republican candidate, was depicted by the Democrats as a warmonger whose election would lead to a nuclear holocaust. The Democratic Party television ads against him always included the background of an atomic mushroom cloud. Thus Lyndon Johnson, the "Peace Candidate," was elected. His line of negotiations, halfhearted fighting and hope for peaceful solutions all failed, leading to another 10 years of war with more than 50,000 American soldiers killed and, in the end, a Communist takeover of the south. Nixon and American politics were heavily involved in the final collapse of our stand, but it started with Presidents Kennedy and Johnson.

In 1964, the future was uncertain, but life had to go on. There was no room for excessive concern about a future that could be bleak, to say the least. The unsettled issues of WWII, Germany, Korea and Vietnam were real, and my generation knew we might be doing military service that could include yet another combat zone. I had volunteered for the Army and was now ready for active duty and on my way to Washington to speak with the men in charge of my destiny. I had been told the Pentagon was the place to find the person overseeing orthopaedic surgeons, and that was my first stop. By comparison to life 60 years later, it is amazing how, without any security clearance, special identification or searches, I could simply walk into the Pentagon, go to an information desk and be directed to an office where somebody would be able to deal with my questions and assignment preferences. Everyone was very helpful, but when I got to the office that was supposed to be dealing with Berry Plan assignments in the main Pentagon, I was told I had to go to the "Navy" buildings on the other side of the Potomac River, not too far from the Halls of Congress. When I got there and found the office of the lieutenant colonel in charge of my future, I found him reading a paperback book with both feet on the desk. He seemed like a nice man and we had lengthy conversation about my training, my interests in academic medicine and my hope to be serving in the Southwest or California. There were no promises, but when my orders arrived a couple of months later, I was to report to the William Beaumont General Hospital in El Paso, Texas, without any extra time in San Antonio for training in the basics of military life (I had that covered while in the active reserve during the weekly drills and the four weeks of summer camp). I could not have been happier, since I was going from my position as clinical instructor at Yale and Chief Resident at the Grace New Haven Hospital to the teaching staff in one of the Army's orthopaedic residency programs in El Paso, on the Mexican border in the sunshine of the Southwest.

THE ARMY

For the time being, our life in Connecticut was coming to an end. The years of residency had been rewarding professionally and life on Killam's Point had been good for the whole family. Thanks to Julie's father's generosity, we had been members of the Pine Orchard Club in Branford, where Julie had been able to play golf and win the club championship. During her last month of pregnancy with Mara, she continued to play while scaring most of the membership with the possibility of a birth on the golf course. I played whenever possible, was pleased if I broke 90, but, above all, I enjoyed hitting long drives, reaching the par fives in two and wining a driving contest. Thinking now about my own musculoskeletal problems and arthritic hips, I remember how even then my left hip ached, clicked and crunched when I pivoted on it.

The Army made it relatively easy for us to pack up and move to El Paso. Movers were arranged and there was little to worry about except for the details of our own transportation. We had to make plans how to get out there and decided I would drive out first, and then Julie would fly out with the two girls once I had gotten there and found temporary quarters. On my way, I would also visit some orthopaedic centers, since an academic career after my two years of active military service still was a consideration.

The drive to El Paso would take a while, but I'd

become familiar with residency programs other than those at Yale, New York and Boston, and I was hoping to introduce myself to some of the leaders of these programs in case of a future wish to be in their geographic or clinical specialty areas. The plan was to stop at Johns Hopkins, Vanderbilt, The Campbell Clinic in Memphis, Ochsner Clinic in New Orleans and the University of Texas in Galveston.

Determined to do some research on the cervical spine, I went to the anatomy department at Yale and was allowed to excise and take with me at least 15 cervical spines. It did not require any special authorization from clinical research committees or other administrators. The cadavers the first-year students had dissected were, at the end of the academic year, routinely cremated together, with the ashes then buried somewhere in "holy ground." The cadavers and tissues dissected now, 60 years later, are cremated individually and the ashes, if desired, returned in an urn to the family. This latter way of handling human remains is dignified and best, but certainly more complex than their disposal in 1964. The cervical spines had been well embalmed, and it was simply a matter of wrapping them in plastic baggies for transportation to Texas in the trunk of our new white Pontiac station wagon with its Connecticut plates.

My drive went as planned with its scheduled stops, the first being The Campbell Clinic in Memphis. It was a Saturday, and I had a great morning attending rounds, spending time in a clinic and having lunch with some of the attending surgeons. As quickly as possible after lunch, I got on the road to New Orleans. The interstate highways had not been finished and my route was to take me over lesser state roads, through many small towns in Mississippi and Louisiana to New Orleans. It was a very "uneasy" drive. The days of Freedom Riders and their confrontation of "Jim Crow" segregation were a reality, and driving through these small southern towns in a white station wagon with Connecticut plates and a trunk full of human spines was a matter for great caution. I was very conscious of the number of trucks with gun racks I saw. They seemed to fit the image I had of the segregated south and its armed "rednecks." The last thing I wanted was an unofficial visit with one of them on a Louisiana back road or a formal detention by one of their sheriffs, who would make a very special issue of my presence, not to mention my cargo. I drove carefully and stayed well within all posted speed limits and made it to New Orleans around 8 or 9 at night. After finding a modest hotel on Canal Street, I checked in, showered and decided to have dinner in this town known for its superb cuisine. I got into a taxicab and asked the driver to give me a quick tour of the city and to drop me off at a good, but not too fancy, restaurant. The quick tour was good and my dinner excellent, complete with French wine. There was also time to see Bourbon Street. It must have been around midnight and life was in full swing. I was not going to be shortchanged and miss one of the town's main attractions, Blaze Starr, the Queen of Burlesque, the hottest stripper of her and any other era who was performing on Bourbon Street that night. I was not shortchanged, and I would have stayed for an encore if it had not been for my meeting, the following morning, with Mary Sherman, who resided at the other end of the femininity spectrum.

Doctor Mary Sherman was one of the early women in orthopaedic surgery with a special interest in bone pathology. She was a stern, no nonsense, somewhat strange looking woman. She was also an examiner on the orthopaedic boards and had a reputation of being hard on tall male residents. I had met her with Dr. Southwick once before, but knowing her, I could excuse myself from having her as an examiner. Bone pathology was not one of my favorite subjects and it made sense now to solidify my relationship with her. Dr. Southwick had written general letters of introduction to all of the orthopaedic programs I was to visit but a very specific one to Mary Sherman, who was definitely expecting me. I was looking forward to seeing New Orleans and spending some "pragmatic" time with her.

Upon arrival in town, I had called Dr. Sherman's office to announce myself and my scheduled visit with her in the next day. Dr. Southwick had arranged it, but when I called before dinner (and Blaze Starr), she had not been available, and her personal answering service took my message. I went to bed, certain of a meeting with her the following day.

The next morning, after breakfast, I called Dr. Sherman's number again and once more was told she was not available. I proceeded to pack up and was still hoping for our meeting, but after yet another call, it seemed obvious there was something wrong. While hoping for the best and an answer to my calls, I decided to visit the famous Charity Hospital. I went over and contacted the orthopaedic resident on call that Sunday morning. He was very pleased with this unexpected visit and was familiar with Dr. Southwick and our work on the cervical spine at Yale. They had several major cervical spine cases on service, and I enjoyed being there with the resident to discuss their management. By the end of my Charity visit, it was close to noon. After leaving another message with Mary Sherman's answering service, I decided it was time to start my drive west to Galveston and the University of Texas.

On the way out of town, I did, however, make a final

attempt to reach Dr. Sherman by stopping at the Ochsner Clinic where she worked. It was on the way out of town and it made sense to make that easy stop. I went to the front desk and asked them to call Dr. Sherman's hospital office and to voice-page her if there was no response in the office. She was not in her office and did not respond to the loudspeaker paging, so after leaving another message on her phone, I got back in the car and headed west. My visit to Galveston was interesting, but brief. I also visited Big Bend National Park, thinking it would be a short detour, but it took hours of driving and was my first experience with the underestimation of distances in the Southwest.

Two days after my departure from New Orleans, I arrived in El Paso. I had to sign into the Army, Beaumont General Hospital and find a place for us to stay. Zeke Ettelson was the orthopaedic surgeon on staff in charge of processing me from civilian to an active-duty captain and orthopaedic surgeon in the United States Army. In the midst of all the details and paperwork, Zeke wondered if I had heard that Mary Sherman had been murdered a few days before my arrival. I told him I had been trying to meet with her at about the same time but without success. We did not dwell on it since we had multiple other problems to deal with, I had many other thoughts on my mind and I had to find a home for Julie, Katie and Mara, who were arriving that afternoon. I found a nice motel with a two-bedroom suite near the hospital. The girls arrived and, as expected, it was a chaotic scene to get unpacked, fed and into bed after their full day of travel from Greenwich to Kennedy airport, the flight west, change of planes in Dallas and getting to the motel.

Doctor Sherman and New Orleans were far from my mind and I hadn't even had a chance to tell Julie about it, when there was a knock on the door and two gentlemen presented themselves with El Paso police badges in hand.

"Are you Dr. Kristaps Keggi?"

"Yes."

"We are here to question you in connection with the murder of Mary Sherman."

My reaction was immediate and surprising to Julie.

"Come in. I'm not surprised to see you."

Their visit lasted more than an hour. It was a good cop/bad cop routine. One of them made it a point of being understanding, the other, much more aggressively, wanted to know every detail of my drive to New Orleans, the exact hour of my arrival, the name of the hotel where I had stayed, the names of persons I had spoken to, the names of the taxi driver I had used, the restaurant where I had dinner, my location at midnight, my departure the following morning, etc., etc., etc. It was quite a session, since, from the time of my departure from The Campbell Clinic in Memphis until the following morning and my visit with the residents at the Charity Hospital, I had been alone, did not know the name of my taxi driver nor anybody else who could confirm my whereabouts at any given time.

"Where were you at ten?"

"I was having dinner at a restaurant in New Orleans."

"What was the name of the restaurant?"

"I don't remember, but it was not one of the famous ones."

"Where were you at midnight?"

"Probably looking for Blaze Starr."

It went on and on and on in that manner. At the end of it, they left, seemingly satisfied I was telling them "nothing but the truth." After the two detectives left, I had to go through the entire story with Julie and that's when I began to feel I needed legal assistance. The following morning, I called Zeke Ettelson, my senior officer. His advice was to see the Judge Advocate Corps Lieutenant Colonel in charge of legal matters at the hospital. The colonel saw me that morning. He was pleasant enough, but for the better part of our encounter, I had a feeling he was not entirely convinced about what I was telling him. I also had the impression he, as a seemingly staunch, western character, had doubts about an easterner and a graduate of that "effete" school called Yale. Later, as we got to know each other, I found out he had already been approached by the police and had been waiting for me to show up. In the course of the next few days, I also found out that the FBI had visited all of our neighbors in Branford and had questioned Dr. Southwick. I had been one of the early suspects in Mary Sherman's murder since I was passing through New Orleans at the exact time she was murdered. I was cleared from the list of suspects, but the case remained and remains unsolved.

The theories about how and who assassinated her abound. She was different, strange in dress and demeanor. She had a tough reputation and as a resident in the days when almost 100 percent of the orthopaedic residents were male, you learned early about Mary Sherman and her ways. She was different from most of the women we knew. We thought she was a lesbian, but our perception of sexual orientation - lesbian, transsexual, sadist, masochist – was minimal at best. We had no idea. One of the early theories of her murder was that she had been a member of a bizarre sex cult in New Orleans and had been stabbed and burned in ritualistic fashion. It was also said that her family was unwilling to talk about her or her way of life and did not cooperate in the investigation. Many years later, there was a book written about her murder. Some people even thought she had a connection with the assassination of President Kennedy, Castro, Lee Harvey Oswald and Jack Ruby. There was also a time when somebody was planning to make a movie about her murder and I was interviewed by the writer who had obtained all of the available documents on the matter and showed me the FBI warrant for the interrogation of my friends, neighbors and Dr. Southwick in Connecticut. It had been a serious matter, but the movie remains in limbo. Sixty years later, the consensus of those in New Orleans who still have an interest in the matter is that she was murdered by one of the male residents, now deceased, in her orthopaedic residency program who could no longer take her "abuse." Nobody knows for sure, but it was certainly an unusual night in New Orleans.

Our time in El Paso was wonderful. I was there for a year and when I was sent to Vietnam, Julie and the girls loved it for another year without me. Under a special military home mortgage program, we were able to buy a comfortable home within walking distance of the hospital. The sun shone every day, the officers' club at Fort Bliss and the Briggs Airbase provided excellent babysitting services and the golf course was good. Julie won a club championship and joined the women's Border Golf Association, playing in tournaments in New Mexico, around El Paso and in Juarez. My game improved to a handicap of 14. We had a Mexican maid at $14 per week which allowed her in turn to have a maid of her own in Juarez. Katie and Mara, who spoke fluently before her second birthday, were both in excellent preschools. We had a great time exploring the area around El Paso with one-day excursions to such places as the White Sands

National Park and Billy the Kid's hangout in Las Cruces, New Mexico. We drove out to Las Vegas to meet, for the weekend, Julie's brother. We spent a lot of time in Juarez at excellent and reasonable priced restaurants and did all of our liquor shopping south of the border, on the other side of the Rio Grande River. We also went to bullfights in Juarez - a major cultural experience. Our parents visited from Connecticut and New York. All of it was a major change from the previous nine years of medical school and residency, and we both loved it.

Professionally, it was also a great experience. The chief of the service, Colonel Lockwood, had spent his entire medical life in the Army and was primarily interested in knee injuries, torn ligaments, torn menisci and degenerated patellas. His wealth of experience with these problems in young soldiers was vast. We all learned from him and many years later could apply this knowledge to our own patients. His unique way of debriding and denervating patellas with chondromalacia was the basis of my future total knee arthroplasties without the resurfacing of the patella. He was also a good trauma surgeon, but not too interested in spine surgery or hip reconstruction. Zeke Ettelson, my senior by two years, like Ben Bradburn at Yale, was a hand surgeon, although he had vast experience with fracture surgery and war wounds, having already spent a year in Vietnam. He had played football at Syracuse and one of his good friends had been a fellow resident of mine at Newington Children's Hospital. He had a great sense of humor and we spent many happy hours together in the hospital and at home with his family, wife and multiple children.

Colonel Lockwood and Major Ettelson left me in charge of the spines and hips. We did a variety of spine operations, including some innovative work with the Southwick spine decompressions and facet fusions using bovine strut grafts rather than the patient's own iliac crests. One of my predecessors on staff had done a number of anterior cervical fusions using the Cloward dowel method. Many of these fusions were now failing and we had a whole series we salvaged with posterior fusions. Peter Keblish was one of the residents (former captain of the Penn football team, great surgeon and a future major contributor in the field of joint replacements), and he and I reviewed these cases and presented them at the Western Orthopaedic Association. Osteotomies, fusions and resections of the hip were also my domain. It was a year of vast experience in adult reconstructive surgery.

My second year, meaning active duty, was fast approaching, and it seemed more and more obvious there would be some major changes in the way we were fighting in Vietnam. The Vietcong and the North Vietnamese were on the move, and one of their main targets was the Bien Hoa Airbase. After one of these attacks on Bien Hoa, in the spring of 1965, President Johnson made a definitive speech about "not being defeated" and introduced regular Marine and Army units into Vietnam to support the South Vietnamese, our American advisors and Special Forces already there. The following morning, I was summoned to appear before our hospital commander, General Blount, and was told I was now on 12-hour alert status and would be deployed to Vietnam in the near future. It meant that, if called, I would have to be ready to go that same evening. There was paperwork to be done, and the first items on that list were a will and a power of attorney. I was also issued a duffle bag to be packed with designated items such as three pairs of socks, three underpants, two shirts, etc. If properly packed, the duffle bag had enough room for all of these and finally a helmet on top of everything. All vaccinations had to be up to date and even though I had had some weapons training while on active reserve in medical school, before going into a war zone, I had to go through the close combat and infiltration courses. It was a full day with M-14 rifles in hand. It consisted of three separate sessions: close combat, infiltration in daylight, and infiltration at night. The close combat course required you to walk several hundred yards and shoot at metal, human-shaped targets as they popped up in front of you. We were given 200 rounds of ammunition and lined up to march. I fired my 200 rounds, the man on my right fired his 200 rounds and the one on my left did the same. We were very close to each other and were exposed, without any earplugs, to the noise of 600 rounds of M-14 rifle shots. After a brief rest, we went through the infiltration course which consisted of crawling 100 (or was it 200) yards on your belly while a machine gun fired live bullets over your head and explosions went off around you as you crawled. Once done with the daytime crawl, you rested until darkness set in and then repeated it with very dramatic tracer bullets from the machine guns flying a foot or two above your head and the explosions as you crawled, rifle in hands, were now bright flashes along with the noise and clouds of sand. It was an interesting day in the life of an orthopaedic surgeon, who woke up the following morning with intense buzzing in both ears. I had passed the close combat and infiltration courses but had left some of my hearing in the Texas desert. In any case, I was now qualified to go do my surgical duties in Vietnam.

I was on 12-hour alert, but my exact orders did not arrive until later in the summer when I was ordered to report to the "3rd Surgical Hospital, Army, Mobile" at Fort Meade, Maryland, during the first days of August for further deployment to Vietnam (MACV - Military Assistance Command Vietnam). During the Korean War, mobile surgical hospitals were called "MASH" units (Mobile Army Surgical Hospital), but somebody in the Army Public Relations Department had decided that the word "mash" had too many negative, bloody, disorganized connotations and had to be changed. Instead of being called the 3rd MASH, we were now the "3rd Surge." MASH, however, had caught on, and we continued to be called the MASH hospital in spite of the official rechristening by the Army.

Before my departure for Vietnam, Julie and I both had decided that we liked the southwest and would continue our lives in that part of the world, although probably not El Paso. We did have the opportunity to stay in El Paso, and two of the major orthopaedic practices in town had offered me jobs, but in spite of our love of it, the surrounding area and Mexico, it was a little too "Wild West" for our East Coast sensibilities. Even the wives of the orthopaedic surgeons I knew, packed "heat" - had loaded handguns in their purses and knew how to use them.

So, it made sense for us to look around at some of the other southwestern and southern California options. We drove to Tucson, Phoenix, Los Angeles, Newport Beach and San Diego. They were all fascinating visits, but in the end, Tucson was our choice. It was a beautiful area, a university town that was about to open a medical school, and there were only 12 practicing orthopaedists, some of them partially retired. The dean of the new medical school was a general surgeon who had trained at Roosevelt Hospital and was very encouraging about our potential lives in Tucson and at the new medical school. It seemed like a solid opportunity to practice and also teach, which was well ingrained in my thoughts of the future and work. Julie was going to stay in our house in El Paso while I was in Vietnam, but upon my return, we would move. It made sense even though Dr. Southwick was quick to express his disappointment, since he was expecting me back at Yale or in a major academic center, preferably in the east.

We also had to deal with the baby we were expecting in August. So as soon as I had my orders to leave for duty in Vietnam, I went to General Blount to ask him if the Army would delay my departure until the baby was born. He was a very nice man, promised to investigate, but was told by Washington that my position as the orthopaedic surgeon with the 3rd Surgical was a critical one and I would have to report as ordered. I was disappointed, appreciative of his efforts and proceeded with the final arrangements. My duffle bag with its military gear and helmet on top was packed and I also had a suitcase for some personal items such as civilian clothing and a few books - *Grant's Atlas of Anatomy*, the latest edition of *Campbell's Operative Orthopaedics* and a text on the management of war wounds of the extremities.

We had some farewell parties, the most memorable one given to me by the orthopaedic residents, which consisted of a dinner in one of the best Juarez restaurants followed by a tour of the town's houses of ill repute. It was a "hands off" spectator tour, but educational in the ways of the world and its most ancient profession. Shortly after the memorable affair with the residents, I was ready to go to Maryland, Fort Meade and the 3rd MASH. I was at home, had finished dinner and was putting Katie and Mara to bed. It was to be my last night with the family. It was a serious, contemplative evening. Julie tells all of her friends that I could not wait to get into the war, but I certainly had mixed feelings about it. I was very sad about leaving the family and even though you put it out of your mind as much as possible, there was always the thought of coming back in a body bag. I did, however, have very strong feelings about the war, service to country and care of the wounded. You think of the history of war surgery and all the surgeons who have gone ahead of you – Doctor Southwick, the Yale Hospitals in World Wars, Harvey Cushing, Esmarch, Brunschwig, Larrey, Pare. There is also the sense of excitement and adventure. You can simplify these thoughts by saluting the flag, and with slogans such as "For God, for Country and for Yale," but there is fear and confusion. "You can do it Kris. You have to do it. Go do your duty." The moment of departure from home to go to war is something all of us had thought about for years. That moment had come. Books have been written on all of those emotions. You no longer need to go back to the Bible, Socrates or Hemingway to read about them, you can simply Google them and then, in eternal manner, put them out of your mind and "press on." My uncles went through it during World War II, my grandmother's brother was faced with it during the Russian-Japanese War of 1904, we had come close to it as boys in Latvia. Millions over the centuries have faced it.

Suddenly, there was a knock on the door and one of General Blount's aides was there to tell me, in person, that I did not have to leave the next morning and was allowed to delay my departure until the baby arrived. This fortunate turn of events had been precipitated by another officer at the hospital who had a pregnant wife, was scheduled to go, but who made a major case of it, including the involvement of a United States senator who was one of his father's friends. As a result of this political meddling, his departure had been officially delayed. General Blount had gone out of his way, without success, to change my orders, and when this other physician got his "political" postponement, he had insisted that I, who had played it by the rules, should also be allowed to await the birth of his child. The next morning, much to the surprise of Colonel Lockwood and the rest of the staff, I was back at the weekly conference, seeing patients and operating. Caroline was born on August 7, 1965, and the morning of her birth I reported to the general's office to give them the happy news. I was told to continue work as usual and to await further orders, which did arrive two weeks later. It was wonderful to be there with Julie and our newborn third daughter. It was precious to see her greeted by her older sisters and Phoebe, our family beagle. There were no changes in the orders of my ultimate destination, but by being delayed a month, I would now be flying to Vietnam by commercial aircraft.

VIETNAM

I was ordered to Vietnam by air from San Francisco on a civilian Pan-American flight. By the time I left, Caroline was at home, although she had spent a few extra days in the hospital because of a mild, benign jaundice due to the interaction of her type B blood with her mother's type O. There is a song, "The Yellow Rose of Texas" and occasionally we would refer to her by that name, but she was the image of health and we could not be happier. Chello, our Mexican maid, was also ecstatic and showered her with absolute and total Latina love and care. It was good to see, and I knew she would be in good hands while I was gone. The situation with Chello and her family was such that when we visited them or when Julie left her with them (unimaginable a couple of decades later), Caroline was hugged and loved by all, never leaving someone's lap or arms. Leaving Caroline without a father also reminded me that I had spent my first year of life with my grandparents and grandmother's sister while Father, Mother and brother Janis were in Copenhagen.

Katie, four years old, was vaguely aware of what was happening. The father of one of her classmates in pre-school had been wounded in Vietnam and at one point she had come home with a picture of a man with holes in him and wondering if I was returning home with holes in my body. She seemed to be dealing with it, although it was hard to understand how much she knew about the reality of the war I was about to encounter.

Mara also knew I was leaving, but men with bullet holes in them had not yet entered her vision of the world. She was the most emotional, with hugs and kisses as we were gathered in the departure lounge of the El Paso airport - "Come back soon! I love you!" I assured her I would be back before too long, although not so far in the back of my mind was the reality of going into a war zone and the possibility of not coming back. The vivid memories of that departure, the hugs and kisses, the promises to be back, were with me throughout Vietnam and made my return to Julie, Katie, Mara and baby Caroline that much more joyful when I had kept my promise.

San Francisco was my first stop. I'd made arrangements to meet with my Scroll and Key classmate, Steve Gurney, who had recently moved to California. We spent a great evening enjoying a good dinner at a fine restaurant and, at Steve's insistence, some time at a lesser spot known for the dancing girls on its tables. Steve was doing his patriotic duty by giving me some dancing memories of my last night in the States. I remember having a chat with one of these feminine memories who was a student at Berkeley, spoke well and danced even better. The next day, I was aboard my Pan-Am jet to Vietnam.

It was a civilian flight and there were a few of them aboard, but most of us had a military connection. The plane was overloaded with our duffle bags and luggage. It took a very, very long run to become airborne and we had to re-fuel several times during the flight to Saigon. I was jammed in the back of the plane between a large colonel in uniform and a middle-aged man with apparent CIA connections. They had no problem exercising the privilege of rank by spreading out in their seats and squashing Kristaps, a junior captain, between them. As I sat there, I thought about my uncertain future, but I was also coming to the conclusion that, should I come back alive, I would, whenever possible, fly first-class. (I did come back and have tried to live up to that promise I made to myself during that 20-hour flight.).

Our first stop was Honolulu. It was late evening and we were there long enough to get off the plane, look around the airport and make a final telephone call home. It was a sad one, since both Julie and I knew all future communications would be by letters, much different from our wars in the modern age of electronic communication, satellites, text messages and Skype. There is something to be said for being able to see and speak to your family from a distant war, but I can also imagine the stress at both ends of these real-time contacts - seeing your daughter in pain with a broken wrist or your wife seeing you during a nearby mortar attack. A reassuring letter that "all is well and there is no need to worry" was the standard before the electronic age.

The next stop was Wake Island, the site of one of the most inspiring battles of WWII. Even though the Japanese captured the island, their first attack on it was repulsed and considered a heroic victory for the Marines who were there in December 1941. I was amazed how small it was. The runway we were on ran the entire length of the island. It was the middle of the night, but we were able to walk around and visit some of the remains of the old WWII fortifications. It was also interesting to see the main airport building, full of troops sleeping on chairs and on the floor, waiting for their flights to Vietnam. They were being flown on propeller-driven C-130 transport planes complete with heavy equipment, and their stay on Wake was going to be longer than our brief refueling one.

Our next stop was Guam, a much bigger island with a normal airport. By this time in our travels, it was daylight, and we were hoping to get off the plane, take a walk and look around, but we had arrived in the midst of a massive tropical rainstorm. Getting off the plane would have been equivalent to stepping under a waterfall. So on to Saigon. A few hours later, the descent into Saigon's Ton Son Nhut Airport was much steeper than the routine, comfortable approaches to civilian airports in the States. It was our first indication we were arriving in a war zone. A slow moving, large jet plane at low altitude would be the perfect target for even the smallest of rifles, and to avoid the sitting duck scenario the descent had to be adjusted accordingly. It was disturbingly steep. As we approached the airport over flat, green fields, I noticed there was an area that looked like a golf course with multiple sand traps, but no - they were artillery craters from a previous shelling of the airport.

We landed safely and were directed to a replacement center where I expected to spend some days, but, much to my surprise, a truck had been dispatched to pick me up immediately for delivery to the 3rd Surgical Hospital, Army, Mobile in Bien Hoa, approximately 15 miles northeast of Saigon. The roads were secure, and we got to my "MASH" in the late afternoon. After reporting to the commanding officer, Major Downs, I was directed to my tent, a GP (General Purpose) Large that was home for eight of us. The hospital had arrived in country just a few days earlier and was not scheduled to be functional until the next day. Since 75 percent of all wound wounds arriving at a surgical facility were wounds of the extremities, the presence of an orthopaedic surgeon was deemed essential, and my absence had been considered a major problem. Our hospital was assigned to the 173rd Airborne Brigade, which had arrived a couple of months

earlier but had not yet been involved in any major combat operations. Its commanding officer, General Williamson, was very concerned about his troops and aware of the need for a hospital with an orthopaedic surgeon. He had been informed about my date of arrival and was ready to plan major combat operations now that he had "his" hospital fully in place.

My fellow 3rd Surgical physicians and surgeons who had reported to duty at Fort Meade in Maryland had had a miserable 6 weeks from the time of their arrival in Maryland to their arrival in Bien Hoa. After the usual Army briefings, paperwork and training sessions, they'd been put on a train and taken across the continent to the West Coast and then placed aboard an old WWII troop transport ship (without air conditioning) for a three-week voyage across the Pacific Ocean to Saigon. Now they had set up the hospital and my late arrival was met with a certain amount of disdain, as expressed by my bunk assignment in the worst corner of the tent. I had arrived after more than 24 hours in the air, though, and the only thing on my mind was getting some sleep, even in my windy, rainy corner of the tent. But rest was not to come for several more hours.

As I was getting ready to bed down, one of General Williamson's aides arrived to tell me I was invited (ordered, without options) to have dinner with the general, who was eager to meet *his* orthopaedic surgeon. He had known about the delay of my arrival and was now wanting to get a good look. Our hospital consisted of approximately 20 tents and had the look of any number of other war zone installations and tents you see in photographs from Korea, WWII and even WWI. Our tents had red crosses on the top of them, but otherwise were the same as those of the 173rd Airborne Brigade. We were at the very end of one of the Bien Hoa Airbase

171

runways, and my tent was less than 50 yards from one of them. General Williamson's headquarters were within two hundred yards and I was told I would not have any problems finding it. As I was leaving the hospital for my special dinner, I was informed that the entire 173rd Surgical area would be on full blackout since Viet Cong patrols had been spotted nearby. That minor detail was of no major concern to the general. Dinner was on and I was able to report to it as ordered.

I was seated to the left of the general in the "dining room" tent of his quarters and next to me on my left was one of his aides or adjutants whose job was to keep me awake by nudging me throughout the dinner. The general questioned me about my education, family and experience with major injuries. He was satisfied with my responses and very pleased that I had arrived and was ready to care for his troops, as he and his staff were planning some major encounters with the Viet Cong and North Vietnamese, who were not too far away and a threat to the Bien Hoa airbase and Saigon itself. After the introductory conversations with me, the officers at the table reverted to "airborne stories" of parachutes not opening, getting hung up in trees, previous practice jumps and combat operations. There were stories they had heard about the general, one of the most decorated officers in the Army, including his past accomplishments and his practice to always be the first out of the plane, be it in practice or combat. Loud voices and loud laughter, interrupted only by a few visits from a junior officer reporting on the enemy patrols in the area. He'd come in, whisper something in the general's ear and leave, but whatever he reported did not interfere with the dinner, one that seemed to go on for a long time. Finally, the general stood up and I was getting ready to leave. That was not to happen. We were all invited to join the general for an after-dinner movie. As "his" orthopaedic surgeon, I had, once more, the honor of sitting next to him and had my "nudger" on the other side. I imagined we would be treated to a light comedy, a western or a war story, but the treat turned out to be a West Point football game. Army won and at last I was allowed, in full blackout conditions, to find my way back to my corner cot in the tent where all the others had been asleep for some time.

I was asleep in a matter of seconds only to be awakened by sudden artillery fire from the howitzers across the road from our hospital tents. I was assured it was nothing to worry about; it was simply the artillery units that, every so often throughout the night, would fire at vague targets in the surrounding jungle or rice paddies for "harassment and interdiction." It was a hell of a surprise, but yet another reminder I was in Vietnam, with the 173rd Airborne, in war zone D and with Viet Cong patrols in the area - nothing to worry about, get used to it, go back to sleep. So sleep it was again until, suddenly, at first light, came the roar of fighter planes taking off from the Bien Hoa runway within a few yards of our tent. It was the start of my first full day with the 3rd Surgical Hospital in Vietnam. It was a day of getting oriented, getting to know my fellow surgeons, physicians and nurses. It was also a day of discovering some very unpleasant problems exposed to me by the sergeant in charge of orthopaedics and orthopaedic equipment.

I inspected the operating room tents – two GP large tents able to hold 3 operating tables each that looked like all the pictures I had seen before. The instrument trays were also familiar looking and would be sufficient to do the basic work of wound debridement – as they had been at Yale under the mentorship of Korean War Marine Corps surgeon Wayne O. Southwick. But there were no internal fixation devices, rods, plates or even simple screws. I knew that there would be very little need for them, but in some severe femoral or humeral fractures with associated major vascular injuries, the vascular repairs had to be protected from being torn apart by inadequate mobilization of sharp bone fragments. It was something I would have to resolve, and did as soon as possible by "liberating" a few rods, plates and screws from the local, civilian Bien Hoa Provincial Hospital where I did some volunteer work. In a frontline mobile surgical hospital, we were not supposed to have them, but it was a situation where the army planners, with WWII manuals in hand, were not necessarily correct, and I felt free to make independent decisions if we were going to save a young soldier's arm or leg from a high amputation. However, the biggest shock came when I asked the sergeant to show me our stock of bandages and plaster of Paris. He took me to a corner of the supplies tent and pointed to one box of plaster bandages that, at best, would suffice for only a few long leg casts. That amount might have been sufficient in the days of WWII or Korea when a mobile hospital, such as ours, was connected to an "umbilical cord" of materials constantly supplied from the rear. But we did not have that umbilical luxury and were sitting in the middle of nowhere, facing potentially large numbers of wounded in need of casts. I did not want to find myself in a situation where arms and legs would have to be immobilized with branches from trees or bamboo sticks. To prevent that type of reversion to Civil War surgery, I immediately got some more plaster from the Bien Hoa Airbase first-aid station and ordered my sergeant to procure a month's supply of plaster and bandages, as his first duty, every Monday morning. He did as ordered. Nothing happened for about three months, but then the ordered supplies started coming in and, by the time I left Vietnam in June of 1966, we had to have a special tent to hold all the boxes of bandages and plaster that kept coming. It might have been seen as a total waste, but in 1966 there were many other hospitals setting up in Vietnam with inadequate supplies. Word got around about our unofficial cache and we had visits from these new units whom we were happy to help "outside of the box or the regular chain of supplies." We would sit with these visiting surgeons, have a few gin and tonics, discuss the possibility of trading bandages for second lieutenant nurses, whiskey or cash - have a few laughs in our world of insanity - then give them what they needed and move on.

On that first day in country, I was also issued an M-14 riffle with ammunition and a .45 automatic handgun to go along with my Geneva Convention card of "not being a combatant." The card was obviously a farce since the Communists in any of their wars had yet to show any type of mercy to medical personnel. In addition to my issue M-14 and .45 automatic, I had my personal snub-nosed, pocket-fitting Smith and Wesson .36 caliber revolver given to me in El Paso by Julie and her mother. It had been the property of Julie's mother's aunt who had been living in Santa Fe. She had had some interesting marriages and divorces in Chicago but had retired from the highlife to the tranquility of the mountains of New Mexico. For years, she apparently had told everybody about her armed status and when old age mental confusion became severe enough, everybody knew she had to be disarmed before she could be moved to a nursing home. Julie and her mother were in charge of the operation and the high-quality revolver they recovered became a present that was by my side from the moment I left El Paso to my last day in Vietnam, when I sold it to a Filipino construction worker for 60 dollars. It was tucked in my belt or pants during all of my operations in civilian hospitals, Montagnard huts and tents, and visits to orphanages. I was very happy with my handy revolver. I knew how to use it, but would I be able to do so in the split second I would have to make the decision that the soldier with the rifle or the young boy with the hand grenade was a threat to my life and had to be shot? I was always thinking about it but feel happy I never had to make that decision.

We also had shortages of other material and in our first month or two we ran out of antibiotics and were supplied by the 173rd troopers, who had liberated some from a Viet Cong underground hospital. The French-made Viet Cong penicillin and streptomycin had to be good enough for our wounded in the fall of 1965. We were extremely frustrated by these shortages of supplies, antibiotics, blood, intravenous fluids, etc., etc. I had no trouble expressing my direct thoughts on that subject to all official visitors, politicians and aging colonels who flew in by helicopter to see how we were functioning. At one point, a group of these "administrators" was outside of the operating room tent where I was working on a mangled leg. I could not contain myself and came charging out in the middle of the operation in a bloody gown and gloves to tell them not to come back again unless they were bringing blood or plaster of Paris. Their response was amazing: "Shhhh, not so loud, there may be a reporter nearby!" What were they going to do with me? Send me to Vietnam? I was already there. Send me into the thick of things in the middle of nowhere? I was there already, so why not say it the way it was for the sake of the poor wounded young soldiers whose lives and limbs we were now trying to save.

The young Army surgeon saw plenty of work and wild days and nights with his Warzone D MASH unit.

The weather, in Warzone D near Bien Hoa, was either hot and humid or hot and raining. We spent most of our time wearing only shorts (underpants). The temperature in the operating room tents or screened-in wooden "hooches" would, on some days, go as high as 110 degrees. In the course of my 10 months with the 3rd Surgical, from September 1965 to July of 1966, it was life and work without air conditioning. Trying to sleep with mosquito netting over my cot did not work and smearing mosquito repellant all over my body was a mess. Luckily, within a month, most of us had equipped ourselves with fans bought at the Airbase PX and were able to set them up at the end of our cots. Sleeping naked with a fan at full blast blowing air over our bodies made the nights tolerable. It also kept the mosquitos away without the suffocating netting or messy repellant. Some moaned and groaned about it, but every so often we had to remind ourselves of how much worse we would be in North Korea, in January, on the banks of the Yalu River. The images of the Marines from that time of the Chinese Communist intervention in Korea made us feel so much more fortunate. If it rained, the ground around us would revert to the mud of the rice paddy it had been for probably 1,000 years before our arrival, but it was not the ice and snow of North Korea. The temperatures in the operating room tents also represented an additional life-threatening hazard to the wounded, who, especially if the operations had been of longer duration, would wake up with very high body temperatures.

If it was the dry season, the mud would turn into dust that would fly throughout tents. The worst of that was up in the Central Highlands, when our hospital (and operating room tents) were next to an unpaved runway. Whenever one of the small planes flew in or out of this remote outpost, we found ourselves in the midst of a sandstorm, a sandstorm that went right through the "operating room" tents, dusting everything in sight and requiring that much more irrigation of the wounds we were dealing with.

There was also the unique smell of canvas in our tents. Even 60 years later, I cannot step into a tent at a fair or party without the immediate vivid recall of Vietnam, the 3rd Surge and its tents. (As I remember it was the French philosopher Camus who had vivid descriptions of that phenomena of sudden, vivid recall of past events precipitated by a passing aroma, smell or scent. I am doubly fortunate, since the aroma of a tent brings back the memories not only of war but also French philosophy).

It was also in a tent that I came the closest to being blown to smithereens. Only a couple of weeks after arriving in country and my having learned about our shortage of plaster, bandages and medications, one of our supply tents caught on fire. We never figured out how it started. It may have been sabotage by one of our local Vietnamese workers or an inadvertently discarded cigarette, but the tent was burning. Without giving it any thought, my orthopaedic sergeant and I grabbed some fire extinguishers and charged into the burning tent. We were able to put out the fire and, having done so, found ourselves standing right next to our supply of anesthetic ether and cyclopropane, both of the highest explosive potential. It is just another tent story now, but it could have been a trip home in a body bag. Lucky, very lucky.

The headquarters tent also deserves mention. Of all of our tents, it was one of the smallest, but its entrance was impressive with the flags of the United States and the Army Medical Corps decorated with multiple campaign streamers, unit citations and other ribbons. They dated back to WWII and deployment in the South Pacific. Papua New Guinea and Luzon were the major battles, and I was very aware of them since the 340th Army Reserve General Hospital (my hospital) had also been involved in the South Pacific Campaign and I knew several surgeons who had served with them during that war. That little tent and its flags were telling a heroic story, and here we were, in September of 1965, the first mobile surgical hospital in Vietnam attached to the first regular United States Army Unit, the 173rd Airborne Brigade - ready to serve our men and add to the distinguished history.

On top of all of our tents were large red crosses, which during more "civilized" wars were signs to identify them as hospital tents not to be bombed as hostile targets. But in the most recent wars, hospitals, physicians, nurses and corpsmen attending to the wounded have simply been targets of great opportunity. In Vietnam, there were no aerial attacks on our installations and the most important function of the crosses was to direct MedEvac helicopters to their hospital destination and the landing zones near the tents designed to receive patients for triage, resuscitation and surgery. The helicopters headed for our red crosses could be identified by the noise of their engines and rotating blades at quite a distance from the hospital. We could tell they were coming straight at us, and without any other warning, you, as the surgeon, knew it was time to go to the helipad and the receiving area to deal with the wounded, their state of shock, their wounds and mangled extremities. As the orthopaedic surgeon, I also knew if there were four wounded aboard one of these helicopters coming straight at us, three of them would be my patients with their extremity wounds and you might as well start dealing with them as soon as they were unloaded onto the helipad.

We had an extremely well-organized process for dealing with the wounded, but there was one "Red Cross arrival" that was far out of the ordinary, dramatic, comic and in the end, lifesaving to the soldier involved. An armed combat helicopter had just left the 173rd Airborne camp and a few hundred yards beyond the outer camp perimeter, was hit by a bullet that had gone through its floor and through the thigh of the machine gunner sitting at his post at one of the doors of the rear compartment. The bullet had caused a partial laceration of the femoral artery of the type that does not allow the vessel to retract into the larger surrounding muscles. In cases of complete transection of a large artery, this retraction controls the bleeding, but in incomplete lesions, the artery continues to bleed in massive spurts. Our patient had an incomplete laceration in a large open wound of the thigh. As the pilot looked back at his gunner, all he could see was blood spurting out of his gunner's thigh, splashing all over the young soldier and the rear compartment of his helicopter. Within a second, he remembered the tents with the red crosses he had just passed, whipped his helicopter around and went straight at the nearest one of them. It was a wise, lifesaving decision, but he had no reason to know that the first of these Red Cross tents was an enlisted men's latrine, so as he went for it, he blew away the flimsy structure, exposing its users with their pants down, in a state of panic running for shelter in every which direction. We, the surgeons, pants on, rushed to the scene, identified the arterial problem, compressed the wound and took the gunner directly to the operating room tent for blood transfusions, surgery, repair of the lacerated artery and a happy ending - another life and limb saved by the quick reaction of the 22-year-old helicopter pilot, the red crosses on the tents and our cardiovascular surgeon, Julie Conn.

The nurses' showers also have a place in this tale of tents. Our showers were buckets of water pulled by a rope attached to the top of wooden poles, too tall to fit inside a tent. In an all-male environment, there was so need for special canvas curtains to surround these buckets on poles, but since we had female nurses, all shower areas were surrounded by canvas "curtains," allowing for some privacy as you washed your sweaty and, in some cases, blood-stained bodies at the end of a working day or night in the reception area or surgery. The "simple" curtains seemed good enough for those of the male sex but deemed totally inadequate by our female nurses. It seems that the helicopter pilots, very quickly, had found the initial, roofless female showers and were amusing themselves by watching the feminine activities from above. It was a situation that had to be corrected with the construction of a special tent covered by a big roof. When we moved to the Central Highlands near the Cambodian border, the special tent was no longer necessary since General Westmoreland felt the area too dangerous for female nurses and all of ours had been replaced by male counterparts. It was life "a la fresca" for the duration of our stay in the mountains, but in the lowlands more civilized ways were the norm.

As an aside, on the average our nurses were older than most of us on the medical/surgical staff and the only one in her early 20s was evacuated two months after arrival with the diagnosis of a "lower abdominal mass." They were a great group and did a fabulous job under difficult circumstances, but there were several occasions when the "older ladies" in charge had conflicts with the younger nurses and young surgeons. One of these caused the male nurse in charge of the admissions tent (a high-stress area) to have a serious and dangerous breakdown, complete with revolver shots in our tent - we'll get to that story in more detail later in this tale.

In normal conditions, we had 60 empty beds/cots ready to receive patients, but we also had a set of tents ready to be set up and receive, if necessary, up to 120 wounded. The mission of our medical frontline unit in Vietnam was to save life and limb, hold the wounded until their condition had stabilized, then evacuate them to a larger hospital for more definitive care and evacuation to the States. Most of our wounded were gone in 24 hours or less. Consequently, we usually had enough empty beds and were able to receive and treat the next wave of wounded in our combat zone. We did not treat Vietnamese troops. Our patients were only Americans, Australians and New Zealanders.

So much for the tents. Now on to those of us who lived, slept, ate, drank and worked in them. There were

14 physicians and two nurse anesthetists on our medical staff. Only two of the physicians were in the regular army. Most of us had been in the Berry Plan, deferred during our year in residency training, but scheduled to serve for two years on active duty in a particular specialty. We had four partially trained surgeons, drafted before entering their specialty training. Typically, they'd had an internship and one year of residency in general surgery. We also had a fully trained obstetrician/ gynecologist and a radiologist. Our commanding officer was a major in the regular army who had completed his general surgery residency in an army hospital a year earlier and was on the same professional level as those of us out of the Berry Plan, although we had completed our specialty training in civilian hospitals. The chief of anesthesia was also an army-trained regular officer. We were in the Army Reserve, "citizen soldiers" giving two years of our lives to the service of our country. With the military draft as it was in the 1950s and 1960s, active duty service was a near certainty for most of us in training. That changed in the 1970s with the elimination of the draft and the creation of an all-volunteer army. As a believer in the benefits of universal service (of some type) to the country and to the young men and women involved, I think that the elimination of the draft without the institution of some other commitment to country is a matter deserving serious review. For all of us, the two years of service were a great transition between the end of residency training and the real world ahead of us. Some time spent in service would be a maturing and educational experience to the average high school or college graduate. It could be modified, deferred or started at age 18. It would be good for the country and all the young men and women learning about service, responsibility, work, discipline, history, our government and basic economics.

There was a lot to be said for our status as "citizen soldiers." We were there to do the right thing for our wounded. We were going to be out of the Army in a year and were not worried about promotions, commendations, awards and medals. Our morale was high, we were trying to do our very best and were not afraid to speak our minds if we felt it would improve the care of our patients. We were totally dedicated to serving the 173rd Airborne Brigade and all other combat units that continued to arrive in our area. I can truly say we represented the best in American surgical education from the University of Washington to Cornell, Columbia, Virginia and Yale. I believe I was bringing to our wounded the best lessons learned from Dr. Southwick at Yale and Zeke Ettelson in El Paso, who had spent a year in Vietnam as an orthopedic surgeon in the stationary Army hospital in Nha Trang, on the shores of the South China Sea, taking care of our wounded military advisors and Special Forces (Green Berets) who had been in country as irregulars for at least 10 years prior to our arrival.

The staffing roster of our hospital was left over from WWII, a time when "general" surgeons were also trained to treat fractures and extremity wounds. But the more modern general surgeons in our hospital had only a cursory knowledge of extremity work, which made my job more demanding than it might have been in 1944 on Papua New Guinea. Three quarters of the wounds arriving from the field of battle in a hospital such as our 3rd MASH were wounds of the arms and legs. To deal with our lack of extremity surgeons, I taught the younger, partially trained docs as quickly as I could to do simple wounds of the arms and legs. Bob Bowden, our obstetrician/gynecologist, also became a fairly accomplished extremity surgeon. Bob was a Southern Gentleman who had graduated from the historic Virginia

Military Institute, a good man, good surgeon and true friend. It was almost like a residency system. I was there to help and look over their shoulders, but they did the work. I took on all the major cases but was very happy about the willingness of the younger surgeons and the obstetrician to do their part.

Our general surgeons were great, but Julie Conn, who had been a resident at the New York Hospital for five or six years, was absolutely the quickest of the quick and the best of the best. He would have the patient's abdomen open and his left hand on the aorta in a matter of seconds. His right hand would then be searching for injuries to other blood vessels, intestines or kidneys. His surgical skills and ability to make the right decisions with precision and speed saved many lives. He and I were a team in all cases of multiple wounds to the chest, abdomen and extremities. He returned the States to be on the faculty at Northwestern but died two or three years later in a scuba diving accident that sounded strange and may have had suicide-with-post-traumatic-stress implications. Another one of our surgeons, our commanding officer, was much more pensive and deliberate in his manner. A good man, but reminiscent of my cardiac surgery professor at Yale with his slow and thoughtful surgery. In cases of multiple injuries that we treated in common, I would have completed the extremity work, be it a debridement or amputation, before he had made the abdominal incision. He did the job, but he was rapidly relegated by his own choice to the simpler cases, with Julie Conn leading the parade of major life-saving chest and abdominal procedures.

I am certain there are many ways of setting up, staffing and running a combat mobile surgical hospital. I am sure there are manuals for that purpose. But in the real world of war, chaos and many wounded, plans of action evolve in a natural, functional manner. The Israeli Air Force comes to mind. On the ground, the chain of command is clear, and the senior officers are in charge, but when flying missions, the best pilot, even if the most junior, leads the flight and gives the orders. Thus, our commanding officer, a major, was perfectly happy to let Julie Conn, a captain, do the big operations. Meanwhile, the triage, or sorting of patients as they were being unloaded from the helicopters, rapidly fell upon Bob Bowden, who was quick in assessing the severity of the injured and had a natural talent to make, without hesitation, decisions about their disposition. He also was tall and had a loud voice that carried over irrelevant chatter, the noise of helicopter engines and all other activity in the admissions tent. If, in his opinion, one of the wounded needed immediate surgery, nobody questioned his loud order of, "Take him to the operating room NOW!" Without access to any manuals on the triage of the wounded, Bob was a natural and knew what to do without schooling, testing and certification. Similarly, one of our partially trained surgeons turned out to be very efficient with rapid resuscitation, insertion of blood lines into the central circulation, starting transfusions in all four extremities and doing whatever else was required to get the patient back to life and ready for surgery. He had obviously been taught all the required details but had a natural ability to get it done efficiently, with speed and without hesitation. We also had to improvise to get the job done. We did not have any special catheters for massive transfusions, so we simply used plastic IV tubing we kept sterile in jars of alcohol. Inserted in the veins of both arms and legs, they delivered the needed lifesaving blood to the worst of our wounded. They did the job, and with them we were able to deliver lifesaving massive amounts of blood to replace what had been lost. Some of the patients who had arrived in our hospital were essentially dead, having bled out to the last few drops. They needed this type of rapid insertion of catheters and massive blood transfusions to survive. One of us had thought of the IV tubing and without asking for special permission we used it with great success.

The wounded, resuscitated patients would next be taken from the admissions area to the operating room tents for definitive surgery. There we were, surgeons one year out of training, all of us under the age of 33, doing operations of extreme complexity. I was 31 and the other two American orthopedic surgeons in country were miles away in the stationary hospitals of Saigon and Nha Trang. The wounded came in and had to be treated. Even though I had been well trained at Roosevelt Hospital in New York and at Yale, at times it was a challenge. I was alone. There was nobody to consult or ask about alternate treatments or operations. I was had to make major surgical decisions based on my, and only my, judgment, experience and skill. Years later, in a civilian setting, the decision to amputate a leg because of a badly infected total knee would be discussed with other orthopedic surgeons, infectious disease specialists, vascular surgeons, social workers and prosthetists. Family members would also be a part of the process until finally, after lengthy discussions, the patient would sign the consent for the operation. In the tents of the 3rd Surgical (MASH), a 31-year-old was making the decision to amputate a leg all by himself, hoping it was the right decision and in the best interest of that 19-year-old private on his operating table. Afterwards, you could spend hours thinking about it, and you did so frequently. Your job was to save life and limb. If at all possible, you leaned in the direction of saving the limb in spite of the risk of fatal infection or a life of pain, multiple other operation and misery that could have been avoided by an amputation and a functional prosthesis.

There are patients you remember in vivid detail, and I immediately think of a case that exemplified all the above dilemmas. He arrived with both legs already blown off by a mine. He was the radio operator of a platoon hit by the North Vietnamese. There were many casualties in need of rapid evacuation from their remote jungle location. Their exact location and status had to be reported, and our patient was the only one who was able to do it. After applying his own belt tourniquets synched down with bayonets, he calibrated his radio, called in helicopters and stayed in place until all of the other wounded had been picked up. His selfless and heroic actions are beyond comprehension. He arrived in our hospital and we had to make surgical decisions that I still think about. Were they affected by the heroic deeds of this 20-year-old? Was the spreading of infection from his thighs and his subsequent death related to my decision not to do high amputations immediately in an effort to preserve enough of his thighs to give him a better chance to have functioning prostheses and a chance of being able to walk rather than lead life in a wheelchair? I still do not know if it was my well-meaning surgical decision, some very malignant bacteria or a combination of the two that was responsible for his fate. We were not equipped to identify the organism that seemed to be destroying his muscles and life. We only had a limited amount of antibiotics. It was not gas gangrene. It did not respond to more radical surgery. I do not think and hope it was not my "timid" approach to his legs. I think about it frequently and talk about it in surgical conferences. The one thing I know for sure, this wounded American, whom I tried to help, was a boy from the Midwest, a great man, a true hero. He is resting in peace back home. His name, Steve Laier, is on the Memorial Wall in Washington and he remains vivid in my thoughts. The Black Wall. I can be calm and give lengthy lectures about war wounds, but a visit to the Wall is an extremely emotional one.

As surgeons and physicians in a civilian setting, we have all had similar situations. We have all had disastrous cases and wondered about having made the right, or wrong, decisions. But reviewing the post-operative death of an 80-year-old with multiple comorbidities and a fracture of the hip is different. My thoughts about the dead and wounded in our 3rd Surgical, and the names on the Wall, range from the philosophical about wars in general to the Vietnam War specifically - tragedy, duty, honor, valor - all meaningful, yet sad. Plato's dictum, "The good die young," does not help much. A sense of religion can be a comfort. My grandfather was a theologian and minister and my grandmother's brother was the Lutheran minister with the Czar's Army in Vladivostok during the Russian/Japanese War in 1903 -1905. In Vietnam, in our frontline hospital, we also had a chaplain who, as well as he could, did the Lord's work among us and our wounded. What was said during WWI was also true in Vietnam: "There are no atheists in the trenches."

Speaking of chaplains, I was privileged to take care of ours, James Hutchens, the chaplain of the 173rd Airborne, who was shot by a sniper while helping to rescue and giving last rites to one of his mortally wounded men. He lived to have many years of selfless military service, was discharged with the rank of brigadier general and has continued to serve the Christian community in Israel. A true hero and a Man of God. Fifty-three years later I felt honored to be able to help get a posthumous Navy Cross to Waterbury-born Thomas Conway, the WWII chaplain of the USS Indianapolis, who lost his life after floating for four days with the survivors of the ship, helping them physically and spiritually until the end. He, like so many others, represents the important role our chaplains have played in all wars.

I can ramble on in thoughts and words about war, heroes, chaplains, life and death in battle, the cold facts and the emotions we deal with, but the reality is hard to describe. Having lived it, it is with me forever, and the year in Vietnam is one of the most significant in my life and career as a surgeon. It is more than being proud of my "service." It is respect for all those who served, gave their lives and limbs in Vietnam, especially those from the major units that were ours - 173rd Airborne Brigade, the 1st and 25th infantry divisions and the Special Forces. I wear their insignia to honor them. The sacrifice could be staggering at times - one company of the 173rd counted some 220 men when it arrived in Vietnam in 1965 but left a year later with only 17 of the original group, the rest having been killed in action or evacuated home with major wounds. It is these men, their units and their flag that I honor.

You were supposed to be tough, calm and able to do your job without emotion, and I did that. The only time I came close to an emotional edge occurred on a dark, windy, rainy night. I can't imagine the courage and skill of the MedEvac helicopter pilots who, in total darkness, through rain and wind, were bringing us the wounded from yet another bloody encounter with the Cong. I was acting as the triage officer that night. I was at the helipad, directing the seriously wounded to the resuscitation and operating room tents, the lesser ones to a holding area. It was dark, it was raining, the wind was blowing, the helicopter motor and swirling blades just a foot or two above our heads just added to the strange scene and shouts of all involved. There was a sense of urgency. The wounded had to be brought into our tents as quickly as possible, the helicopter pilots were anxious to leave since others were circling us, trying to deliver their wounded.

We had to move, we had to act fast - another had just landed, and I approached it with flashlight in hand. I could see the body of one of four soldiers on a stretcher near the helicopter's rear door. It was dark, it was eerie. I aimed my flashlight at him and his hand with a wedding ring was the first thing I saw. In a split second, the images of Julie, our three girls and this man's family passed through my mind. Here, there was something wrong, though. The soldier was not moving, his upper body was covered with a poncho and as I reached to remove it, my hand slipped into remnants of his skull and brain. It took a truly major effort to stay calm, under control and move to the next patient and the operations of that night.

As mentioned earlier, we did not take care of the Vietnamese troops. Their wounded were taken to Vietnamese Army hospitals, but their American advisors were brought to us. Thus, one morning, I was faced with a tall American captain on duty with a Vietnamese Marine unit. Both his ankles and feet had been shredded by a land mine. He had been spared wounds of the upper legs and trunk by the Vietnamese Marine next to him whose body had taken most of the blast and metal fragments. As we were getting ready for surgery, we established he was a Yale graduate and rower. I came close to amputating both his legs, but after extensive soul searching and close observation of some blood flow to the toes and the intact major nerves of the ankle, decided not to do it. He was the only patient I had to deal with that morning, and I had the time to think about it at length without the pressure of 20 more wounded waiting for their surgery. (With 20 more wounded waiting for their care, the decision to do amputations would have been the answer for the greater good of all involved.) My decision is one I have debated in my mind for five decades. The patient himself is now one of my most respected good friends. He thinks it was the right decision, but I wonder if his life would not have been better with modern prostheses. He spent three years in the Philadelphia Naval Hospital, had an untold number of operations then and in the course of the ensuing years, has continued to have infections and reoperations, but has his own feet and likes them the way they are. He is glad it was a quiet day when he arrived at the 3rd Surgical and applauds my highly debated decision to leave him with his shredded feet, but he does criticize me for cutting off his pants. One of our routines in order to examine the patients as quickly as possible and not miss other wounds or fractures was to cut off the patient's pants. His Vietnamese Marine pants had been custom tailored, since most of his Vietnamese comrades were at least a foot shorter and their standard issues were much too small. He was also forgetting they were as shredded as his skin and bones, but, to put the matter to rest, on one of my visits to his home on Cape Cod, I presented him with a brand-new pair of shiny United States Marine trousers, pants, bottoms or whatever they call them in their Corps. Once he was able to walk, the Marines wanted him to stay on active duty and become a lawyer. After a few months in law school, he decided the law was not a profession for him and retired from active duty. He then went on and had a very productive life, establishing a school for delinquent boys on an island off the coast of Massachusetts, working as a lobsterman and raising two sons, who, in family tradition, also served in the Marines. He is certainly one of Yale's finest graduates who, in spite of major disabilities, has had an extremely productive, constructive life.

The next patient I want to talk about was from Wisconsin and grew up in its woods, hunting rifle in hand. When he got to Vietnam with the 25th Infantry Division, the "crazy bastard" was volunteering to be "on point" with his patrols since going after hidden enemies was just like hunting deer back home. It was only a matter of time. He was shot, in 1966, by a North Vietnamese sniper while "on point" of a patrol in the jungles not too far from our hospital. His life was saved by the metal ammunition clips he had on his chest, but the bullet that ricocheted from the ammunition clips hit his right arm and shoulder. I would possibly not have remembered him, but he remembered me and found me through the Yale Medical School Historical Library website. He was eager to come to New Haven to see me again. We arranged to meet, had a wonderful day in New Haven and have been the best of friends ever since. We went through my Vietnam File at the Yale Medical School Historical Library and found his records, which I had kept and given to the Library. He has had a successful career in finance and has conservative views in line with some of mine. He is still an active hunter whose goal in life is to have successfully hunted every type of mountain goat on every continent. We have had a fun time with almost daily email exchanges. I am proud to know him and to have had a part in his life and in the lives of all the other 20-year-olds brought to us at the 3rd "MASH."

Jack Price is one of these men and has a very special part in this story of Vietnam. A lengthy book could be written about Jack. It would range from the jovial to the tragic, but heroic would be the best descriptions of his life from Oklahoma to West Point, then Vietnam and finally the back woods of Southwestern Virginia. A platoon of the 173rd Airborne had suffered casualties and they were being brought to our hospital. The last one to walk off the MedEvac helicopter was its leader, First Lieutenant Price. In a matter of minutes, he was on my operating table for treatment of a high velocity gunshot wound (probably AK-47) involving most of his forearm near the elbow. I was operating on him under nerve-block anesthesia and talking with him throughout the procedure. He was somewhat concerned about his arm and was hoping he would not need an amputation in spite of very marginal blood supply to the hand, major bone loss and probable nerve injuries. But his biggest concern was the probability he would be evacuated out of Vietnam before the arrival Jo Collins, *Playboy*'s Playmate of the Year, whose visit he had arranged upon his arrival in Vietnam. He and the "men/boys" in his platoon had collected enough money to order a lifetime subscription to Playboy and the first issue was to be delivered by a Playboy "Bunny." That lifetime subscription, coming from Warzone D in Vietnam, apparently caused major turmoil at the magazine's headquarters in Chicago. In due course, Hugh Hefner himself made the decision to have the first issue of Jack's lifetime subscription delivered by the Playmate of the Year instead of the promised ordinary "Bunny." Jo Collins was flying to Jack's platoon in Vietnam and was due within a few days, but by then Jack would have been evacuated to a hospital in Manila, Japan or the States. It took some "doing" with the Army establishment, but we were able to get a special dispensation to keep Lieutenant Price at the 3rd Surgical until Jo Collins' arrival. It worked out about as well as could be expected, although Jack had neuralgia of his forearm and hand from the contusion his nerves had sustained from the bullet that had passed through. It was fun for all, but it was sad to see Jack in severe pain throughout that special visit. He was with us long enough to have some skin grafts, which I did without plastic surgeons. As orthopedic surgeons in the 1960s, we were trained to do partial thickness skin grafts and full thickness skin flaps to cover wounds that could not be closed with standard closure techniques. Sixty years later, there are many more plastic surgeons and our orthopaedic residents seem unable to consider even the simplest of these procedures on their own. It is probably progress, but way back then we did most of the standard "plastic" closures and skin grafts on our own. Anyway, Jo Collins came and was an absolute sensation no matter where she went. She was the nicest, most sympathetic visitor we ever had at our hospital. Jack was with her for the entire stay and I was the official doctor in charge of such medical issues as giving her the shots she needed to return to the States - in the arm, much to the disappointment of the photographers who followed her every move. They had to settle for a view of her deltoids, having hoped for bared gluteus maximus muscles, which she definitely had and would have been worth visualization.

As soon as she left, Jack was evacuated to the Brooke Army Hospital in San Antonio, where I had the opportunity to visit him and his future wife, Sam, who worked there. He underwent some 30 operations in all - special full thickness skin grafts, bone grafts and multiple tendon transfers - but as soon as he could move his hand, he was volunteering to go back to Vietnam. It took special intervention by a high-ranking general to allow him to return to duty with the limited motion of his elbow and forearm, but back he went and served another year-and-a-half as a long-range patrol ranger and airborne company commander. Upon his return to the States, he was assigned to the Ranger School and, as one of the most distinguished young officers in the army, was advised to continue his career by attending command staff schools or similar institutions to be headed for higher command, responsibility and rank. At one of his annual physicals, the orthopaedic surgeon who examined his stiff arm was amazed at what he had done with it in combat but also told him he could at any time, based on the physical findings, get out of the army on full disability. He was not inclined to be an "administrator" and retired from military duty to get a degree in ocean engineering from MIT. After spending some time building and racing ocean-going motor yachts, he got involved in the diamond business with a friend from South Africa whom he had met while at MIT. His shop was in the Los Angeles area and all was well until some poor soul had the misfortune to attempt an armed robbery of the premises. It did not go well for the robber, but it also ended Jack's career in South African diamonds. He and his wife then ran one of the first electronic medical-transcription businesses in the country, with clients from coast to coast. They had also moved to live outside of Washington D.C. until they decided it was too close to Ground Zero in a potential attack on the United States. As far as Jack was concerned, a big or little dirty bomb on the District of Columbia was only a matter of time. Being the ultimate survivalists, they then moved to the mountains of southwestern Virginia where they built a house designed for long-term survival. They seemed totally happy in this remote part of the world, devoting their time to family, garden, beekeeping and the memory of his fellow West Point graduates, Rangers and members of the 173rd Airborne Brigade. We kept in touch through the years. I was made an honorary member of his West Point class and given their Honorary Saber. Attending his son's West Point graduation and joining him at an Army-Navy football game were very special events. It was also fascinating to visit him and Sam in their remote Virginia abode. Sadly, while taking care of his wife, who had developed early Alzheimer's, he contracted fatal pneumonia and died in the spring of 2018. Books can and should be written about Jack and his life of service, loyalty to country, his friends and family.

We were the hospital for the advance party of the

1st Infantry Division when it arrived before we had become fully operational. Their first KIA (Killed in Action) died tragically in our hospital. A West Point graduate, he had set up listening points around their position and, against all good sense, decided to check on them in the middle of the night. The 18-year-old trembling draftee on duty in one of those outposts, his loaded M-14 rifle in hand, was frightened by the large dark shadow approaching his post and fired, only to discover it to be the commanding officer. Severely wounded in the abdomen, the captain, married and with a child back home, was brought to us, where Julie Conn was able to save his life. But his kidneys failed, he developed an infection and died a slow death over the course of the next two weeks. It was in the very early phases of our presence in Vietnam and there was no way we could evacuate him to a larger hospital in the Philippines or Japan, where he might have survived. It was frustrating and sad. Our nurses sat with him, tried to console him, and helped him write letters home as he was awaiting death. If I have to, I remember it well, but it is such a sad story it is easy to repress it.

These are the stories of but a few of the many wounded who passed through our tents and whom we helped. I am certain most of these men went on to have full, productive lives, and have been proud of their service, good fortune and above all of their fellows who did not come back. But I am also sure that among them are men who had difficulty dealing with the grim reality of war, such as the three members of our 3rd Surgical Staff who committed suicide shortly after getting back home. We also had two episodes of major mental collapse while still in Vietnam.

In November 1965, two months after our arrival in Bien Hoa, the 173rd, the Royal Australian Regiment and the New Zealander Artillery, started major combat operations. One of them, called the "Hump," flooded us with casualties. We operated nonstop for two days, ran short of supplies and blood and were tested physically, mentally and emotionally. It was a major victory for the 173rd and we had done our part of the job. It was over and it was time to put it all in the back of us and move on. The senior medic of the Royal Australian Regiment was retiring and going home. It seemed like the appropriate time to have a celebration in his honor. We invited him to come to our tent, where one of its corners had been set up with empty ammunition boxes as a living area and lounge. It was time to have a few drinks. We listened to the Australian's stories, dating back to WWII, Korea and the jungles of Malaysia, then had a few more drinks. Toby, one of our nurse anesthetists, who had lost two of his wounded in the midst of their operations, and had been, like the rest of us, upset by our supply problems, was doing a good job of drowning his sorrows. We stripped him naked, put him face down in his cot, expecting regurgitation and hoping to avoid aspiration problems. Having done so, the rest of us returned to our "lounge" to complete the evening on a less alcoholic level.

The evening ramped up suddenly as we saw our "buddy," stark naked except for jungle boots, M-14 rifle in hand, coming in our direction, mumbling something about getting our commanding officer who, in his eyes, was responsible for all of our supply problems and the death of the men on his operating table. Our response was dramatic. The area was cleared in a second and the wobbling Toby passed through the empty "lounge," continuing his mumble about "getting" Major Downs. Outside, he immediately got lost in the dark and stumbled into the rice paddy next to our tent. I followed him, crawling on my stomach, hoping to jump him. I thought he wouldn't see me in his inebriated state, but that was not the case. I heard him trying to chamber a round of ammunition in his rifle - click, click, click - and yelling, "I see you, Keggi! I see you, Keggi!" Suddenly, there was a very young military policeman on the ground next to me, who, in a matter of seconds, assessed the situation, stood up and walked calmly straight at our Toby. "An officer and a gentleman does not behave this way, Sir! Give me your riffle, Sir!" He did, and I suddenly felt brave enough to join that amazing M.P. to grab poor Toby. He was putting up a struggle, but joined by several others, we were able to restrain him and strap him between two stretchers with a hole cut out over his nose and mouth and evacuate him as a "stretcher sandwich" to Saigon where, in a stationary hospital, there was a psychiatrist.

That was the end of our party. I don't remember if we had another drink that night, but all of us felt lucky that in that rice paddy the rifle had jammed. Two days later, Toby was back, sober, subdued and able to function without any obvious psychiatric problems for the rest of his tour. All of us were very understanding, we all had been through those bloody days, and having two young soldiers die on your operating table is tough. We all thought highly of Toby as a man, he was a superb anesthetist, but for a few minutes he had been a major life threat to himself and the rest of us. His anxieties may also have been aggravated by radio broadcasts from Hanoi and their English-speaking female voice who while we were in the midst of surgery was describing the scene outside our hospital: "Doctors of the 3rd Surgical Hospital, we see those wounded soldiers lying on stretchers, in the rain, outside of your tents. They lost the battle." Some of the Vietnamese workers who were working in our hospital area were obviously passing information to their comrades in touch with Hanoi radio. We were hearing the real "Hanoi Jane." Her American version came a little later and should be remembered, forever, as the voice of absolute treason – "Hanoi Jane Fonda."

Another one of our male nurses, another best of men, had a similar gun-in-hand breakdown. Alexander was the only one on our staff who had served in the Korean War, where he flew on medical evacuation planes with the nickname "Alexander the Flying Nurse." Unfortunately, he had a difficult time with our head nurse. Alexander was in charge of the admission and resuscitation area. He was extremely effective, organized and worked well with us as we were dealing with the wounded upon their arrival in various states of shock, hemorrhage, total exsanguination, pain and confusion. I considered him a close friend and we had spent a few days together on a weekend of R&R on the South China Sea beaches near Vung Tau. He was entertaining, and the highlight of many of an evening with tales of Korea, Japan and the details of his days in a Geisha House. He was on the heavy side of the scale and was bald, except for the rest of his body, neck, arms, and hands, that were covered with tufts of dark hair, which added something special to the "visual" aspects of the Geisha stories. Hairy Alexander with cute Geishas all around him - great stories and much appreciated by those of us in the midst of the daily insanity of our war. In the hospital, he was totally dedicated to the lifesaving details of his work.

Our head nurse was a nice "little old lady" who was of minimal practical assistance and made Alexander's life miserable by her insistence on a variety of superfluous details and nursing routines. After a confrontation about the handling of large glass containers full of alcohol sponges for rapid cleansing of the patient's skin for IV's, cut downs, chest tubes, catheterizations or tracheostomies, Alexander returned to his bunk in our tent. It was the middle of the day, but since the tents were dark, there was always a string of lightbulbs lit from one end to the other. I was in the tent when he returned from his encounter. He was not saying much, and the tent was hot, as usual. I was quietly reading when all of a sudden there were gunshots from his end of the tent. There he was, in his bunk, lying on his back, firing his revolver at the lightbulbs. He was calm and did not seem to be interested in shooting me. He did not need to be jumped, nor did he require "a litter sandwich." He gave up his weapon without a struggle and was shipped off to the Saigon psychiatrist without any major objections. He, too, was back two days later and did not seem to have any further mental problems - until his alleged suicide shortly after getting back to the States. He did a great job in our hospital, he truly cared for the wounded, he was a friend, we felt sorry for him and the problems he was having with the head nurse and I was glad he was taking out his frustrations on the lightbulbs instead of his tent mate.

We were in a combat zone and there were moments of potential danger and potential infiltration or attack. There was one occasion when the situation was very "uncomfortable." It was nighttime and I was in the middle of an operation, a major wound debridement, when suddenly there was gunfire, a firefight, less than 100 yards from our "operating room." It seems ludicrous to compare our situation in the operating tent in the middle of the 3rd Surgical/173rd Airborne Compound to the daily dangers of the young soldiers in the field. We knew we were as safe as you could be in a combat zone, surrounded by the troops of the 173rd Airborne, yet suddenly there was the possibility of someone charging through our tent with a satchel charge, ready to blow us to smithereens. It was alarming, but at the time there was only one thing we could do: "stay calm and carry on." I was more concerned with the possibility of an unexpected event while doing my volunteer surgery in a Vietnamese civilian hospital or when I was with the Special Forces out in the field. I did the work, I felt it was important, but was very much aware of the risks. I was always happy when I got back to the relative safety of the 173rd Airborne. As extra insurance, I always had that private Smith and Wesson Chief's Special revolver with me under my operating gown. I am glad I never had to consider using it.

When there were no combat missions in the area, or during the month of December 1965, when President Johnson declared a ceasefire in Vietnam and a "Peace Offensive" throughout the world, life could be fat and easy. Sleep late with the blowing fan, have breakfast and linger over coffee, then return to the bunk to write letters to Julie or read *Campbell's Operative Orthopaedics*. The writing of letters was an integral part of daily life and most of us spent at least an hour or two at that task each day. The letters from home arrived in the afternoon "mail call" – by far the most awaited event of each day. The nap after lunch was frequently followed by gin-and-tonics in preparation for the unappetizing dinner ("slop"), then some more letter writing, reading or more napping while awaiting poker at the 173rd officers tent and the gin-and-tonics that went with the game. I participated in those late-night games for a few weeks, managed to keep most of my money and quit after an evening of high returns ($200 comes to mind). I saved all of the letters from Julie and, much to my surprise, when I returned home found out she had saved all of mine. Many years later our granddaughter Julia Hunter spent a month of one of her college (Duke) summers putting them in order. They are now in the Yale Medical Historical Library in the Keggi File. When I gave these letters to Yale, I didn't think anybody would be looking at them for years, but when the library announced them in their bulletin a Yale College class studying the Vietnam War used them in their course immediately.

"Rest and Recuperation" (R&R) was an entitlement after you spent a certain number of days or weeks in a war zone. I decided to take my R&R in Bangkok, Thailand. It started at the Saigon airport, from which our R&R group was to be flown to Bangkok. While waiting to be "processed," I met a Navy lieutenant who seemed like a good guy and we decided to room together. It worked out well and we had a wonderful time visiting spectacular Thai temples, buying temple rubbings and some fancy silks for the girls back home. Shortly after our visit to Thailand the temple rubbings were no longer sold on the streets, their production ("rubbing") being forbidden since it was destroying the carvings on the temple walls. When we were there, though, they were still sold on street corners for minimal dollars and I bought at least a dozen that remain among our family art possessions.

I had a special evening in Bangkok with a Thai Army colonel and orthopaedic surgeon who had been our guest in El Paso while he was getting some training at Beaumont Hospital the previous year. He came to my hotel with a bottle of Scotch whisky and we went to some Thai restaurants featuring meals that seemed to be pure curry. The Scotch helped to get that curry processed. As the evening progressed the colonel made it clear that according to all Thai customs of hospitality and culture, my visit with him could not end until we had found a woman to complete my night and visit to Bangkok. We went to several clubs where I could select my companion for the night, yet in spite of my insistence I did not want to turn my R&R into I&I ("Intoxication and Intercourse"), the colonel insisted on continuing the search for my woman. He would not take me back to my hotel without a Thai companion for the night. Finally tiring of the visits to Bangkok's finest hot spots, I made a choice and the colonel dropped us off at the "special visitor" rear entrance of my hotel. After the appropriate bowing and courtesies, the colonel left and as soon as he was out of sight, I dismissed my "date," who expressed disappointment, but, having been paid at some point of the evening by my gracious host Colonel Sirichai, left without further ado. I went to my room and my sleeping Navy roommate.

In the course of our few days and evening together, I told my roommate, who was the third or fourth highest ranking officer in charge of the Port of Saigon, about all of our tragic supply problems. He was duly impressed and assured me he could help, since the Navy warehouses in Saigon were full of everything we needed. Upon our return to Vietnam, he said, I should visit him to pursue the matter. That was exciting news and as soon as I got back to the 3rd Surgical I reported it to our commanding officer. He had no objections to reaching out to the Navy for whatever supplies and equipment we needed. The following day our supply officer and I drove down to the Port of Saigon headquarters and found my Bangkok roommate in his air-conditioned office (not one, but two air conditioners blowing at him from two different angles). He assured us we could have anything we wanted as long as the paperwork was completed. He gave us triplicate requisition forms and told us to fill them out for any and all items we needed from the Navy warehouses. We were then to come back with the forms and trucks to pick up the requested supplies. He would sign one copy of the requisitions, indicating the items involved had been transferred to the Army. We would then have to get an Army supply officer to sign the second copy of the requisitions, indicating the items had been duly accepted by the Army. With the two signed forms in hand we could then proceed to the warehouses to load up our trucks and return to our hospital. The third copy of the requisition forms, which normally would go to some central accounting office, would have to disappear. The Navy would have their signed papers documenting the "official" transfer of materials to the Army, which in turn had their signed papers showing their acceptance. With the third copy missing, that would be the end of the story. It was all in the family and the fog of war. "Big Brother" probably did not care and did not need to be bothered about such minor problems as inadequate equipment in a mobile hospital.

We returned to Bien Hoa in the afternoon and our supply officer and his staff spent the rest of the day and evening filling out a stack of the triplicate forms requesting refrigerators, freezers, desks, typewriters, chairs, sheets, fans and a variety of medical supplies. The following morning, with the appropriately filled-out stack of forms in hand, we returned in trucks to the air-conditioned office of my Navy friend. He signed all of our forms, indicating the Navy was transferring our requested items to the Army. It took him what seemed like a half-hour to sign the stack of our forms. When he was done, we headed to the Army section of the port to get them signed by one of their officers, whom our guy knew. He would be willing to do his official part of signing the acceptance forms, allowing us to proceed to the Navy warehouses to load our trucks. But a major surprise awaited us. The officer who was to sign our forms was no longer there and had been replaced by a stern looking full colonel who blew his top when asked to sign our forms. Our supply officer and naval companion seemed to fade into the background, and I was left to take the full blast of anger from the colonel.

"Captain Keggi, what do you think you are doing? You are totally out of order!"

And on and on. Asking the colonel to call me Doctor Keggi just got him more agitated. Finally, after at least 15 minutes of ranting and raving, I was able to tell him the story of our shortages of medical supplies and how it affected the care of our wounded men. In due course he seemed to calm down, "understood our problem," and, from the bottom of his generous heart, sign one of our requisition forms for the item we needed the most. I shuffled through the stack of requisitions and picked out the one for a refrigerator for blood storage which he signed before telling us to "get the hell out of my office."

Once outside, the first words out of the mouth of our Navy benefactor were, "Fuck that bastard! I know somebody in the Army PX system who owes me a favor and will sign the forms." Lord knows what that favor might have been, but off we went to the central PX, where in one of the offices in the far back of the store, a young 2nd lieutenant, signed all of our forms indicating the Army was accepting the equipment and supplies we were requesting from the Navy. We were then off to the naval warehouses where we loaded our trucks and headed home to the 3rd Surgical and the much-needed gin-and-tonics. No idea what happened to the third copy of the forms. I presume they burned well in the latrine barrels. The items we brought back from the Navy were all of use, starting with that refrigerator for storing blood and finishing with toilet paper. With refrigerators in place it was also the beginning of much happier times with our gin-and-tonics, which could now be served with ice. It is a strange story, but in line with so many other war stories of improvisation outside the rules and regulations - for the good of the men in the field, the good of the wounded and the greater cause. Could have received a medal, might have been court-martialed, but all of us at the 3rd Surgical felt good about it and were certain we could better help our wounded with the supplies and equipment we had "liberated."

The troops, the wounded and some of our surgeons were starting to sport moustaches. It seemed like the perfect time for me to try one on my own face. Being less than hirsute, it took a couple of weeks to grow one that I could curl up in the frisky manner of a 19th-century British or Prussian officer, and I thought it was worth a few photographs and long-term consideration. It did not work out that way. One morning, during an operation in our hot and humid operating room, the perspiration running down my face was soaking that frisky appendage to the point where I no longer could stand it. At the end of the case, I went straight to my bunk and shaved it off. The next operation was as hot as the first, but I no longer had to deal with a moustache dripping hot sweat into my mouth while I was operating.

CENTRAL HIGHLANDS

T hus "moustacheless," I was off to the Central Highlands in January 1966. There were North Vietnamese regiments operating along the Cambodian border near Buon Ma Thuot that were a major threat to all of central Vietnam. General Westmoreland had decided to deal with them with a multidivision operation (1st Air Cavalry and the 101st Airborne). The operation also needed medical support, and we, the "mobile" 3rd Surgical Hospital, were elected for the job. The area was supposed to be dangerous, and in Westmoreland's judgment, too dangerous for our female nurses. They were all replaced by male nurses from other hospitals in Vietnam and the States before we were flown, by large C-130 transport planes, to the Central Highlands, the mountains of Vietnam. We had our tents, our medical equipment and our trucks. We were all armed with M-14 rifles and .45 handguns, but also carried Geneva Convention cards declaring us "noncombatants."

We set up our hospital tents next to the runway of an old airfield, which was the gathering point for the various combat units involved in trying to engage and destroy the North Vietnamese who were said to be there. When we left Bien Hoa, our hospital had been undergoing construction and the tents we had lived and worked in were gradually being replaced by wooden barracks with the promise of screens and air conditioning (something I never did get to experience). Up in the Highlands, it was back into the tents, but the good news was that the air temperatures were cool and there were even nights cold enough to require a blanket for comfort. Even though we were generally next to useless as true soldiers, we had to set up our own security perimeter with medics, scrub techs, nursing assistants and truck drivers acting as sentries. It was less than reassuring to see some of them patrol the area with helmets on their heads, rifles over their shoulders and a portable radio blaring music in their hands. It was not a problem as long as the 101st Airborne, the 1st Air Cavalry and the Special Forces were around, but a couple weeks into the campaign there were sudden changes that in a matter of hours made our situation precarious, to say the least.

I was having an after-dinner beer in the one of the doctors' tents when the brigade surgeon of the 1st Air Cavalry arrived late to announce the combat units were moving to another location at "O-five hundred" (5 a.m.) the next morning. The North Vietnamese units in the area had vanished, probably across the border into Cambodia, thus the operation we were sent to support had been completed. Everybody was leaving the area within a few hours. It was stunning news to say the least. I immediately went to our commanding officer's tent, where the major was half asleep with a beer in hand. I informed him about what I had heard and wanted to know our own orders. He had no clue, no orders, nothing. I informed the rest of our physicians about the news I had heard and our commander's total lack of information about it. I had done my job, there was nothing further I could do, so I went to sleep, soon to be awakened by the rattle of tanks, trucks and jeeps as our troops departed the area. The last armored personnel carrier to leave was headed by the colonel in charge, who, sitting atop his tank, pulled up to our tents in a cloud of dust, looking like Patton himself, and gave us the word: "I don't know what you guys are going to do, but if I were you I'd get the fuck out of here." Message delivered, his armored personnel carrier spun around and took off. All of a sudden it was silent. We, the 3rd Surgical Hospital, Mobile, Army, were alone, close to the Cambodian border, on an isolated runway in the middle of nowhere, an area too dangerous for female nurses, and with North Vietnamese regiments somewhere nearby.

We had no orders, but we knew we had to get "the fuck out of there." Our commanding officer, Major Downs, managed to get on a plane that had landed for a brief inspection of the departure of the fighting units and was gone. He was clueless and had no idea of what we were supposed to do. He said he was leaving to get orders about what to do next, but most of us felt he was abandoning the ship for his own safety. It was a beautiful, sunny morning. The peace and quiet were in total contrast to the activity of the combat troops with their armored vehicles and helicopters that surrounded us less than a few hours before. We were walking around the area wondering what to do next. The vague, mild mannered, nice guy, profoundly religious regular army anesthesiologist left in command was of zero help. Julie Conn, Art DeSimone, our internist from Columbia, and I seemed to be a committee of sorts, trying to help our anesthesiologist/acting commander make a decision about our next move. Our deliberations were interrupted by a small plane circling above us and then coming in for a landing. It was a CBS News crew on its way back to Saigon from a mission in the northern part of the country. They had spotted our isolated tents with their red crosses and a C-130 transport plane that had crashed a few days earlier. After making sure it was safe to land, they'd decided to stop to take a look at the upended plane at the end of our runway. Julie, Art and I approached the video crew and told them about our predicament, our lack of orders and need for help. We described ourselves as having been lost. We quickly became a "Lost Hospital" that had been moved from one command area to another and then left behind without orders. The video crew was friendly and assured us they would report our story to Peter Kalischer, their boss and the CBS correspondent in Vietnam, who would then have to decide what to do with it. They left. We had sent a message to the outside world, but we did not expect to see them again. Our acting commander and anesthesiologist had stood by, did not object to our conversation with the video crew, but did not want to participate in it. Meanwhile, we still had to get "the fuck out of there," and after several more hours of hanging around without further orders or communications of any kind, we decided to pack up and move to a nearby Special Forces camp just outside of Buon Ma Thuot. By the time we were "packed," it was getting dark and had started to rain. We sat on our trucks with rifles at the ready. We had no idea what to expect on the five-mile journey. There were no other vehicles on the road. We were passing through some dense jungle without any protection and thought of ourselves as a target of great opportunity to any Viet Cong or North Vietnamese unit in the vicinity. We made it through, and once in Buon Ma Thuot were directed to an empty soccer field, part of that Special Forces camp. It was dark and raining hard as we set up our tents. Finally, the generators kicked into gear and the lights came on to give us a view of the ground around us. Wet grass, mud and dead rats. No problem with the mud, but the dead rats were a major concern, since we knew Buon Ma Thuot had had some recent cases of the plague, a disease spread by fleas and rats, the rats dying from the killing bacteria they were carrying. We had all been vaccinated against the plague and no ill came of our dead rats, but they were an unpleasant surprise when the lights came on.

The next day, Major Downs, our commanding officer, was back, approved of our decision to "get the fuck out" of our unprotected airstrip and explained how we had been lost between the commands of two Army Corps. The following day, as we were getting settled in our new surroundings, we had an unannounced visit from Peter Kalischer, who, with his CBS crew, had flown up from Saigon to record and report the story of the "Lost Hospital." Major Downs, safe and sound after his return to us, was not happy, but could not order us to keep quiet about a major administrative error by the Saigon Commandos that could easily have cost our lives. Julie Conn, Art DeSimone and I, who had spoken with the video crew a few days before, were willing to speak for the hospital and the greater good of future mobile hospitals assigned to combat missions without specific orders in the case of changing plans for their companion combat units. Major Downs and other members of our staff watched as the three of us told our story. It did not take too long. The crew did not seem to be eager to spend any more time than absolutely necessary in our camp and left as soon as we were done. We did not know what to expect next and had plenty to do getting settled in our new surroundings. It was totally different, and we had much greater contact with the surrounding inhabitants than we had in Bien Hoa. We became acquainted with the Special Forces as well as a Protestant missionary group, an orphanage run by a French nun with a Ph.D. in English literature, and, above all, the Montagnards who thought of themselves and their mountains as a separate nation that did not belong to the Vietnamese lowlanders. The town itself was also scenic, with the imperial palace of the former emperor Boa Dai as its centerpiece.

Back in Washington, Robert McNamara, the Secretary of Defense, was being briefed about the multidivision operation in the Central Highlands along the Cambodian border. The operation was going smoothly even though the North Vietnamese units they were chasing seemed to have vanished into Cambodia. The situation seemed under control until they happened to see Walter Cronkite's CBS Evening News with Peter Kalischer reporting the "Lost Hospital" story. That apparently was worthy of a direct red telephone call to General Westmoreland in Vietnam, who apparently had not been told about our plight and flight. One can only imagine the scene and conversations at the General's headquarters, but the aftershocks at our end of it were dramatic.

We were sitting around in our shorts, flip flops and T-shirts as a helicopter landed on our helipad. It discharged several colonels from Saigon headquarters who were looking for Captains Keggi, Conn and DeSimone. We came out of our hot tent to meet them, and, after a sharp exchange of military greetings that ended with our insistence on being addressed as "doctors" not "captains," we invited them into our tent to sit down, have a warm beer and hear our story starting from lack of supplies to being lost in enemy territory. What started as a seemingly hostile confrontation ended as a friendly discussion of the events and the surgical work we had been doing and were ready to do again. We did make a strong point of our shortages of medical supplies and surgical instruments. The scene was somewhat comical. We the civilian soldier surgeons in shorts, flip flops and T-shirts - the Saigon Commando colonels fully equipped for their flight into a war zone, in full jungle fatigues, .45 automatics with extra ammunition on their belts, sipping warm beer and resolving the problems at hand. We thought it had been a good encounter with the high brass, and as they were getting back on their helicopter their farewell words to us were: "Yes it was a fuck up, but officers and gentlemen do not go to the press." Once more it was a situation where we had done what seemed to be the right thing for our hospital and wounded, but the Army was once more in a situation where they did not know whether to give us medals or to court-martial us. They could not discipline us by sending us to Vietnam - we were there already. Even in Vietnam, they could not discipline us by sending us up into the jungles of the Central Highlands - we were there already. We all pressed on and hoped the men in command learned something from our actions as citizen soldiers, doing our duty as best as we could think of it.

Up to this point, our hospital had been a showpiece for the Army Medical Corps in action. We were proud of our service and care of our wounded. We had the highest academic and professional qualifications – the senators, congressmen and others who came to visit were all impressed with our work, dedication and morale. Their visits had been frequent. But after the "Lost Hospital" episode, they stopped. We were to be kept out of sight. We were not to be visited by politicians nor the press. We had been bad boys and were to be kept isolated. We did however go from C-rations (in a can) to A-rations of meat, fresh vegetables and ice cream. All of a sudden, the instruments and supplies we had been waiting for started arriving in triplicate. Our new friends in Washington and Saigon had been given the word to give us anything we wanted as long as we were kept from causing more bad publicity with stories to the press and politicians.

At that time, there were no major regular army combat operations, and we were getting only a few casualties from the irregular troops in the area. This gave us time to get involved with some other work. The Special Forces had a makeshift tent hospital a few miles out of town where I operated on their mercenary and Montagnard wounded. In the eyes of the local Rha De tribe, this work was sufficient to warrant my initiation into their tribe. I was taken to one of their villages of wooden and straw huts on stilts in a Special Forces Jeep with a guard, machine gun in hand. The ceremony was supposed to have an animal sacrifice, but in my case, it consisted of simply drinking putrid rice wine from a large clay ceremonial jar while the men of the tribe chanted in the background. They had a very precise way of serving the wine. It was sucked up through a long straw from the jar which was kept full to the very top by one of the tribesmen who knew exactly how much wine was being drunk by the initiate by watching the level of the liquid in the jar and then refilling it. One cup, two cups, more chanting, three cups, more chanting and then cheers from the village boys who had gathered around the hut, waiting for vomiting out one of the windows (holes in the wall of the hut). I disappointed them. It was interesting to note there were no women or girls in sight anywhere. As I sucked up the wine, some of their special spices and debris at the bottom of the jar also came up into my mouth - it was anything but a fancy French vintage and hard to keep down. I managed to do so, but as I was sucking up this Rha De brew the thought of every tropical gastrointestinal disease passed through my mind. Luckily, I was spared the parasites, worms and bacteria, but for the rest of my life even the slightest sip of even the fanciest of rice wines brings back the memory of that initiation and my Montagnard "brothers." At the end of the drinking and chanting, I was given a wooden crossbow with arrows, a simple brass bracelet, a black turban like head dress and a Rha De loin cloth (which some 20 years later I gave to the Yale Peabody Museum of

Anthropology). I was driven back to our hospital in my new loincloth, which in my happy frame of mind I showed off with a vague imitation of some tribal dancing (well recorded in many photographs taken by my uninitiated colleagues). I did not adopt some of the more interesting habits of my tribe such as men squatting to pass water and the women doing it standing up, legs spread, long skirt pulled to the waist, but I am proud of having helped them and be one of theirs.

All was not surgery in Vietnam. Here, I show off the gifts I received from a Montagnard tribe after being initiated into their ranks.

A follow-up to the initiation was another Montagnard "cocktail party" at a remote Special Forces outpost called Camp Alpha reached by armed jeep over roads through jungle and coffee plantations. The mission of the camp was to police the area, gather information about enemy activities and, in the case of a major confrontation, to hold out as long as possible, then "fade into the night." After a formal military review of the 20 Montagnard troops ranging in age from 15 to 50, I was seated between two Rha De chieftains who did not speak English but had served with the French. I spoke enough of my high school language to carry on a modest conversation. There was some food, but the main event again was their rice wine concoction. I did not have to suck it out of a jar; it was served in regular glasses. The chief on the right would tap me on the shoulder to do a "bottoms up toast" which would be followed by a tap on the left shoulder and the toast from the chief on that side. It did not take long to understand their plan of celebrating my visit, and from then on, we all drank together – bottoms up on the right, bottoms up in the middle, bottoms up on the left. I could handle that since my Montagnard brothers were at least a foot shorter and 50 pounds lighter. At the end of the festivities I was less than steady on my feet, but my chiefs were under the table. I was taken back to the 3rd Surgical in that Special Forces jeep with its guard and machine gun in the back. It had been another interesting day. Had it also been a foolish day? Probably so, and, as a matter of record, none of my peers were comfortable about such excursions to the outposts of our Special Forces in the woods around Bhan Ma Thuot or remote Montagnard villages. I would probably go again, but there would be my tentmates who would advise me to stay in our guarded camp.

Bhan Ma Thuot also had a major Christian Protestant mission complex devoted to helping the sick, spreading the Christian Gospel and translating the Bible into Rha De. These missionaries were the most admirable human beings I have ever met, and one of the greatest horrors of the war was their slaughter by the North Vietnamese troops during the Tet Offensive. It is my understanding that 30 years later some missionaries were allowed to return to the remnants of their homes to resume their good deeds and the translation of the Bible. I hope that is fact.

One of our major efforts with missionaries was helping the lepers in this part of the Highlands. Leprosy was endemic among the Montagnards, with estimates as high as 60 percent of them being affected by the disease in its various forms. Foot and hand deformities were among the most disabling manifestations of the chronic disease, and since some of these deformities could be corrected by tendon transfers, I was encouraged by the Army Special Forces colonel in charge of the area to consider performing some of these operations. It was also an interesting project from an academic, surgical-experience perspective. I was more than happy to do it, but before starting any of the operations I insisted that the colonel would get me back to Bhan Ma Thout for follow-up care of the patients should our hospital be ordered out of the area. Having obtained this absolute promise from the colonel, we set up a makeshift operating room in one of the missionary shacks that had probably been a chicken coop in the past. There, with the help of volunteers from our hospital and the missionaries, I did a series of hand and foot tendon transfers. I was pleased to have had some training to do these operations at Roosevelt Hospital (Dr. Bill Littler) and Yale (Dr. Bob Chase).

There was also a Catholic orphanage nearby. It was run by a very genteel French nun who in her younger years had obtained a Ph.D. in English Literature from the Sorbonne University in Paris and spoke fluent English. She had also trained as a nurse, and when I consented to some corrective surgery on one of her orphans, she insisted on helping in the operating room. It was all good, but when she joined us, we had a major communication problem. Her English, as stated, was perfect, but our vocabulary was suddenly cut by about a third. During the weeks in the Central Highlands without our female nurses, most of us had degenerated to talking "Army talk," with its colorful copulatory, excremental or ejaculatory adjectives. It was an absolute privilege to work with this dedicated woman and to adjust our language accordingly. I have no information about her fate at the hands of the North Vietnamese, but I hope she survived the horrors of war to continue doing God's work on earth.

All was well, and we seemed to be learning a lot about missionary work, the history of the Montagnards and their diseases, which included waking up with their numb and necrotic leprosy-afflicted toes chewed off by rats during the night. Eventually came the inevitable orders to return to our home base outside of Bien Hoa and the care of the wounded of the 173rd Airborne Brigade, the 1st Infantry Division and such other combat units as the 25th Infantry Division that were arriving in Vietnam. I could not, however, forget my lepers in the mountains, and, before leaving, made sure once again that the Special Forces colonel in charge was going to live up to his promise and have me brought back to finish taking care of them. He had under his command a couple of two-seater Cessna L-19 forward-observation planes, and he assured me that one of them would be dispatched to pick me up in Bien Hoa at a prearranged time.

When the time arrived, I was brought to the Bien Hoa Airbase in my travel outfit of jungle fatigues, some minor personal items, helmet, M-14 rifle with its double load of ammunition and a box of supplies including some plaster of Paris. The pilot who had been assigned to this Civic Action operation and had flown down from Bhan Me Thuot to pick me up at the Bien Hoa Airbase, was fuming. The lightweight L-19 was not designed to fly long distances at high altitudes and in bad weather. We did have bad weather, and the 150 miles we had to fly was over enemy-controlled jungle and mountains. We could not fly too low since that would expose us to all types of enemy ground fire, but at the safer altitudes we were in worse weather. The pilot had survived a year of combat duty with his L-19, was due to go home in a week and now here he was, exposed to all kinds of potential problems having to fly a crazy "doc" to take care of a 'bunch of fucking gooks." Was I supposed to give up our mission? Listening to his diatribe about the weather and the flight over enemy jungle, I certainly considered it. But since he was flying back north anyway, I decided to go. As I was getting into the tight rear compartment of the plane, I noticed a sign on its door, "Maximum Load in Rear Compartment 205 pounds." I thought it was worth mentioning to the angry pilot since I weighed 210 pounds naked and there I was in full uniform, with helmet, rifle, ammunition, medical supplies. "Get in," was his only reply. I managed to do so and was able to put on the safety belts. The box of supplies, the rifle, its ammunition and my personal items were going to be held between my legs and on my lap. Just before our departure we also had the unique experience of watching one of the famous, or infamous, U-2 long-distance, high-altitude "spy" planes take off at high speed and a rocketlike angle. We took off at what was very slow speed by comparison as the pilot tried to reach altitude high enough to be out of gunfire range by making our ascent as steep as possible. As he leveled off and we were bouncing along in the bad weather, the pilot, who had not said a word since my squeeze into the rear compartment, suddenly issued another order: "Put on the parachute that's under your seat." I managed to get it strapped on, but it did not add much to the overall sense of security while flying at 10,000 feet in bad weather over the dense jungle below with an angry, uncommunicative pilot. Then all of a sudden, the plane seemed to be in a steep, spiraling fall which seemed like the end of ends, until the pilot started laughing. As it turned out, it was the only safe way to land at our destination. A smooth, gradual, slow, straight line approach to the short runway outside of Bhan Ma Thout was simply an invitation to be shot at by the Viet Cong or North Vietnamese. The pilot was amusing himself, celebrating his safe return to home base and getting some jollies out of scaring the "doc of the gooks" in his rear compartment.

The follow-up care of the lepers with their tendon transfers went well, and the operations I had performed on them seemed to be successful. I had a nice visit with our missionary friends and spent a couple of nights in one of the bedrooms of the spectacular hunting lodge, or palace, of the former Emperor (Bao Dai) of Vietnam. My roommate in the lodge was a Special Forces lieutenant who, on both days I was with him, went out on patrol. Every morning before leaving, he wrote a letter home – "All is well up here in the mountains of Vietnam. I am safe etc., etc."

Based on what the L-19 pilot had reported to the colonel in charge it was decided not to repeat that small-plane adventure. The trip back to Bien Hoa took me instead through the coastal city of Nha Trang and then a long helicopter ride along the coast of the South China Sea, over beautiful blue waters and sandy white beaches framed by dense green jungle. Future sites of resorts and golf courses for sure.

After our 3rd Surgical Hospital had been moved back to Bien Hoa, the time for me to go home was approaching rapidly. The flow of wounded continued at a steady pace, but we were no longer the only hospital in War Zone D. A stationary evacuation hospital had been set up in Long Binh, just a few miles from us, and other hospitals were also arriving with the massive influx of combat units into Vietnam. Life had settled into a routine with few unexpected events. The patients were brought in, we knew what to do, we were well supplied, and our primary thoughts were devoted to plans beyond the Army. For all of us it was a complicated process negotiated through handwritten letters that took several days to reach home. In this manner even the simplest of problems would take almost two weeks to resolve. In the case of an absolute emergency, we could make a call by radio, but that was a complicated process and I attempted it only once. It was prearranged through the USO in Saigon, scheduled by mail with Julie in El Paso, and frustrating as you went through the radio call routine of "Is this you Julie?" "Over." and "Over and out." - all of it barely audible through the interfering crackle and noise of the radio waves.

Our biggest family problem arose with a letter from Dr. Southwick asking me to return to Yale and the academic career we once had been planning: "You owe it to Yale. You will be the first academic surgeon back from the war in Vietnam. Your experiences have to be shared. You are too valuable to be a community surgeon in Arizona. At $20,000 a year you will be the highest paid Assistant Professor in Yale history." Etc., etc.

I had loved teaching while in training at Yale, and the year with residents at Beaumont General Hospital in El Paso had been fun. It had been exciting to think of new operations and ways to improve the lives of disabled patients. Education and teaching was a family mantra. Grandfather, Father and Mother had all been teachers. But prior to my leaving El Paso, Julie and I had decided to live and practice orthopaedic surgery in Tucson. We both loved the Southwest and Mexico, it was going to be a good life and now thousands of miles away from her, the decision to go back to Yale was a very, very hard one. After much soul searching, sitting in the midst of war in remote

Vietnam, I finally decided to go back to Yale. We would be amidst our many old friends and live up to Dr. Southwick's expectations of a productive academic career. At first Julie had a very difficult time accepting it, but it had to be. It was a decision made by the Kristaps shown in jungle fatigues in front of the tent marked "Surgery," staring into the distance, having to deal with the wounded, the flights over the jungle, the uncertainties of each day - yet trying to see the future in the most optimistic and idealistic terms. A future with Julie and the family, but also a productive future in the field of orthopaedic surgery.

I was convinced the war we were fighting was justified to stop the influence and spread of Communism, but at the same time I was eager to get back home to be with the family. It was war but was not fought like a true war. Every step of it seemed to be micromanaged by President Johnson within his political agenda. We could not pursue hardcore North Vietnamese regiments when they vanished into Cambodia, where they could regroup and return to fight again. I talked to pilots who were totally frustrated by not being allowed to bomb missile sites as they were being built in North Vietnam. They had to wait for special orders from Washington, and even then they were not allowed to attack until actual missiles were being fired at their planes. Supplies and personnel from Russia and China were flowing in, but the ports of entry, major targets indirectly responsible for the loss of many American lives, were off limits to our planes. Having seen and survived the bombings of Germany during World War II, the "carte blanche" the North Vietnamese were getting was incomprehensible. The taking and retaking of the same terrain, at the cost of many lives, was sad for all, including those of us taking care of the victims of these battles. It was frustrating and it was going to be years before the realistic bombing of Hanoi and the port of Haiphong, planned and ordered by President Nixon and his Secretary of State Kissinger, brought the North Vietnamese to the conference table - more than seven years after my departure from Bien Hoa.

It was strange to be leaving the 3rd Surgical Hospital, Army, Mobile. I had been the last to arrive and among the first of the original staff to be going home. We had been together for close to a year and had shared some very unusual experiences. We had spent days and nights together. Together we had been concerned about our safety. We had worked together and had learned war surgery under the duress in a combat zone. We knew each other as well as we knew our brothers. We *were* brothers, but when it was time to go home the farewells were brief. We were returning to the real world, the world we had left, the world that for a year we had occupied only in our thoughts and letters. The letters had been a sacred ritual and a contact with the world beyond the reality of the one we were living - the next helicopter and the bloody young men it was bringing. Sitting on the side of my bunk, reading about the children, imagining them in school and at play and then writing them about the life we were living and trying to report with some assurance that we were safe and all was well – it wasn't always easy. Somehow, along the way, Julie and I managed to communicate and solve the problems of changing career plans, the sale of the house in El Paso, moving arrangements and the fresh start in New Haven and at Yale. It was all a much different scenario than our present-day instantaneous contacts and exchanges of information.

Before leaving we had to hand in our jungle fatigues and jungle boots (I don't know why) and make sure all paperwork and orders were completed. My issue M-14 rifle and .45 automatic pistol, with all ammunition, were returned to their owner, the United States Army. I also had to dispose of my personal Smith & Wesson Chief's special snub- nosed pocket revolver. It didn't take long for word to get around that I had it for sale. It was bought by a Filipino contractor for $60, and I was ready to fly home without the fear of being delayed, stopped or arrested for trying to smuggle weapons out of Vietnam. (Hort Spitzer, a good friend and Yale College classmate was trying to convince me to bring out an M-16 automatic rifle to add to his collections of arms certified to have been used by Americans in actual combat. I hope he has been able to add an M-16 to his collection, but I was not going to be one of his contributors, no matter what the price. Absolutely nuts.)

Throughout the months with the 3rd Surg, I had taken many photographs of our life and surroundings. I had also made it a point to document the primary surgical management of severe, contaminated war wounds in preparation for lectures on the subject once home. The decision to return to a full-time academic teaching position made that project even more significant and productive in terms of podium presentations and publications in the long run. The photographs were to be the basis of my lectures, scientific exhibits, movies and publications once home. Most of the photographs and 36mm slides are now an integral part of the collection of my letters home, Julie's letters to me and other materials in the "Keggi File" at Yale. We took the photographs and have given the lectures with professional efficiency and minimal emotion, but there have been times when talking about the mangled arms and legs of the wounded in these pictures has been "emotional." Such was the case when I participated in the West Point project of a video history of the Vietnam War and started speaking about our wounded. Suddenly there were tears in my eyes. One of my visits to The Wall in Washington also produced the same "choked up" effect, as I was remembering the men of the 173rd, the 1st and 25th Infantry Division and all the others. I think of them, honor them by wearing their unit pins on my lapel and shedding that sudden tear.

My official time was up in the middle of July 1966, but I could leave earlier if my replacement arrived ahead of schedule. It was essential that all the paperwork, travel and discharge orders were completed to allow an instantaneous departure. Fresh out of residency, my replacement arrived. I showed him around the hospital, gave him a 15-minute course on my experience with the management of extremity wounds and was gone. Gone to Saigon to catch the first available medical evacuation plane to California. It was a large four-engine jet with more than 100 wounded aboard. I was assigned to a forward seat next to the cockpit and could visit with the pilots in the course of our flight. We made quick stops in Manila and an airbase in Japan and were on the ground in California in a fraction of the time it had taken me to fly to Vietnam almost a year earlier. A day after my arrival I was discharged from active military duty at the army base in Oakland.

Julie, who had come to terms with my decision to return to Yale and an academic career, met me in San Francisco to get reacquainted before we returned to El Paso. I was discharged in Oakland and within a few hours we were reunited. It was a joyous occasion. We were staying with Julie's Aunt Freddie and her husband George White in their San Mateo house, outside of San Francisco. It had a swimming pool and could not have been nicer after 10 months of living in tents. Freddie was there for some of the time but had made a point of leaving us alone for most of it. We had fun in San Francisco, although the fog and the temperatures in the 60s made it seem like winter in Connecticut to me. My body, acclimated to the temperatures of Vietnam and its steaming operating room tents, had to deal with it, but survived. We saw our Yale Scroll and Key friend Steve Gurney, who had seen me off the previous September, and met Patsy, his wife-to- be. Steve had had an epiphany and was now a "left liberal" with strong negative views of the war in Vietnam. We did not dwell on those issues in 1966, but in the years since then we had multiple debates and discussions ranging from Vietnam to President Donald Trump. Next, we were off to El Paso and the reunion with Katie, Mara and Caroline. What joy! What joy to be back to see them again. There was also Phoebe, our family beagle. Even before my departure Julie was allowing her to sleep on our bed when I wasn't home, and every afternoon as I returned to the house from the hospital, the first thing I heard was Phoebe getting off the bed. Now, she apparently had been on the bed during my entire absence, but as I entered the house there was the welcoming "plop" of Phoebe rolling from the bed to the floor. She seemed somewhat offended as she walked slowly to her assigned spot on the living room couch and I was allowed to get into my side of the bed. What fun for all to see.

VIETNAM EXTRAS

Two General Purpose Large tents housed the male medical staff (physicians and male nurses). One of the tents held the bridge-playing types, the other the rest of us. We resorted to humor whenever possible, off-color jokes, erotic stories, gin-and-tonics, but above all, we had the willingness and ability to operate as long as possible and to take all the difficult cases. We called our tent "CUF" and had a sign at its entrance that spelled it out. When visitors such as U.S. Senators or Congressmen asked about it, we would tell them CUF was the Vietnamese word for tent. None of them had the presence of mind to read it backwards, right to left. Ah well, boys will be boys and with our Ivy League educations we thought ourselves entitled to have a little fun in the "fog of war." We were the "Cuffers" and proud of it. Proud to be there and proud to be doing our job saving life and limb. Having a laugh to keep us sane in an insane world all around us.

Our internist, a bright Columbia graduate, missed the research activities he had been involved in at that famous university – he had to have a project. The best he could find was an attempt to correlate the color and consistency of our bowel movements with the food we were eating and the anti-malaria pills we were taking. In the tent that served as the officer's latrine he installed a box and expected us to describe our output on a ballot giving us check boxes for color, consistency, rapidity of excretion and the times of each event. The research project failed because some of the staff (not me, of course) stuffed the ballot box with unacceptable accounts of hard pellets, color purple, four times a day and twice at night. More of the insane to stay sane.

On Wednesdays we ran a clinic for injuries of another nature. Love and war are here to stay. We were willing to help on all fronts, and the waiting line at our Wednesday morning venereal disease clinic was substantial and confirmation of General Patton's view that an Army "that does not fuck does not fight." Our troops were doing a good job of fighting and Vietnam provided them with options on keeping up their Patton-inspired fighting strength. Very familiar was the "four-for-one" item - for one Yankee dollar you could get the four most common wounds of these encounters – gonorrhea, syphilis, chancroid and lymphogranuloma venerum. That was more than plenty then, and I imagine a few wars later you could add HIV and herpes. The stories that went along with these special wounds were also interesting. "I caught it in my zipper" was always a good one. I didn't take any photographs, but a few pictures from our work in the Wednesday clinic would add to the insanity of the entire story of war and war medicine on all fronts.

Then there was Lieutenant "Jungles" Rutledge of the Australian Regiment attached to the 173rd Airborne Brigade. Rutledge had been involved in some previous combat encounters with Communist guerillas in the jungles of Malaysia and it is there he had earned his nickname. The Australians were proud of their performance and went into the jungle with one rifle and only 20 rounds of ammunition, each one to be fired to kill an enemy. They did not share the enthusiasm our American troops had for automatic weapons with hundreds of rounds to be sprayed at an unseen enemy hiding in a tree or bush. True or not, it made for good war stories. Instead of fighting in Vietnam, Jungles would have preferred to be a tank commander in a desert duel with an enemy tank and its commander. But instead of getting blown up in the desert, he was shot in the arm while on patrol in our jungle. The wound was superficial and his humerus was solid on examination. Jungles was eager to stay in Vietnam to complete his tour of combat duty, and after the initial management of the wound we arranged for him to stay in country by moving him into our tent, where he entertained us with his ability to drink Australian Foster's beer by the case, disdaining the American brands as "piss." His stories were complete with marches on a table, Australian salutes, slamming of the feet and his strong accent. He was a "fahking good tent mite." In the manner of old-fashioned armies he also had his own batman, an Australian aborigine ("Abbo"), who came with his rifle one dark night in the back seat of the jeep Jungles and I drove to the Bien Hoa Airbase officers club. All was well with Jungles' recovery until his seemingly solid humeral shaft broke with a loud crack one day as he was throwing a football outside of our tent. The bullet that had gone through his arm must have grazed the bone, causing a weak spot ("stress riser") which gave way as he was throwing the ball. He was lucky. It could have given way upon his return to combat duty while throwing a hand grenade at the enemy. Anyway, it was the end of his tour in Vietnam. He was shipped back to Australia where, we later heard, he was continuing his military career – hopefully in one of the tanks of his dreams.

On the subject of hand grenades, one of the most dramatic pictures in my war-wounds slides is the shredded remnants of a hand. In the high humidity and heat of Vietnam there was always the fear of a rusting grenade, unexpected explosion and death. To prevent it, some of the troops would tape the handles of the grenades with adhesive tape to avoid the sudden catastrophe of a rusted pin. Before pulling the pin and throwing the grenade the adhesive mechanics tape had to be stripped. Our patient thought he had stripped the tape and had pulled the pin and was about to throw the grenade when he discovered the tape was stuck both to the grenade and his hand and no matter how he tried to deal with it he could not shed the grenade about to explode. At the final second he grabbed the grenade in his fist and pushed his arm over a sandbag. The grenade went off, his life was spared, but there was nothing left of his hand.

A visit from *Reader's Digest* led to one of my nicknames in Vietnam and at Yale. *Reader's Digest* was planning a story of a wounded soldier from the moment of being hit by enemy fire in Vietnam to his final destination in one of the major hospitals back in the United States. It was to include first aid in the field, helicopter evacuation and the initial surgical care in the tents of our hospital. When the day came, the writer of the story arrived with two wounded soldiers. The patient I was scheduled to treat had a gunshot wound of the knee. I had him in the operating room tent ahead of the other patient, who had more extensive injuries and needed greater preoperative care. The operating tables were in the same tent, and, as I was working on my patient, the other table was being prepared by a registered nurse who rarely, if ever, functioned as a scrub nurse or operating room technician. On this day of *Reader's Digest*, she had decided to become a participant in the story and was trying hard to act important and super professional. She was lining and realigning the instruments on her table while awaiting her patient and surgeon. The writer, out of the way in the corner of the tent, was watching the scene and taking notes. In the course of the operation I was performing I needed an instrument that was not on my table but was on the other table in our nurse's special arrangement. I asked her to pass it to me to complete the excision of a shattered patella, but she immediately got agitated, refused to do it and launched into an incomprehensible, screeching tirade. I tried to calm her and be nice to her, but the more I tried, the worse her screeching. I finally lost my temper (one of the very rare times in my years in the operating room), walked to her table and took the instrument I needed to excise the badly damaged bone which I then dropped into the bucket at my feet. The event later appeared in the magazine story, where I was described as sullen, angry and throwing, with a "crunch," a bone into a bucket. Consequently, my sweet, kind and sensitive Vietnam fellow surgeons renamed me "Crunch" Keggi. When back at Yale, I told the story to a group of our residents, who without any concern for my feelings, perpetuated that name and upon their graduation presented me with a silver bowl thanking "Crunch" Keggi for being their mentor. Times have changed, and as I these days glance at the weekly emails from Yale administrators about sensitivities, comfort levels and professional behavior, I would probably not have been accorded that crunching accolade.

BACK HOME

Katie, who had pre-school classmates whose fathers had been killed or wounded in Vietnam, was glad to see me without the holes in my body she had imagined, Mara was talking up a blue storm and Caroline, now 11 months old, was as happy and responsive as could be. Julie was also pleased to have me back in one piece, but there was much to do.

We managed to sell our house in El Paso at approximately the same price we'd paid for it two years earlier. The Army moved our furniture and other belongings to Connecticut. Julie and the girls were going to fly east, and I was to drive our station wagon, with its new Texas plates, but with a detour through Phoenix where I was scheduled to be interviewed for an Arizona Medical License. Even though I was on my way to a university life, it made sense to complete the Arizona license requirements in case of another change in plans and a return to the Southwest. I passed the interview and was licensed to practice in Arizona until five years later, when our roots in Connecticut were too deep to consider any changes and I stopped paying the substantial fees to maintain it.

After my brief licensing interview in Phoenix, I immediately turned north to go east. I was planning a quick look at the Grand Canyon and a short stay in

Colorado to visit my Berzins cousins, uncles Ansis and Andris, their wives and multiple children. It was a fast drive and the visits were quick, but it all worked out as planned with only a minor encounter with the Arizona State Police. On a highway without speed limits I was stopped for a chat with one of their finest who thought I had been going 100 mph. It was a friendly encounter. "Welcome to Arizona! We want you to come to Arizona, but we also want you to leave it alive" was the gist of it, and, after a short conversation about my tour in Vietnam and destination in Connecticut, I was back on the road at a somewhat slower pace. Arizona was and is a great state. We would have been happy there in life and surgical career, but Yale (and Doctor Southwick) were calling and the decision to answer that call has been one I have not regretted. Many years later it was an absolute delight to provide a house in Scottsdale as Caroline's golfing "headquarters" and our family fall and winter vacation destination, as well as a setting for blue skies, starry nights, spectacular sunsets, dramatic thunderstorms and lightning bolts. But back in 1966, it was goodbye Arizona and back to Connecticut.

I reported for "duty" at Yale in July. It was a relatively minor process. I signed a few papers, the professor of surgery, Doctor Lindskog, assured me that I had hospital privileges, and I went to work.

My re-entry was, once more, typical of Dr. Southwick and the trust he seemed to have in me. On my first day back, I drove up from Greenwich, where were staying while looking for a house in New Haven and walked into the offices of the Orthopaedic Section of the Department of Surgery. It consisted of three rooms: Doctor Southwick's office, a middle room for two secretaries, and the room that was to be mine. It held a bare desk, a telephone, two chairs and an empty bookcase.

There was a piece of paper on the desk, a handwritten note from Doctor Southwick: "Welcome back Kris! You are in charge! See you in September. Wayne." It was the second week of July, I was 31 years old and in charge of Yale Orthopaedics, resident teaching, student teaching, clinics, private patients, elective surgery, emergencies and the West Haven Veterans Administration Hospital. Immediately after I read that note, the telephone on the bare desk rang. It was Dick Linburg, whom I had last seen as a fourth-year medical student and who, having completed two years of general surgery, was now in his first year in the orthopaedic residency at the West Haven VA. He was about to start a Putti Platt shoulder stabilization and I was to help him as the responsible attending. It was Linburg's first major case, similar to my hemipelvectomy at the VA five years earlier, and off I went to supervise him, walking into the hospital and the operating room without any previous paperwork, security checks or special badges.

Caroline, Mara and Katie were ready for a family life again with their Dad.

It was the beginning of three very exciting, productive and once more life-changing years. Doctor Southwick had left for two months in California to do basic research and learn electron microscopy. Jim Albright, who had been a year ahead of me in the residency program, was in New Haven studying biochemistry and related subjects in preparation for an academic career, but was staying away from any clinical, administrative or teaching duties. Don Nagel, who had also been ahead of me, was around, too, but like Albright was staying away from us. Ulrich Weil, who had been on the full-time faculty for several years, was now in a private practice with Ben Bradburn and was willing to help with some of the teaching and resident supervision duties, but during those first two months of my life in orthopaedic surgery, I was almost as alone as I had felt in Vietnam. When Doctor Southwick returned, the "work" was a little lighter, but I was still in the operating room almost every day supervising residents and taking care of my first private patients. I was also in the operating room at night several times a week taking care of the emergency cases. I enjoyed the work with the residents and students then and continued to do so as I am writing this memoir all these years later. We worked in all areas of orthopaedics - spine surgery in adults, scoliosis in children, hand surgery, foot surgery, sports injuries, reconstruction of the hip and knee, and all trauma. One of my favored photographs from those days shows me working with an old-fashioned hinged cast to correct a flexion contracture of the knee in a young girl, under the watchful eyes of residents Chuck Edwards and Fred Tiley (one of two Princeton football captains I taught at Yale). The photograph may well have been taken shortly before or after some major spine surgery, which was to become Chuck's area of specialization in his very accomplished career in Baltimore. Fred moved out to Oregon and also specialized in spine surgery.

With a Yale University-sponsored mortgage we were able to buy a house in Westville on Westwood Road, only a few blocks from the Yale Bowl. It was a grand old brick house which we bought "as is" with some very classical furniture that is still with us. It was a friendly neighborhood. Katie, who was starting first grade, was able to walk to the Edgewood School, Mara was in our Congregational Church kindergarten and Caroline had plenty of play space in the house and its basement (where, among other fine activities, she managed to paint one of our Guinea pigs orange). Bart Giamatti, whom I knew well from our common days in Scroll and Key, lived around the corner until his appointment to the presidency of Yale University and a move to fancier quarters in the president's mansion on Hillhouse Avenue. Our closest neighbors were John and Andriana Thompson, he a former Bellevue Hospital nurse, now professor of Public Health and Hospital Administration, and she a general surgeon, with a family that would grow to seven children. Professor Thompson was an interesting, earthy character and very productive in the area of health-care planning and management. We enjoyed sharing time and some drinks as we planned our common research activities in the field of accidents and their management. He was very involved, at the highest federal levels with the implementation of DRG's (Diagnosis Related Groups) for the reimbursement of medical services and the introduction of Medicare. At the state level of medical planning, one of his projects was the division of Connecticut into two areas of influence and control. Yale was to be in charge of the western and southwestern part of the state and the University of Connecticut of the rest. It is a plan he was promoting in the 1960s and, amazingly enough, it continues to evolve along John's lines. He was an inspirational teacher, and two of my best friends received their PH.D.s with him - Bill Kissick, who was two years ahead of me in medical school and after a surgical internship decided he was best suited for a career in Public Health and Hospital Administration, and Sam Webb, an old Scroll and Key friend who, as manager of the Yale hockey team, met Kissick, the team physician, and decided to follow in his academic footsteps.

Back from Vietnam, with a multitude of ideas on the management of severe wounds of the extremities in war and civilian settings, I was looking for funding of these ideas and happened to hear of the new Insurance Institute of Highway Safety (IIHS), established in Hartford. It had been created to promote highway safety and safer cars, but I didn't think they'd object to hearing about some of my aspirations and hopes in related areas. I called the president of the organization, who was willing to meet with me. We made plans to do so on a summer afternoon at their offices in Hartford. I did not have any written proposals or budgets, but was willing to tell them about Vietnam, war wounds, the work of corpsmen in combat, helicopter MedEvacs and how it all might apply to the injured in a civilian setting.

It was to be a preliminary meeting. My major preparation for it was to look as professional as possible. I'd recently purchased a white linen jacket and that was the uniform of the day as I started my drive north on the recently completed I-91. It was a sunny day, the traffic was light and smooth, yet all of a sudden, near the Middletown exit, there was a car in the ditch with its unconscious driver collapsed and bleeding over the steering wheel. I was the first on the scene. I stopped and pulled the semi-conscious driver out of the car, bandaged his head wounds with his shirt and stayed with him until the police and ambulance arrived to take him to the Middletown hospital. In the rush of events, I had not removed my fancy J. Press jacket, and it was now stained with blood. I was faced with the decision of what to do next. With the help of police radios, I was able to communicate with the Hartford executives who were willing to delay our meeting but still expected me to come. Half an hour later I walked into their office, hoping they would forgive me the blood-stained jacket. Our meeting could not have been more positive, and at its conclusion I was given, without lengthy forms or precisely written plans, a $20,000 unrestricted grant to be used for the work in trauma I was doing and hoping to do.

This money allowed us to pursue such studies as the documentation of first aid at the scene of accidents using the latest available technology: a bulky but functional portable television camera. Two medical students made it their summer project to go to accidents with the first responders from the fire or police departments and record dramatic cases of very primitive care at the scene of these accidents, emphasizing, beyond any doubt, the need for better training of firemen, police officers and ambulance attendants. It was all in line with the nationwide effort to create special courses and certification requirements for EMTs, which over the years has saved an untold number of lives. With the help of John Thompson and one of his graduate students, we also did an analysis of motor vehicle accidents in the New Haven area using very early computers. It was interesting to be involved with these computers and learn enough terminology to sound informed about this new science. It was pioneering work, and our data was cited in research projects for several years. Another one of these computerized data "banks" was our analysis of all the trauma-related visits to the New Haven Hospital Emergency Room over a period of 30 days.

The grant from the IIHS also allowed me to prepare lectures and a scientific exhibit on the management of severe extremity wounds in both wartime and civilian settings. The core of this work consisted of six tableaus by Leon Schlossberg of Johns Hopkins University, one of the greatest medical illustrators of his era. These large color illustrations were based on photographs of a major gunshot wound of the humerus I had treated at the 3rd Surgical Hospital in Vietnam. They depict the wound and its management, from the initial debridement to the delayed skin closure. To get it done I made several trips to Baltimore to work with Schlossberg, who did an amazing job. These tableaux are truly great works of art and they do tell the story of wound care.

That exhibit was shown at the annual meetings of the American Medical Association, the American College of Surgeons and the American Academy of Orthopaedic Surgeons. The photographs and illustrations became an integral part of the Academy's instructional course lectures in 1969 and were published in 1970. They are preserved in the Cushing Whitney Medical Library at Yale along with the letters my wife and I exchanged during my tour of duty, photographs and other materials. These illustrations would not have been possible without the grant from the IIHS that covered Schlossberg's work and my expenses related to the time I spent in Baltimore. Overall, the work we accomplished with the initial grant led to a multimillion-dollar grant to Yale to establish a Trauma Service, start the School of Physician Associates and build a research facility for its Surgery Department

I was also being drawn into administrative and committee work at the local and national levels, including meetings and administrative work at the medical school and hospital in New Haven and the chairmanship of the American College of Surgeons' Connecticut Trauma Committee. I worked with the American Academy of Orthopaedic Surgeons.on training requirements for EMTs and was a member of its Emergency Room Committee. I made multiple trips to Washington to attend a variety of trauma-related meetings and spent several days in Detroit working with a Trauma Committee of the American Automobile Association. Initially all of these trips were interesting and could potentially bring funding for greater trauma projects. But with time I came to the realization I was happier teaching residents in an operating room than sitting at a committee table, be it in Washington, Detroit, Chicago or Las Vegas. I was also becoming aware that a "successful" career in academic medicine would require ever greater involvement in this sort of administrative work, and less work with students and residents in clinical research and, of course, surgery itself. That conflict became more and more acute and eventually led to my decision to leave the full-time faculty and go to Waterbury while maintaining a Yale teaching affiliation.

But in the meantime, the surgical training we had as residents with Doctor Southwick was inspiring, and all of us in subsequent years would try to pass on his skills and confidence to the residents we taught. I was even more fortunate in this teaching capacity, having had two extra years of surgical experience during my two years of active military duty. A year of complex reconstructive surgery at Beaumont General Hospital in El Paso and 10 months of war wounds at the 3rd Surgical Hospital in Vietnam had given me additional experience which I was now able to pass on to the Yale residents. While taking care of the wounded I had approached every joint and every bone from the front, the back and the sides. It was fun to share this experience with the residents as we were working on the uninsured clinic patients and the victims of major accidents.

Being back at Yale after Vietnam was a lot of time spent with residents, students and patients. I never did then, nor have I since then, thought of what I was doing as "work" - it was a productive and fun way of life. With Dr. Southwick's encouragement, I was also doing some innovative spine procedures such as combined posterior fusions and anterior decompressions in cases of severe degenerative disease, trauma or tumors. As a result of this work I was one of the early members of the Cervical Spine Research Society, met some great surgeons and was exposed to some novel ideas on the management of cervical spine problems. It also led to some exciting adventures, such as being flown to Illinois to treat a high school student with a crushed body of C5 and quadriplegia. It had been a wrestling injury and the patient, who had been accepted at Yale, was now paralyzed. His pediatrician knew Jim Marks, one of our Yale vascular surgeons, and had called him for advice. Doctor Southwick was consulted, but I was given the job. The boy's father was a prominent attorney in Chicago and wanted to make sure his son was getting the best and latest thinking in the surgical management of crushed vertebrae.

I was flown to Chicago, and, as I got off the plane, I was met by a limousine driver who told me he was assigned to me for as long as I was in the area and would take me anywhere I wanted or needed to go. But Highland Park Hospital, just north of Chicago, was my only destination. After the examination of the patient and discussion of the anterior decompression with all concerned, I met with operating room staff, looked at their instruments and outlined the operation to them.

They seemed like a competent group and ready to work with me. There was no question but that they were miles ahead of the chicken-coop operating room, the missionaries and Montagnards in the Central Highlands of Vietnam. Everything was going to go well. I could hear Dr. Southwick: "You can do it, Kris!" The following morning, I excised the crushed vertebral body and the bone fragments pressing on his dura and spinal cord. Having done the decompression, we inserted ("wedged in") a block of the patient's own iliac crest to fill the space from C4 to C6 and fuse the spine. We did not use any plates, screws or pins, the iliac crest graft was fashioned to have cortical spikes at each end which were then imbedded into the vertebral bodies of C4 above and C6 below to achieve solid fixation of the graft and spine. It was a concept we (Ben Bradburn and I) had been working on at Yale in simple cases of two-level degenerative disc disease.

Amazingly enough, the morning after the decompression the patient was starting to move his toes. The prognosis looked good and I flew home. He did not have a total recovery of function, but progressed to independent ambulation and was able to enter Yale the following year. Several decades later he wrote a book about his injury, operation, education, life and career as a lawyer. I was extremely pleased and do believe the removal of the bone fragments pressing on his spinal cord was the key to his recovery. The moving toes the day after our operation were the source of immense satisfaction. I had not thought of surgical fees, and when asked by the family pediatrician how much I would charge for the operation I had to make a major readjustment, since the initial number I had quoted was a third of what the pediatrician was planning to bill.

It was a situation I would encounter on several

occasions in the years to come, when, for example, my fee for revising a failed total hip replacement would be less than the surgical charge for the primary, failed procedure. Perhaps I should have been more realistic in these financial matters, but during the five decades of active surgical practice, surgical fees and reimbursement schemes always seemed secondary. I was operating and teaching for reasons far beyond the dollars involved. I was, however, somewhat more realistic than my father, who never billed his patients and accepted whatever amount the patient chose to give him for a simple visit to the office or major surgery. Years later, it would be the same scenario for me, with a bottle of Armenian brandy being the most tangible or potable payment for the hips I would be replacing in the Soviet Union. In the long run, the rewards of good will, education, the satisfaction of having helped somebody, have made up for any number of lost dollars by being away from the office and the operating room in Waterbury. Of course, there are the medals and honorary degrees - and they look good.

Lectures, exhibits and articles on the management of major extremity wounds occupied large segments of my time, but I was also active in giving talks about the war in Vietnam to interested groups in Connecticut and Yale alumni in venues such as the Yale Club of New York. They were stories of our arrival in Vietnam, the lack of supplies and being lost in the Central Highlands, but they also included my views on the march of Communism and the validity of the war. In the Yale groups there were many of my fellow graduates and classmates who worked in Washington, in the White House, the State Department and the Central Intelligence Agency. I was aware of them but did not expect to be used by them. It was, therefore, a surprise when I received a call from U.S. Senator Everett Dirksen of Illinois and was, as a recent veteran of the war, invited to join a Committee for Peace with Honor in Vietnam. The committee consisted of Sen. Dirksen, the former United States Ambassador to the United Nations Mary Lord and General Omar Bradley. I accepted the invitation with enthusiasm and flew to Washington to appear at the National Press Club for a public appearance with the committee, followed by an informal luncheon. I believed in the Vietnam cause and considered it a duty and honor to be there. It was a memorable occasion, and being with Gen. Bradley was its highlight. He lived up to every historical image I had of him - soft spoken, polite, a true officer and gentleman. At the time, I thought my invitation to be on this committee as a young Vietnam veteran was simply based on my public statements, a feature story in the *New Haven Register* and my reputation among Yale graduates. But there was more to the story than that. When the "Pentagon Papers" were made public, in large part due to the work of James Goodale, Yale College classmate and an attorney with *The New York Times*, it became clear that the committee and my presence in the group was the creation of the Central Intelligence Agency and especially my classmates in that institution (one, a fellow Keys man, served in various worldwide positions before a premature death from cancer; the other, a fellow French Literature major, was in charge of clandestine operations for most of his career). It was an interesting committee, but it had no effect on the events in Vietnam and its ultimate collapse. I felt strongly about our presence there and was happy if I could support it at any level. I felt happy about it then and my views have not changed over the course of years. I debated the issues with William Sloane Coffin and Benjamin Spock back then and continue to do so whenever the subject of Vietnam comes up in conversations in the liberal environment of Yale and New Haven. I feel sad as I read the history of the war and the stories of so many young soldiers who lost their friends in combat but were not allowed to pursue those who had killed them because of the micromanagement of these battles by President Lyndon Johnson and his Washington politicians.

No matter how busy we were in our clinical and academic work, the war was a constant presence at Yale, the evening news, the daily discussion of the news, the demonstrations, the members of the faculty who were supporting the North Vietnamese, the student strike in the spring of1970 and the military occupation of the town to protect it from mayhem by radical antiwar groups (Hillary Clinton) and the Black Panthers. Those were not the happiest days at Yale and they also played a role in my decision to leave the full-time academic and administrative world.

I had told Dr. Southwick I would definitely give that academic world three years but would move on if it did not fit my plans and hopes for the future. Approximately a year before my final decision to leave, I had dinner with him and during the evening expressed some of my frustrations with the university and my determination to leave if changes had not occurred by the end of my three years. I do not think he took it seriously, nor did the rest of the leading members of the faculty. I was a success by all of their standards, and they could not imagine I would give up a seemingly brilliant academic career at the end of the first three years. I did though.

Westville, where we lived, was a beautiful section of New Haven inhabited by many Yale faculty families and New Haven professionals. Politically it was liberal, and many of its residents acted on their views by participation in various demonstrations for racial integration or stands against the war in Vietnam. Julie and I were not involved with them but supported causes we believed in. Ours were in some cases quite contrary to the actions of the ladies who organized marches on the New Haven Green only to return home to toasts of wine in celebrations of their good deeds. Integration and support of minority groups at Yale were causes our neighbors all talked about, but we were the only family who responded when it came time to act.

Yale had started a special program of classes for minority students with inadequate high school educations to give them access to colleges and a brighter future. The boys in this special "prep school" were quartered in university housing, but the girls were to be placed in families throughout New Haven. We were the only ones in our liberal neighborhood to accept the challenge, and, in the course of an academic year, had three girls move into our family and home. It was interesting, frustrating yet productive, and exposed us to many of the problems we are still facing 60 years later.

The first of our resident students was a girl from the American Samoa whose father was a tribal chieftain. She was intelligent and attractive with a happy personality but felt very uncomfortable in the primarily African-American school and returned to her Pacific home in a matter of a few weeks.

The woman who followed was from the Los Angeles area, of Mexican background, tall but significantly overweight. Education did not seem to be her goal. My memory of her is coming home from work to a house smelling of marijuana and finding our resident student dozing on the couch in the den. Her tour at Yale ended when she was found to be dispensing sexual favors on the New Haven Green.

The third was an African-American girl from the Midwest and an Evangelical Christian community. She was bright, motivated, and a solid member of our family. She finished the prep school, was accepted at Swarthmore and pursued a career in journalism. We could not have been happier about her; she more than compensated for the frustrations we had had with her Latina predecessor.

We also had parties for all of the students in the program. They were fun but frowned upon by our neighbors who were concerned by the sudden appearance of a "bunch" of black kids in their all white Westville.

There were also a variety of neighbors who would go from door to door soliciting signatures on letters to Congress expressing support or opposition for any one of many causes. One of these was a man who appeared at our front door and wanted me to sign a petition against gas warfare in Vietnam. It was all in line with some Communist propaganda at the United Nations, totally absurd, yet causing enough of a reaction at the political level to petition President Johnson to issue an order to ban the use of tear gas or vomiting agent to clear enemy tunnels and prevent further American casualties. The practice was to blow one of these non-lethal gases into the tunnels and force its occupants, be they active soldiers, women or children, to come out vomiting or in tears, but alive. As a result of President Johnson's political order, that practice became no longer possible, and in order to disarm a tunnel, some poor soldier, at the risk of his life, would have to crawl in to face the waiting enemy or deal with the booby traps that would have been left behind if the North Vietnamese or the Viet Cong had abandoned it. "Poisonous gas" was no longer allowed, but white phosphorus was permissible, and now, instead of vomit or tears, burning bodies were the alternative. Having been in Vietnam and having heard some of these stories from our men in the field, who had to survive some of these politically motivated orders, my reaction to the man seeking my signature on his petition was close to rage. That was the end of the knocks on our door and liberal solicitations.

The most interesting consequence of my neighborhood image as a conservative Vietnam veteran was the member of the Yale faculty who dismissed me from taking care of his son's broken femur because of my views on the war. I knew that person and his connections to some old, well-known, former card-carrying Communists in the Yale/New Haven community. Some of my friends still find it hard to believe that one of "theirs" would dismiss me in this manner.

Drugs were also coming into the world, especially among the young. Until the late 1960s alcohol had been the pervasive mind-altering substance in use. There were occasional stories of marijuana, but I can only think of one incident told to me by Jerry Storm, a close friend and good musician familiar with a professional jazz pianist who smoked it and thought he played better with some of the drug in his system. Jerry did not think it did much for his mentation at the time. But now there was LSD, with its potential of total alteration of the mind. There were at least two Yale students who, under the influence of LSD, thought they could fly, but died trying it. I took care of a fellow Vietnam veteran who had returned to New Haven and its Yale-related drug culture. He, too, while sitting around with fellow "druggies" in a third-floor apartment on High Street, smoking pot and dropping acid, had the same fantasy and without any warning went out the window in the best Superman style. His life was saved by a steel picket fence three stories below. His pin wheeling flight was witnessed by several people and, as it was coming close to its end on the sidewalk, his thigh caught one of the steel spikes of a very sturdy old fence. His head was within an inch of the concrete sidewalk, he hung there like a side of beef, but alive. I met him in the Emergency Room. "High" on his LSD and whatever else he had been smoking, drinking or injecting, he was feeling no pain, mumbling to himself and every so often expressing his appreciation of the operating room lights with loud exclamations of "Wow! Wow!" and "Wow!" The wounds of his thigh were identical to a high velocity gunshot, complete with dirt, shreds of torn clothing and old paint from the steel picket mixed into the highly comminuted fracture fragments of his femur and the blood clots from the transected femoral artery. We treated his injury in a manner identical to similar wounds I'd encountered in Vietnam - extensive debridement and irrigation followed by internal fixation of the fracture with Rush rods and cerclage wires before the arterial repair. Even though we were in a civilian setting, I thought it wise to leave the wound open and do a primary delayed closure and skin graft two days later. It worked, and after a few days, when he had cleared the drugs from his system, this fellow Vietnam veteran turned out to be a fine young man who went on to a productive life of hard work, a happy marriage and wonderful children. It was good to meet him again 40 years later to share a few war stories and to see his leg that was still operational. His had been an unbelievably dramatic story and he had been so much more fortunate than the many others who had their minds and lives altered by LSD or died from it.

The feeling was that New Haven was slipping into turmoil at the street level, and then, from the higher political levels came a redistricting of schools, which meant sections of town such as Westville no longer had any control of over their local primary schools. Crime seemed to be on the rise. Our neighborhood high school students were expressing safety concerns. There was an exodus to Woodbridge, Hamden, Branford and other suburbs. There was a sense of unrest. All of it naturally played a role in our thinking about our own future. The old Hillhouse High School, which sent a large percentage of its students to Ivy League colleges, was dismantled. Private schools would have to be considered, but their costs would be out of reach on the salaries I would be making on the Yale faculty.

In short, it was time to move on, and we were ready to go. I was developing a busy private practice of reconstructive surgery. It was primarily with problems of the spine and major joints, but it also included some simple hand surgery and work on children with clubfeet, congenital dislocations of the hip and scoliosis. Orthopaedic subspecialties were yet to evolve and I was fortunate to be working in all its areas. My private patients were primarily from the New Haven area, but many came from northwestern Connecticut. With my resume building, I was soon in the running for chairmanship jobs in Washington, Texas and Rochester, although I had serious doubts about the administrative work involved and our willingness to deal with the potential moves from one university to the next.

The chairmanship of the Orthopaedic Department at the University of Rochester was a job that did have appeal for both Julie and me. The search committee had interviewed me twice and I'd gone up to Rochester for what was to be a final discussion of the details of my appointment. Julie had been invited to come along to meet the family members of the academic community and to start looking at houses. But at the last moment, all plans came to a sudden end. The private practitioners of orthopaedics in Rochester had vetoed my appointment. In their view, I was too "liberal" for the job. It was the first and last time in my career I have been honored with a "too liberal" label.

My interview for the position in Texas is also worth telling. I was invited to the University of Texas School of Medicine and its Orthopaedic Department in Galveston, on the Gulf of Mexico. I had been interviewed by a variety of physicians for two days and the final interview was with the chancellor of all Texas medical institutions and a very close friend of his fellow Texan, President Lyndon Johnson. He was a plastic surgeon of international renown, a southerner and Texan by all standards - solid stature, demeanor, dress and drawl, he had it all, and his was to be the final pitch for us to return to Texas and its universities. It was 1969, and the interview was historic and would have been unimaginable just a few years later. We had a good conversation about my background, El Paso, Vietnam, Yale and a potential future in Texas. We then started to talk about the unrest throughout the land, the anti-war demonstrations, "flower children," drugs and the rock musical "Hair."

"Boy, I understand you have three daughters," he began (and I'm paraphrasing here). "My wife and I were in New York last month, went to see this thing called "Hair," and on the way out of the theater saw a black boy hand-in-hand with a white girl! I dare say that if such a thing happened around here, we would run that son of a bitch right out of town. We like big, blond, blue-eyed boys around here and New York is no place to bring up daughters such as yours. So come on down, you hear?"

I don't think he was appealing to my liberal instincts as had been identified in Rochester, New York.

We did not go down to Texas, and Julie made it clear that if I were to accept the Galveston offer, I would be going there by myself. Fewer than 14 years later, one of our Yale College and orthopaedic residents, Ron Lindsey, did go to Galveston and Houston to become a professor and chair of orthopaedic surgery. He has been there for more than 30 years and ironically is an African-American. One sort of person may have been the foundation of the Texas medical education system in 1969, but it is Ron Lindsey who is now carrying its flag into the future.

These job offers were flattering, and I did enjoy many aspects of the full-time academic life, but a private practice with clinical teaching and research seemed to have the greatest appeal for me. Julie and I considered Arizona, but it seemed far away now that we were back with our families and Eastern friends. I thought of New Haven but decided it would be in direct conflict with Dr. Southwick and his specialties of spine and hip surgery, the two areas of orthopaedics I also considered to be mine. Two major events made the decision to move my practice to Waterbury a relatively simple one. Doctor Alfonso Della Pietra, the busiest orthopaedist in Waterbury, died suddenly while operating at St. Mary's Hospital there, and James Carey, the second busiest in town, was planning to move to the full- time staff of the Newington Childrens Hospital. Jim Carey had been in practice with Doctors Peter Dingman and William Fisher, who were now looking to fill his space. His office was available and Doctors Dingman and Fisher seemed very happy to have me join them. It was a wonderful professional opportunity and Julie was delighted. Life in Middlebury with its excellent schools, rural atmosphere, family golf and country club was going to be, for the entire family, a change for the better. It was also clear the chances of making a better living were there. I was also hoping to maintain my contacts with Yale.

WATERBURY AND YALE

On July 1, 1969 I started working in Waterbury. My first case in town was a reconstructive femoral osteotomy for arthritis of the hip, an operation which had not been done there in a number of years. It was the beginning of a very busy practice of fracture care and elective, reconstructive surgery. Initially Dr. Southwick was upset about my departure and I felt bad about leaving him, but I could not have been more clear about such a possibility back when I'd returned from Vietnam. Our state of "conflict," disappointment and frustration did not last long. Within a few months of my departure from New Haven he was still submitting my name for chairmanship positions to such institutions as the University of Maryland, and within a year residents were coming to work with me, unofficially and on their own time at first, but within two years we had a formal rotation of Yale residents at Waterbury Hospital.

My first weekend on call in Waterbury was most unusual. We had not made our move to our new residence in Middlebury and I was staying with the Dingmans. It was an amazing time with them, as we were watching the first man on the moon and Senator Edward Kennedy's aquatic adventures at Chappaquiddick. It was a small step for mankind on the moon and a deadly plunge into the ocean, here on earth, for our senator from Massachusetts.

Middlebury seemed to be the logical choice. Doctor

Dingman lived there and we also knew the Goss and Upson families who were longtime Middlebury residents. Julie had known Hiram Upson and Dick Goss since their days at Hotchkiss in the same class as her brother Joe, and I knew them at Yale, where they were my classmates and lived in Saybrook, my residential college. Jerry Storm, who had also gone to Hotchkiss, dated one of the Goss "ladies," and as a senior at Yale I had spent a weekend with them in Middlebury. The town's public schools were good and the private schools excellent. There was the potential of membership at Highfield, a private, family-oriented golf and tennis club, with swimming pool of course. Middlebury was less 10 minutes from the Waterbury and St. Mary's hospitals, which meant I could come home for dinner before undertaking a late-evening fracture operation. I was determined to start my private practice by doing as much as possible, accepting all patients and willing to operate at all hours of the day and night. It was also my intention to continue academic activities at Yale, which would be only a 45-minute drive.

A home in Middlebury was our destination. It was only a matter of finding one and selling the one in New Haven. We settled on a house with approximately five acres of land, two blocks from the Middlebury Green and the Westover School for girls. Our house had been built by the Bronson family in 1910 and was in line with a number of other houses in Middlebury that were summer "cottages," located above the heat and polluted air of their main homes in Waterbury or Naugatuck. The house had three stories, 17 rooms and a carriage house complete with very Spartan accommodations for a chauffeur or gardener. The price seemed reasonable and Julie was very happy with the house itself and the gardens she could create around it. We rented the third floor to a very nice couple of newly married teachers which helped with the expenses of maintenance and heating. At first we were not too concerned about the lack of insulation and the loose windows of this "summer cottage," but shortly after we had moved in, the world was hit with rapidly rising oil prices (OPEC crisis) and the cost of neutralizing the fall, winter and spring breezes passing through our rooms was literally going through the loose roof. We had to proceed with total insulation, plastic siding of all exterior walls and the replacement of all the loose windows. The price of the house had been reasonable, but the insulation project was almost a quarter of the purchase price. Another costly surprise was the sudden malfunction of the antique cesspool which started to overflow into the back yard of our neighbor's carpentry shop. The overflow was not totally catastrophic, and we did not have to abandon our house. We stopped the overflow, drained the "pool" and installed an elaborate septic tank with drainage field which, luckily, lasted until the town connected us to their sewage system some 20 years later. We also discovered a large fuel tank buried close to the house. It had to be removed and we were lucky to dig it out without any contamination of the soil on our property nor the one below us. Last but not least was the town ordinance, passed some 20 years after we'd moved in, that required the removal of all and any asbestos in the house. All of our basement pipes had asbestos insulation, and its removal was another major, costly project. The best part of that story was our feral cat, brought up from Grand Cayman, who had lived in a nest on top of the old furnace, inhaling, for years, asbestos fibers without any ill effects.

I could write a book on the perils of buying a charming old house, but in the long run we were extremely happy in it, even though the cost of the repairs and improvements exceeded the original purchase price by many thousands. We loved the house, we loved its location, its five acres of land and, with the purchase of the six-acre meadow across the street, it was a life in the fields. The meadow was later purchased by a community-minded group with the major contributions made by us and our close friend George Goss. Once bought, it was deeded to the Middlebury Land Trust to be preserved as open space in perpetuity.

A heated swimming pool we added a few years after our arrival made home life even more fun and gave us aquatic exercise from April until November. The addition of a three-car garage and rerouting of driveways also made life easier, as did the renovation of the kitchen, installation of a first-floor toilet and a deck extending from the kitchen into the garden area. The final project was the renovation of the old carriage house, which was a major cosmetic gain with added living space for family or rentals. With Julie's love of plants and horticulture, the land had turned from neglected bushes and wild grass into beautiful gardens of flowers, woodland plants, vegetables, raspberries and specimen trees.

As we were moving to Middlebury, we tried to sell our New Haven house, but the market was "down," and we decided to rent it while awaiting better times. After three years of waiting, continued mortgage payments to Yale, taxes to New Haven, significant sums to insurance companies and the monthly maintenance expenses, it was an ongoing loss and I felt lucky to dispose of it at a price I would not have accepted earlier. It was a lesson in real estate which I relearned with some of our other properties later on and share with all interested friends and family. Take the first offer, avoid more taxes, repairs and legal fees - move on.

The expenses associated with our house in Middlebury were far beyond my expectations, but no matter how I look at it, the money was well spent. For 40 years we had many happy times there. We hosted dinners for family and friends. My 40th birthday comes to mind, with Bill Pierpont of the Waterbury-based Mattatuck Drum Corps playing his bagpipes as we listened from the house and new deck. Christmas, preceded by the selection, cutting and transportation of the tree from its farm to the house, was always a major event. We celebrated three marriages in the house. The first was my brother Andrej's to Wendy, followed by daughter Katie's to Howard and Mara's to Chip. Having been on good terms with the Mattatuck Drum Corps by replacing their worn-out hips to keep them marching, they consented to play at Katie's and Mara's weddings. It added a historical dimension to the events since they are the oldest fife and drum corps in the land, having been established in 1767. The role of the house in the funerals of both my father and mother was equally significant.

But above all, we lived there. Katie, Mara and Caroline were eight, six and four when we moved into it, and, years later, their children have also had some joyful moments in the old place, its swimming pool and gardens.

The dogs - Phoebe our Texas beagle, Lolo and Riga our German shepherds and Schatzie the "Little Lion Dog" - added immeasurably to our lives. In the days before strict leash laws, Phoebe was familiar with most of Middlebury, and Middlebury knew her from such mishaps as getting stuck in a water drainage pipe, being rescued by the fire department and publicized in our newspaper. She had been bred in the Texas desert to be a tracker and hunter, and her sense of smell was so intense that once she was on track nothing else mattered. As a result of this blindingly strong natural gift she was hit by cars on four occasions. She survived all four, but the last one left her with a dislocated hip and a limp for the rest of her life. She once created a sensation when on a sunny, summer morning we walked to church only to have her appear, halfway through the service, sniffing her way through the open church door and up the aisle to our pew. She was a delight and very friendly, but always growled at Caroline who in the first years of her life had tormented her.

The shepherds were also great dogs, but most of our friends were cautious when coming to the house and wanted to make sure we were there to guide them in safely. They did have the appearance and demeanor of watch dogs and I am certain kept some undesirable visitors at bay.

All of them had puppies in the house. It was a life lesson to the girls and delivering them all was my last chapter in obstetrics.

Lolo, our first shepherd, was special. We were keeping her for the Kaman Foundation to be bred to a male of their choice to produce the best of the breed in temperament and eliminate the gene of congenital hip dislocations. We could have kept Lolo after she produced a litter of their choice, but the foundation thought so highly of her, they wanted to take her to Germany to be mated with a very special male of the breed. We had no objections, and one of her puppies, which we named Riga, stayed with us for the rest of her life.

Riga was followed by Loewchens ("Little Lion Dogs"), discovered by Julie and beloved by all.

We were always a dog family, but we became unexpected cat owners one morning in Grand Cayman, when two very sickly-looking kittens appeared on our doorstep. We have no idea where they came from, but there was no other choice than to nourish them back to health. With special care by Julie and the girls, they survived and thrived to become family members that could not be left in the feral Caymans and had to be brought to Connecticut. They were vaccinated, certified as healthy by veterinarians and processed according to all rules and regulations to be flown with us to the United States. They were "legals." I had named them "Grouper" and "Breadfruit," and they made it to Middlebury to resume their feral instincts in the great outdoors, with their living quarters in our basement. Both had been neutered, which did not cause any problems with the female Grouper, but poor Breadfruit, having lost his testosterone, did not fare as well and was killed by the other male cats in the neighborhood, not having the juice to fight and survive. Grouper lived for another 15 years, but was not too friendly, spending most of her time to herself.

Julie was busy running the house and the gardens - they were spectacular. She also devoted much of her time to volunteer work. The Mattatuck Museum was a major project. She was the co-chair of a campaign that raised enough money to move it out of its 19th-century house on the Waterbury Green into new facilities. They were able to purchase the former Masonic temple on a corner of the Green and, under the supervision of Cesar Pelli, famous Yale architect, convert it into a major museum, complete with lecture halls and cafe. It is today a major art museum, but also devoted to the history of Waterbury and Connecticut.

Golf had been in Julie's life since childhood in Wisconsin and within a year we became members of Highfield, followed by the Country Club of Waterbury, with its wonderful Donald Ross-designed layout, to enjoy the game for years to come. I was happy to hit the long drives, but it was all muscle and pounding of the ball without Julie's smooth swing. I played the game, but it is Julie who won the club championships at Highfield and Waterbury, and various regional and state titles.

Daughters Catherine, Mara and Caroline also seemed to be enjoying their lives in Middlebury from childhood, through college and beyond. Katie was a good athlete but did not have her sisters' spirit of competition. She swam well, played golf and tennis, but intellectual matters were more her domain. After finishing Saint Margaret's middle school in Waterbury, in the last class without boys, she moved on to Emma Willard in Troy, N.Y., then Tufts and Harvard for graduate school (Education). Emma Willard was a very academically oriented all-girls school that Julie had attended 25 years earlier. Katie applied to Tufts for college since she wanted to be in Boston and felt her chances of arranging for major time in Athens, Greece, would be easier from Tufts than from some of the other schools. I was somewhat disappointed, since she had the qualifications to be at Yale or Harvard, but she was a determined young lady who had a plan that was not to be changed by a father who thought he had ideas about her education. It all worked out. She did well at Tufts, spent more than a year in Greece and in the end went to Harvard, where she met her future husband Howard Hunter from New Orleans and the son of David Hunter who had roomed across the hall from me in Saybrook College at Yale. They were married in our Congregational Church on the Middlebury Green in 1988 with a major celebration in our old house a block away.

Mara, after surviving some disorganized time at Saint Margaret's that had just merged with McTernan, a boys' school, went on to boarding school at Northfield-Mount Hermon in Massachusetts. Her academic work was good, but her athletic performance superb on the soccer field, in the swimming pool and in a boat. Her swimming coach tried to persuade her to continue swimming, but she chose rowing as her major sport and moved on to the University of Wisconsin, where she majored in Art History and was the captain of a crew that won the NCAA Championship. She was on the United States national team for four years, rowed in the first Goodwill Games in Moscow in 1986 and finished her active rowing life as a finalist (fourth) in a straight pair at the 1988 Olympic games in South Korea. After getting her Master's degree in Business Administration from Emory, she was in charge of rowing at the 1996 Olympic Games in Atlanta and was a vice president of the Amateur Women's Basketball Association until her marriage to Don ("Chip") Ford and the arrival of the mirror image identical twins, Christopher and Alexander.

Caroline, an equally talented athlete, followed Mara at Northfield-Mount Hermon. Golf was her main sport, starting very early at Highfield, where on the third hole she had her first par at the age of four and her first birdie at six. I was playing with her on both occasions and feel fortunate about having witnessed it. At Northfield she played on the boys' team, then, after spending three frustrating semesters at Ohio State with a coach who was less than inspiring, she was able to transfer to the University of New Mexico, where she was second in the NCAA championship her junior year and won it all the next. Her amateur career extended from coast to coast with a multitude of victories, trophies and titles. She was selected for the Curtis Cup team and represented the United States against England and the British Isles in the spring of 1988. She went on to a great professional career that ended prematurely with a lingering intestinal infection.

We have many happy memories of Katie's education

in Greece and Harvard, Mara's rowing and work at the Atlanta Olympics, and Caroline's golf as an intercollegiate athlete and a professional. The summer of 1988 was, however, the ultimate in our family life in Middlebury. In the late spring, Caroline represented the United States on the women's Curtis Cup team against the British Isles in Sandwich, on the North Sea shores of England. Julie and I were able to go and watch her play Royal Saint George's, one of England's historic links courses. It was also meaningful to have Caroline's teacher and Country Club of Waterbury professional, Floyd Gensler, come with us. Unfortunately, the United States lost, but our ladies gave it their all on a tough course in extreme British seashore weather. It's how you play the game that counts. Well done. Sorry about that. Good show.

Katie was married a month later, on Memorial Day weekend. She had met Howard Hunter at Harvard where they were both getting advanced degrees in education. Howard was from New Orleans, a city Katie loved then and has continued to enjoy ever since. It was a great wedding, complete with the Mattatuck Drum Corps and many guests from New Orleans. Then, two months after Katie's wedding, Mara went to the Olympic Games in Seoul, Korea. She had had a successful four years on the United States rowing team but lost her seat in the "Eight" and qualified in a pair a month before the Games. She was the last athlete to qualify for the United States 1988 Olympic Team in any sport. It was tense but she made it, and in September, Julie and I were in Seoul to watch her row, reach the finals and place 4th in the end.

1988 was a summer that, as a family, we can celebrate for generations to come.

We also were fortunate to have a winter home in Grand Cayman. We had always hoped to get away from the winter with a vacation in the south. It was a must in Julie's mind, and I was happy to consider it. Having spent the entire first year after my return from Vietnam in freezing cold New Haven and many feet of snow, it was time to find a place to warm up come January. We discovered Grand Cayman in its very early development. I had gone to a committee meeting of the American Academy of Orthopaedic Surgeons in Atlanta, where one of the surgeons from Johns Hopkins had arrived with a snorkel and spear gun since he was going from our meeting to a Caribbean island before returning to Baltimore. He described it as hard to reach but worth the effort. He also thought it was relatively inexpensive once you got there. I returned to New Haven and immediately went to our travel agent to ask about this island, but she had never heard of it. She was, however, able to find someone in New York who was the Caymans-only agent in the United States and found us a house to rent there. Getting there meant flying to Miami and waiting for a LACSA Costa Rica flight that would stop in Georgetown, Grand Cayman, on its way to San Jose. You flew to Miami, checked into a hotel and hoped to get on the plane the next day. It was a major inconvenience, but once there it was worth the effort. Seven Mile Beach was pristine with only a few houses and practically no people in sight. We had a house with a full-time maid less than 100 yards from the beach, at a price less than any hotel in Florida. The next year we came back, and, when we returned after I had started working in Waterbury, Peter Kellogg and his family joined us.

Peter was an entrepreneur at heart and was immediately convinced we had to buy something on this island with an obvious great future. So he and I started to look at beach properties and found one on the south side of the island. It had 125 feet of beach, two inhabitable native shacks, a cistern, electricity and working toilets. It was a go at $15,000. We did some repairs, added a deck to the main house (shack) and shared expenses until Peter's divorce a year later. I then became a very happy sole owner, and for more than 20 years we had wonderful winter vacations there. When all the daughters were in boarding schools or college, Julie was able to spend substantial portions of the winter there. The rest of us came and went for Christmas, winter breaks and shorter vacations. Many friends and relatives joined us. We snorkeled, fished, went scuba diving and became members of the local church. We had the best of times.

We built a real house to go along with the shacks. This house was supposed to be hurricane-proof, positioned on top of a huge underground cistern. It was all good until Hurricane Ivan in 2004. The original old Cayman shack was gone except for some of its original stilts. The gazebo which we had built had collapsed and was leaning over the old native kitchen house, saving it from the huge waves that for more than 24 hours had been rushing in from the sea. Our two-story, reinforced-concrete house was standing on top of its cistern, but the sand had been washed away from its hurricane proof base and the entire construct was now tilting at a precarious angle with holes in the walls, no windows and lost furnishings. Son-in-law Chip Ford and I flew down as soon as possible after the hurricane to inspect the damage - it was a sad sight, a total loss. We'd been looking forward to being there with the grandchildren, but rebuilding a new home made no sense, since for more than 10 years we already had a place in Desert Mountain, AZ, which I had purchased as a "winter headquarters" for Caroline who at the time was playing golf at the highest professional levels. We were able to collect insurance on the destroyed houses and our neighbor bought the land to build a new hurricane-proof house. Our old kitchen house, considered a historic structure by the Cayman government, is still there next to the modern structure build by the neighbors. It had been the best of many winters, but all things come to an end.

Professionally, life was going well in Waterbury. I was seeing patients, operating and teaching. There were some who felt I was doing too many major reconstructions and major trauma cases at what they considered a small country hospital, but having done them in New Haven I saw no reason why I should stop doing them in Waterbury, where the patients were well handled, we had good support from well-trained internists and the operating rooms ran more smoothly than in the larger New Haven hospitals. I was also encouraged by the votes of confidence I was receiving from some of my former referring physicians in New Haven, who continued to send me their major cases, and the ones in northwestern Connecticut, who were pleased I was now closer to their location.

It was the best of both worlds for me. I was doing what I truly enjoyed and was able to support my family. I was seeing patients, I was helping patients, doing surgery and teaching surgery. I was able to contribute to our field of surgery with new procedures, surgical approaches to hip replacements and a variety of other clinical studies. I was contributing to the surgical education of two generations of Yale orthopaedic residents and eventually established the Keggi Orthopaedic Foundation that would bring to Waterbury Hospital and Yale University over 250 orthopaedic fellows from the Baltics, Russia, former republics of the Soviet Union, Vietnam and Germany. We were also able to establish a program for Baltic orthopaedic nurses at Waterbury and Oxford (England). The funds contributed to the Foundation by orthopaedic manufacturers, such as the Richards Company, friends and many of my patients allowed me to lecture and operate from Riga to Vladivostok. Many of these former fellows and residents are now professors in the United States and their native countries. Two of our former fellows from Latvia are now professors in Dallas and Richmond. One of them, Valdis Zatlers, became the President of Latvia and another has been the longstanding speaker of the house in the Latvian parliament.

Having talked about it for many years with Gary Friedlaender, the long-term Chair of Orthopaedics at Yale, I returned to the full-time faculty and accepted the appointment of professor of orthopaedics and rehabilitation in 2008. In 2010, after the funding and establishment of the Kristaps Juris Keggi Professorship of Orthopaedics and Rehabilitation, I was made its recipient and named Elihu Professor, since I could not very well be "Keggi, the Keggi Professor." Amy Rich of the Yale Development Office, who had been instrumental in putting together all the details of the professorship, and I had to come up with a temporary name for the professorship a few minutes before the Yale Corporation meeting finalizing the matter. Elihu, the first name of the college's first benefactor, Yale, sounded good, so we passed it to the Corporation, and they approved it.

THE ANTERIOR APROACH

I have written about the Yale System, my exposure to some fabulous teachers of surgery, and my own evolution as a surgeon. All of this had something to do with it, but the actual process of starting the anterior approach to cemented total hip replacements was relatively simple and in line with the innovative thinking encouraged within that Yale surgical system. Sir John Charnley, who developed the "low friction hip arthroplasty with a cemented metal femur and a cemented plastic (polyethylene) acetabulum," was a British general surgeon who began his career in the 1930s but did not move into orthopaedics until World War II. He started his work on low-friction hip arthroplasties in the 1950s and did his first "total cemented hips" in the early 1960s. By the end of that decade, it was clear to the worldwide orthopaedic community that his method was producing superior results to any of the previous hip reconstruction operations such as femoral osteotomies, simple "ball" prosthesis, cup arthroplasties, fusions and resections. Charnley was pedantic and had developed numerical steps by which the operation was to be performed, using specific instruments presented to the surgeon on special trays. It was his belief that formalizing each step of the operation for the benefit of the average surgeon would decrease infections and avoid complications. He also developed a tent-like device to control air flow over the operative field. This was unwieldy and was soon replaced by "space suits" worn by those who felt them necessary - or abandoned by those, like me, who felt that proper surgical technique with prophylactic antibiotics was the answer to infection control. Charnley also felt that those who wanted to start these exciting new hip replacements should, ideally, spend some time at his hospital in Wrightington, England, and that the introduction of the operation to the world community of hip surgeons should be gradual and monitored in order to avoid catastrophic problems.

The net of it in the United States was that the use of the methylmethacrylate cemented hips was at first restricted to only a few surgeons and institutions. From a purely academic point of view, it made sense, and most of the selected surgeons who were doing and teaching the procedure did so with the highest principles in mind. But there were those who, having a "monopoly" on this new, extremely successful operation, were suspected of delaying their universal use for their own financial gain. The situation was finally handled by the American Academy of Orthopaedic Surgeons, which sponsored coast-to-coast seminars on the key element of the procedure and the safe use of the methylmethacrylate bone cement. I attended one of these cementing seminars in New York at the Hospital for Special Surgery and was also fortunate to be invited by Dr. Stinchfield to spend a day observing him do Charnle- type total hip replacements at New York Presbyterian Hospital. It was a good day in New York with one of the leading orthopaedic surgeons of the era, whom I had met on several occasions and whose residency I had considered before returning to Wayne Southwick at Yale. Interestingly enough, Dr. Stinchfield also asked me to become one of the founding members of The Hip Society, an invitation I did not accept based on my naïve perception that hip surgery already had a solid place under the direction of the American Academy of Orthopaedic Surgeons and did not its own need special "Society." I was also extremely busy with my practice and was trying to divest myself of some of the administrative roles and committee memberships I had assumed while on my full-time academic track. A few years later, as The Hip Society became an important leadership organization, I had reason to regret that decision as I was rejected from membership by one of my Harvard colleagues.

Having been "certified" in the use of bone cement, having spent that day with Stinchfield and having done multiple other hip reconstructions during the previous nine years, I now felt qualified to proceed with this new "miraculous" operation. There were those in Connecticut and Waterbury who still felt we should not be doing it without a few days with Charnley, but I did not feel that necessity and performed my first cemented "total" hip at Waterbury Hospital in 1970. The implant was not of the Charnley type. Having done cobalt-chrome ("vitalium") alloyprostheses in the past, I thought a prosthesis of that type would be more comfortable than the Charnley. On the day of that "first," I had the choice of Howmedica or DePuy devices. The Howmedica were brought from Boston in green velvet pouches by their New England salesman Jack O'Mahoney, and the DePuys in transparent plastic boxes from Cheshire, Connecticut, by Ron Wood. They looked very similar, but there seemed to be some powder or debris in the boxes, so I chose the Howmedica and performed the operation as had been demonstrated by Dr. Stinchfield, using the Charnley transtrochaneric approach. Jack O'Mahoney went from being a salesman to worldwide president of Howmedica, Ron Wood also had a very successful career with DePuy and was of great help in my later activities in the Soviet Union. We frequently joked about that first hip and the "rust" I was seeing in those little plastic boxes. It was not the first total hip in

Connecticut, but a first in Waterbury. (A few months later, I did, however, do the first total knee in Connecticut.)

For a year or more, I continued to use the transtrochanteric approach to do these new cemented hips. The skin incision was a long anterior lateral one and the joint was exposed by doing an osteotomy of the greater trochanter and reflecting it, along with its abductor muscles, proximally and out of the way. The thigh was then placed, with the knee flexed, in maximum external rotation and left in that position during the acetabular preparation and cementing. Some of the post-operative thromboembolic issues associated with the operation were probably related to the twisting of the femoral veins with the leg in this extreme position. It was a problem recognized by most of us and was but one of several reasons for considering alternative approaches. The greater trochanter osteotomy was another problem. Even though its retraction allowed excellent visualization of the acetabulum and proximal femur, at the end of the operation that piece of bone complete with its muscles had to be reattached. It was a nuisance. We all tore gloves on the wires used and no matter how we did it there were delayed or non-unions of the osteotomy. It also took extra time and increased the potential for infection. There had to be a way to improve the operation by avoiding the trochanteric osteotomy. I discussed it with other surgeons such as Rod Turner, my contemporary and one of the early total hip surgeons at the New England Baptist Hospital in Boston, and started doing it through some "old fashioned" anterior lateral approaches.

The anterior lateral approach worked fairly well, and I continued to use it until I decided to try to split the anterior hip muscles more medially, through the internervous interval we had used to perform some cementless Smith Peterson cup arthroplasties. I had assisted Fred Thompson at Roosevelt Hospital with the insertion of his prostheses from the front. We had used it for a variety of other procedures such as the open reduction of femoral neck fractures, reduction of dislocations, denervations, drainage of infections and had been in that area with gunshot wounds in Vietnam. The anterior approach to a variety of hip procedures had also been described by many surgeons in the past, but nobody seemed to be using it for cemented hips in the United States. To start doing so was a relatively simple decision, no different than so many others we make over the course of a career. It was much less stressful than the hemipelvectomy from the first year of residency or the first-ever vertebral artery decompression two years later. It made sense to be excising and replacing the hip joint through the internervous, intervascular, Smith Petersen interval between the sartorius, quadriceps and adductors medially and the tensor fascia lata and the abductors laterally; muscles innervated by femoral nerve medially and the gluteal nerves laterally. The skin incision was relatively short and most commonly slightly curved (upside-down "C") to facilitate femoral instrumentation.

From the very beginnings of our direct anterior attempts, the acetabular visualization, exposure, preparation and cementing were a relatively simple process. The femur however, from the very beginning of our anterior approaches, was a challenge and, as we learned, could test the best of surgeons. To expose and prepare it, capsular releases had to be performed and circumflex vessels controlled to prevent sudden bleeding in a "deep hole." Initially, this process was especially challenging since the only femoral instruments we had were relatively short-handled, straight rasps of only one length. We resolved that problem when we started using the Zimmer T-28 devices, which were the first to come in a variety of stem sizes and neck lengths. I was able to convince the company to provide me with rasps of three lengths in each size. The shortest, the easiest to insert, would be the "starter rasp" to create a path for the next longer sizes to enter the femoral canal in proper position and a direct line with its long axis. That was the first step in making a path for the safer preparation of the femur. The next step was to take these instruments to a Waterbury tool shop to bend the handles for easier insertion and rasping in line of the femur without extension of skin incisions or releases of the tensor fascia lata from the iliac crest. It took a couple of trips to the tool shop to get the right angle, but these variable-length, bent rasps made the procedure easier.

We also thought of a simple, minimally displaced "fold back" trochanteric osteotomy to be used for femoral exposure in cases of extreme difficulty and tight, soft tissues. The greater trochanter was osteotomized (front to back) without releasing any of its soft tissue and muscle attachments. Without displacing it superiorly or inferiorly it would then fold back to give some more mobility to the femur for visualization and safe preparation of its canal, for insertion of the bone cement and the prostheses. At the completion of the procedure, the anterior trochanteric osteotomy cut would then be repaired by some wire or heavy nylon sutures giving it the stability of an undisplaced trochanteric fracture. Its posterior soft tissues were intact, the abductors balanced by the vastus lateralis and the final repair of the tensor fascia late split giving it some anterior stability. It made the femoral part of the operation safer in cases with rigid soft tissues and it worked nicely. The greater trochanters were relatively pain free, functioned well from the start and healed. We were doing the operation with the patient in an anatomical position, through an area with less fat between the skin and the hip joint itself, we were not going through the buttock, splitting the gluteus maximus, and we were avoiding damage of the hip abductors and their nerves. The initial operations went well, and we continued to use it with enthusiasm. I remember one lady, whose hip we had done through an incision of less than ten centimeters, who refused to believe we had done the replacement until she was allowed to look at her X-rays.

The clinical results were dramatic by comparison to the other approaches we had used. Post-operative pain was minimal, weight bearing could begin immediately and the return to excellent function was very rapid. All of this was happening in the early 1970s, before our present age of advertising and self-promotion. At that time, professional ethics were still the number one rule. If you were thought to be involved in promoting yourself as being better than your fellows, you were immediately dismissed from the American College of Surgeons. Good results, however, spread by word of mouth, and the results of our anterior approach were such that within a matter of months I was getting referrals from all over Connecticut, and by the end of 1973 I was doing all of my total hips through the anterior approach. I was also starting to do revisions through the same anterior approach, with extension of the skin incision, fascial releases and muscle splitting as indicated.

My patients were playing golf in a matter of weeks while their playing partners, having had replacements through one of the other approaches, were still on crutches. If properly done, these other approaches also recovered, and at the end of six months or a year the results were the same. But there was a major difference in the early post-operative period. Our experience of patient satisfaction with the anterior approach was experienced and reported by many other surgeons who switched to it or witnessed it in their communities.

The bent rasps were a major asset and made the anterior approach easier to perform and teach. A few years later, I helped Howmedica make similar rasps, and for several years these were featured in their catalogue as the "Keggi Anterior Hip Rasps." I even received a few hundred dollars in royalties. Bent rasp handles are now the norm, and every instrument company has them, but they were first developed in that Waterbury tool shop in the early 1970s

As long, straight stems were being introduced for some primary procedures and most revisions, we also started using a short secondary incision ("puncture wound!") over the gluteus medius muscle mass to prepare the femur and insert the prostheses if necessary. To do it, we had to revert back to straight rasps with long handles after the preliminary reaming with straight reamers. At one point, the Zimmer Company was attempting to get a patent on this two-incision approach, claiming their minimally invasive sponsored surgeons had "invented" it. I had to disappoint them by showing definitive podium presentations and publications of having done it years before.

Terry Light was a resident on my service as I started to do more and more total hip replacements. Terry was a Yale College graduate and had been captain of the wrestling team before the sport was discontinued. Terry was a superb resident and was willing to work with me on a scientific exhibit to be presented at the 1977 annual meeting of the American Academy of Orthopaedic Surgeons in Las Vegas. The Zimmer Company, whose implants we were using at the time, was willing to pay for the production of the exhibit, its illustrations, its transport to Nevada and Terry's expenses while there.

That scientific exhibit on the anterior approach was a Yale "first," presented by two former Yale athletes, both captains of their teams (Keggi/Fencing and Light/ Wrestling). I stayed at Yale. Terry went on to a brilliant career as a hand surgeon, chair of the Loyola University Department of Orthopaedic Surgery, and president of the American Orthopaedic Association. The exhibit was followed by multiple published articles on hip surgery through the anterior approach in "simple" primary cases and a multitude of other complex situations. The first of them came in 1980. Although learned by most of the residents who worked with me, the exposure and replacement of the femur had been too much of a challenge to many others. Even now, more than 50 years later, some of the greatest enthusiasts of the procedure keep talking about the steeper learning curve associated with anterior femurs and continue with their posterior approaches. We recognized this problem early on, and by the early 1980s were starting to use a secondary short incision ("stab wound") over the origin of the gluteus medius muscle to instrument the femoral shaft and, if necessary, insert the implants themselves. I was reporting this in my articles and had my first formal presentation of this "K-spot" approach at the Yale Orthopaedics alumni meeting in 1986.

Our anterior approach is also related to the first successful use of ceramic-on-ceramic prostheses. Non-cemented total hips were being introduced to the American orthopaedic community in the early 1980s and I elected to use the ceramic Mittelmeier device marketed by the Richards Company. Professor Mittelmeier came to Cincinnati in December 1982 and gave a course on his non-cemented ceramic hip inserted through an anterior approach. He showed, with Germanic precision, the evolution of the prosthesis over a period of 10 years, had laboratory information on the superior wear and friction characteristics of ceramic and excellent clinical follow-up studies. All of this was in marked contrast to other companies who were hurrying into the non-cemented market with only a few implanted joints and no follow-up studies.

The Mittelmeier hip with its screw in ceramic acetabulum was technically difficult through any approach and essentially impossible through the most common posterior one. We were able to do it through our approach and had its only successful series in the United States. We became strong advocates of the use of ceramic in younger, active patients. We showed our work with an educational video (1985), a presentation at the American Academy of Orthopaedic Surgeons (1988) and formal publication (1991). More than 30 years later, we could show excellent long-term survival of these devices at the Connecticut State Orthopaedic Society (2018). This ceramic story is another Yale Surgery "first."

Approximately 10 years after I started doing the anterior approach at Waterbury Hospital, my joint replacement practice had become so busy I no longer had time for any other orthopaedic procedures. Over the course of years, I had given up pediatric work, hand surgery and trauma, but continued to consider myself a spine surgeon, in Dr. Southwick's footsteps. Ben Bradburn and I were among the first to excise vertebral bodies to treat degenerative cervical disc and, based on those operations during our residency, I continued to work on variety of spinal decompression and fusion procedures. We were using methylmethacrylate to stabilize the spine and this work was published with participation by numerous residents on my service (1976-1984). John Barrasso, who 25 years later became U.S. Senator from

Wyoming, was one of them, with our publication of "Vertebral Body Excision in the Treatment of Cervical Disc Disease, Spondylosis and Spinal Stenosis" (1985).

The residents who participated in all of it seemed to love it and several times I received their annual teaching award. It was and is a wonderful feeling to have participated in their surgical education. It was hard work. I was up at five in the morning to run or row, in the operating room or office by seven-thirty and did not get home until dinner time. My elective surgical practice had grown to the point where I had to give up trauma call, but even then, I was back in the hospital after dinner with regularity. It was an extremely busy professional life, but I did find time for family, vacations, school visits and a variety of trips at home and abroad. I played golf on weekends during the summer, ran those marathons, then, as mentioned earlier, found myself rowing in races in Holland, England, Sweden and Croatia. I was also able to organize the first Yale-Harvard four-mile veterans' race on the Thames in New London (we lost) and the first veterans race between the United States and the Soviet Union in Riga, Latvia (we won). I had fun, I was in shape, and it allowed me "to work, eat and drink in the manner I was accustomed to." But, finally, at age 63, I simply no longer had the time to continue with rowing – not with following the daughters and grandchildren, working and teaching at Waterbury/Yale, not to mention trips to do surgery and give lectures in Latvia and the rest of the Soviet Union.

Based on the effective anterior approach, primary total hip replacements were the core of my surgical practice, but I found myself doing more and more complex revisions of failed hip replacements as well. I was also accepting cases that nobody else was eager to deal with, such as congenital dislocations, neurological problems or arthritic joints in the obese. I continued to do primary and revision knee replacements until the age of about 70, but then decided to concentrate only on the hip for the rest of my career. I also continued with education and work with our Yale residents and foreign fellows.

Family life was also moving at high speed. Katie and her children, George and Julia, were to be visited in New Orleans, brought into the family in Connecticut and accompanied on vacations in Grand Cayman and Arizona. The birth of Mara's twins, Christopher and Alexander, followed by Eliza, the last of our grandchildren, was to be celebrated. Caroline was playing golf at the highest professional levels and following her was a must whenever possible. Julie was winning club championships in Waterbury, which were memorable events, and I was eager to play a little more golf of my own.

I was working hard and spending long hours in the operating room, but the rewards of it were such that we were able to live well, educate our children and find time to take some exciting family trips and excursions. Early on, when the three daughters were in their mid-teens, it seemed like a good time for a European tour. I also felt it would be educational for them to do a trans-Atlantic crossing by ship and to experience an old-fashioned railroad trip. We scheduled Julie and the girls to go from New York to Le Havre in France on the *Queen Elizabeth II* and then by train to Milan, where I would join them, having spent my time seeing patients and doing surgery in Waterbury. They had a grand time and I allowed myself the luxury of a New York-to-Paris flight on the supersonic French Concorde at the height of its history. It lived up to all expectations: Champagne in the departure area, no waiting in a line of other airplanes for departure, caviar and frozen Vodka upon take-off, followed by the various "salads," fish and meat courses served with appropriate wines. The flight ended as we were finishing French brandy with Cuban cigars. It remains one of the finest of dinners I've ever had – with most of it at twice the speed of sound. After a night in a Paris airport hotel, it was catch-up to the girls in a rented minivan, through France, the tunnels under Mont Blanc to Milan, from where we continued our travels through Italy, the Dolomites and the Alps with a flight back to New York from Switzerland. Our Alaskan cruise was memorable, too, as was our voyage by private motor yacht from Stockholm across the Baltic Sea to the island of Saarema, the home of the last of Eastern Vikings and Keggi ancestors, the Gulf of Riga, Latvian family sites and the city of Riga. I also felt fortunate to be able to contribute to our Congregational Church, the Middlebury Land Trust, the Mattatuck Museum in Waterbury, and Yale, where I ended up as a Sterling Fellow. It's always been a busy life, but it became especially so as I and my surgical skills were drawn to Latvia and the Soviet Union.

ABROAD

It was 1986 and President Ronald Reagan was restoring prosperity at home and "peace through strength" abroad. Three years earlier, he had stopped the spread of Communism and its wars of national "liberation" with a definitive military intervention on the Caribbean island of Grenada and firm confrontation of the Soviet Union throughout the rest of the world. He was also able to initiate positive negotiations, from a position of strength, with Mikhail Gorbachev the new leader of the Communist party and President of the Soviet Union, who had hopes of restructuring (perestroika) with transparency (glasnost) to his party and his land. Some of the treaties Reagan and Gorbachev were signing were encouraging, but nobody could imagine the collapse of the Communist Soviet Union in a matter of a few years. The Goodwill Games organized by Ted Turner in 1986 were perestroika and glasnost - the entire world was celebrating this athletic encounter between the United States and the Soviet Union on the playing fields of Moscow. Our daughter Mara was on the national team, stroking the women's eight that was to row in the Games. As a lifelong anti-Communist with close friends in the CIA who had been responsible for my membership on the Committee for Peace with Honor in Vietnam, I had serious doubts about visiting the Soviet Union. Had I gone, been arrested and sent to Siberia as a spy, all of my friends in the United States would not have expressed surprise. ("Kris Keggi? Why of course he worked with the CIA.

Think back to everything he has said about Russia. Look at his friends in the White House and the CIA.") I'd be sitting in a gulag, claiming innocence, but would probably have little support from these "friends." Anyway, the Goodwill Games seemed like a safe, once in a lifetime opportunity to visit the "Evil Empire," so I decided to fly to Moscow to watch Mara row.

Don Henry, a Yale graduate of the late 1930s and a lawyer in Waterbury, was also eager to go and his presence added an extra sense of security to the trip. We flew to Moscow, were processed by the border guards without any problems and got to the Games to see Mara row. As a parent, I managed to get a pass that allowed me access to the dock where she and her team were getting in and out of their shell and socializing with the Soviet crews. All of a sudden, two of the "Russians" standing next to us started speaking Latvian. They were both ranking officials and referees in the Soviet rowing world. Daina Sveice had been on several Soviet teams and had won a European championship, the equivalent of a world championship in the days before women's rowing had spread beyond Europe. Juris Tiknuss had also rowed for the Soviet Union but came from a Latvian family heavily involved in the sport long before the war and was familiar with its history, traditions, rules and regulations. I immediately spoke to them in Latvian and spent time with them during the festivities after the Games. I introduced them to Mara, and they expressed their earlier suspicion that with her name, height, blond hair and blue eyes she might be a Latvian. They could not have been nicer and spent much time telling me the Soviet Union was changing and I should come to Latvia. They were also proud to talk about Viktors Kalnberzs, a Latvian who was the leading academic orthopaedic surgeon in the Soviet Union and director of the Latvian Institute of Orthopaedics and Traumatology, somebody I should know and work with. I assured them that if invited I would come, knowing full well it was less than likely to happen. Then, in November of 1987 it did happen.

A phone call came in the middle of the night from a Professor Haralds Jansons of the Riga Institute of Orthopaedics and Traumatology inviting me to participate in the first Latvian International Orthopaedic Conference just a few weeks later. Once I was in the Soviet Union all expenses would be covered. All I had to do was get to Moscow, the port of entry to all of the Soviet Union. An official invitation followed, and the visas were processed with amazing dispatch. After an 11-hour flight on Pan American to Moscow and a shorter one on Aeroflot, I arrived in Riga in the darkness of a barely lit airfield, setting foot on Latvian soil, ready to participate in the historic conference, the first that was allowing foreign lecturers to join their Soviet counterparts in a major medical meeting. It was all in the spirit of glasnost and perestroika and the beginning of a new era throughout all the Republics of the Soviet Union.

The conference was supposed to be on Orthopaedics, but Viktors Kalnberzs, a "Hero of the Soviet Union" known for his reconstructive work with external fixators, also chose to use it to demonstrate two other operations he was performing – breast augmentations with frozen human fat and penile implantations of plastic splints. He was especially proud of his penile implants, which he had performed on the Soviet elite and some of its aging generals. One of his most famous patients was a Fidel Castro bodyguard, who had come for help with his erectile dysfunction and left with an organ that in its test run with Riga's ladies of the night had left them terrorized. A picture of this erotic hero appears in Viktor's autobiography, a book that tells his story of a childhood among his father's Bolshevik comrades,

283

medical education and progression into the Communist elite, followed by leadership toward perestroika and an independent Latvia. I count Viktors Kalnberzs as one of my great friends and give him credit for the work we were able to accomplish in Latvia and the Soviet Union. His external bone fixator system was far more versatile than the Ilizarov one that was receiving much attention all over the world, and I was willing to help with its promotion. Alas, but I could not help him with fatty breast augmentation and plastic male organs.

Bertrams Zarins of Harvard University and the Massachusetts General hospital was another American Latvian participating in the Conference. Our families had enjoyed close ties for more than 100 years and it had been Bertram's father, the Latvian Lutheran Minister of New York, who had sponsored us to the United States. We and our families had been members of the fraternity Lettonia for several generation with a strong history of service to the country in education, the study of its history, linguistics, collection of its folk songs and the Lutheran Church. Bertrams was more connected with Latvia than I and encouraged me to join him on a path that he hoped would lead to its greater freedom and national independence. He insisted I should give my lecture in Latvian, even though all of my previous presentations on surgical subjects had been in English. He felt the importance of Latvian as the vehicle of my talk was far more important than my shortcomings in its scientific and surgical vocabulary. None of us could foresee the events about to unfold throughout the Communist world and Latvia, but that conference was one of them, and, without expecting it, all of a sudden in December of 1987, I was right in the middle of things.

To help with my presentation on total hip replacements in Riga, the Richards Company (Bob

McEneany, my Waterbury sales representative) had given me a small box of hip prostheses and some bone cement. The prostheses were labeled "Samples. Do not implant," but seemed of perfect quality, probably rejected for clinical use because of some minor scratches. Almost immediately after my lecture, Viktors Kalnberzs asked me if I would be willing to use one of these devices and perform a cemented hip replacement through the anterior approach which I had presented at the conference. We discussed the "samples" issue, but that did not seem a problem in his mind and I consented to the operation. It was another one of those Dr. Southwick "You can do it Kris" situations, in a foreign country, with strange instruments, poor lights, bizarre drapes, overheated operating room, unknown assistants and nurses - Why not? It was going to help Latvian surgery as well as the director of one of the major collective farms, who had volunteered for the operation. We completed the operation in good time, and the professors from some of the other Soviet Republics, Uzbekistan in particular, who watched it seemed impressed. Interestingly enough, the only surgical instruments of any western quality had been inherited from German military hospitals at the end of World War II. The patient did extremely well immediately after the operation and for many years thereafter.

The operation was the first of well over 100 hip replacements I'd go on to perform in Latvia and throughout the Soviet Union. Professor Kalnberzs was pleased, and the next morning I was invited to the office of Professor Haralds Jansons along with his deputy director in charge of all administrative details and the director of the only biomechanical research institute in the Soviet Union. No sooner had I been seated with them than out came the glasses and the Armenian brandy.

It apparently was time to celebrate the success of the conference and the operation we had performed. After two of the traditional "bottoms up" toasts, Haralds came to the point. It was his hope that we could establish an academic exchange program between the Riga Institute of Orthopaedics and Traumatology and Yale University/ Waterbury Hospital.

An educational nonprofit foundation came to mind. It was all in the category of a dream, but worth considering. It was, above all, an academic venture, but it came to us at a time when the Soviet Union was ready to work with the rest of the world, and with the western commercial enterprises eager to explore these potentially vast markets. My contacts with the major orthopaedic manufacturers were very positive. I had been on the surgical advisory boards of several of these major companies and had access to their executives for advice on the funding of a foundation and the start of the educational work Professor Jansons and I had discussed. The companies saw it as academic work with one of their clients and also the entry into the Soviet Union's orthopaedic market.

Upon my return to Connecticut, I established the nonprofit Keggi Orthopaedic Foundation with my own funds in March 1988 and was then able to get some help from several orthopaedic manufacturing companies. It is impossible to put a dollar figure on the charitable non-compensated hours, days and months I'd spend away from my private practice, but it was primarily the Richards Company (later bought out by Smith & Nephew) that was the major financial contributor of hard dollars toward our work. Waterbury Hospital was also of great help by providing room and board to our fellows during their stays in Connecticut, and we were fortunate to be getting regular support from friends and patients. Our quarterly newsletter was a great success and much of the credit for that goes to Laurine Zatorski. She was our only salaried assistant, and the work she did was the core of the success we had with the foundation from its beginning in Waterbury to its conversion into the Yale Fund for International Orthopaedic Education 20 years later. As we recall our lectures, operations and other constructive activities in Latvia, the Baltics and other Soviet Republics, Laurine's administrative work must also be remembered and appreciated. On her first trip to Latvia to start a nurses' exchange, she discovered and recruited Iveta Kelle as our local contact there - administrator, interpreter and friend, who made it possible for us to function from Latvia to Outer Mongolia. At the time of Laurine's visit to Riga, Iveta was the only nurse there who spoke some English in addition to her Latvian and Russian.

The first of our Soviet visitors to Connecticut was Professor Viktors Kalnberzs himself, who came in February 1988 to visit, "evaluate" and finalize the program we had discussed in Riga only two months earlier. Shortly after this visit, we signed the official Academic Exchange Agreement between the Soviet Union and the United States of America, the Soviet Academy of Science and Yale University, the Latvian Institute of Traumatology and Orthopaedics and Waterbury Hospital, to be administered by the Keggi Orthopaedic Foundation. Before signing this elaborate document produced by the Soviet establishment, I called our State Department and Yale administrators to make sure I could sign on their behalf. I was told I could do anything I wanted as long as they did not have to pay for it.

We were now ready to go, and our first two fellows arrived a couple of months later. They were Konstantins Kalnberzs, Viktor's son, and Gundars Lacis, whose father had served with the Latvian units in the German Army, had managed to surrender to the Western Allies and was now living in New York. Both were fully trained orthopaedic surgeons in their 30s, ready to complement their education with total joint surgery in the States. It was the beginning of a program that would last more than 20 years and bring in more than 250 orthopaedic fellows, radiologists, and other physicians to Waterbury and Yale. About 120 of these were from Latvia, the rest from Estonia, Lithuania, Ukraine, Russia, Uzbekistan, Georgia, Belarus, Germany and Vietnam. At Waterbury Hospital their official status was that of "medical students," which allowed them to participate in operations, clinics and conferences. At Yale, they were designated as "visiting scholars" with access to libraries, museums, lectures and conferences.

The nurses' program is also worthy of review. Initially, we had two of the main Latvian operating room nurses involved with joint replacement come to Waterbury Hospital to become familiar with our instruments, implants, surgery and nursing techniques. They were the two who later accompanied me to Moscow, Kiev, Yeroslavl and multiple other locations to help with joint replacements. Laurine Zatorski, with the help of Iveta Kelle, then worked on a program for the education of Latvian nurses. She went to Latvia on her own on several occasions and arranged for Merrilee Albright, the wife of one of our early Yale residents, Jim Albright, to spend several months in Riga, bringing the Latvian nursing practices and education closer to western standards. Merrilee, a nurse and lawyer, definitely left a positive mark on Latvian nursing and was continuing to work with our foundation until her premature death from complications related to atrial fibrillation. With the financial assistance that I was able to obtain from the chairman of the Smith & Nephew Company (at a very elegant dinner meeting in their London headquarters on the banks of the River Thames), Laurine and Iveta established a program for Baltic and Russian nurses to spend time at Oxford University's Nuffield Orthopaedic Centre. I estimate that at least 100 nurses benefited from them that effort.

As our foundation got up and running, Viktors Kalnberzs was eager to have me teach, lecture and operate in Latvia and the rest of the Soviet Union. It was a challenging and interesting proposition that was to take me on surgical trips from Riga to Vladivostok, four to six times a year. That first operation I'd conducted in Riga used prosthetic samples and elementary instruments, but if I was to operate on high ranking members of the Latvian and Soviet establishment, we had to do better. I was fortunate that two of the Latvian operating room nurses were willing to work with me in Latvia and travel to help in Moscow, Vladivostok, Yaroslavl, Kiev, etc. Waterbury Hospital helped by donating some used, but useful, basic instruments for hip replacements in my anterior manner. Smith & Nephew could not have been more generous in supplying the implants of various types and sizes to accommodate the spectrum of joints I might encounter. All of these implants and instruments were kept in Riga by Lolita Misins, our senior nurse assistant, and transported by her during our surgical travels. I was also able to get American antibiotics to take with me for all the operations I performed. Their prophylactic use was routine at home, but more than essential in some of the remote hospitals that hosted us. Having worked out these staffing, instrument and antibiotic details, I felt secure about being able to do my operative part with relative safety.

With a few rare exceptions, my patients were

selected by Viktors Kalnberzs. The first was Neilands, the foreign relations minister of the Latvian Soviet Republic. I met him in Moscow, where he and Viktors had come to meet me and ease my entry into Russia. All flights to any destination in the Soviet Union went through Moscow and its elaborate security process. Being met by a Hero of the Soviet Union (Viktor) and a minister of foreign relations made things much easier. A few months later, when the man meeting me was Admiral Aleksy Stepanovich Shindjajev, the second in command of the KGB and in charge of all borders of the Soviet Union, it was always a remarkably smooth and pleasant experience. I was met by him as I came off the plane, escorted through all security gates to a VIP lounge for brandy or vodka while his underlings took care of the paperwork, luggage or any other details prior to a transfer to a connecting flight or a drive into Moscow in a waiting limo a few yards from the lounge. (More on The Admiral just ahead.)

Neilands was remarkable, spoke excellent English, looked and dressed the part of a West European gentleman. One of the reasons for wanting his arthritic hip replaced was his love of tennis, which he played on the courts for the Party elite in Riga. He took me on a tour of Moscow, I examined his hip, we talked about surgery and he decided to proceed with it. His operation at the Latvian Orthopaedic Institute went well, and he returned to the normal life of a middle-aged gentlemen, complete with his tennis.

One of the more enthusiastic observers of my surgical performance in Riga, in December 1987, had been Hamrayev, a professor of orthopaedic surgery in Uzbekistan. He invited us to visit him in Tashkent to lecture, do an operation and tour the historic Muslim Silk Road cities of Samarkand and Bukhara. Viktor was enthusiastic about the trip and it seemed like a major adventure to me, so, soon after the Neilands operation, we were off to Uzbekistan. One of the interesting parts of the trip was the flight from Moscow to Tashkent. I was amazed at its length and the great distance between the two cities. I knew about the Silk Road and had heard of Samarkand, but I could not have imagined what we encountered. The old mosques, bazaars, minarets and madrassas were spectacular. The history of the area was also amazing, with its place in the world of science and medicine 1,000 years ago, part of a Muslim world that extended from there through Persia all the way to Spain. We visited the home of Avicenna, the 11th-century physician, scientist and philosopher. We heard about the Uzbeks with red hair, said to be descendants of the Greek Macedonians who had reached the area with Alexander the Great more than 2,000 years earlier. There were the stories of the caravans, the Mongols and Genghis Khan – fascinating, absolutely fascinating.

Our experience in the operating room was also fascinating. We had come to the hospital, had met the patient and were waiting to do his hip replacement while he was being anesthetized. As we were getting ready to operate, I had to visit the toilet and was directed to a room within a few feet of the operating room. Within was a toilet with its bowl full to the top with feces and toilet paper. The window was open, and the flies were having a grand time buzzing in and out. I did what I needed to do, came out and expressed my concern about doing a major joint replacement within a few feet of this facility. Viktor, who had also seen it, assured me there was nothing to worry about since in Uzbekistan the patients prone to infection died young and the survivors did not need to fear a few contaminated flies. Okay. Anesthesia worked fairly well, and the pre-operative catheterization was somewhat bloody, but we managed to do our part, complete with the prophylactic antibiotics which I had brought. It all ended well. We were invited to come back, and a year or so later Professor Hamrayev was one of our fellows at Waterbury/Yale.

Minister Neilands and the unknown survivor of infections in Uzbekistan were my first "planned" operations in the USSR. There are a few others that will have to be told, but first to the Admiral, whose presence made so much of it possible.

THE ADMIRAL

Admiral Aleksy Stepanovich Shindjajev was the #2 man in the KGB. His office was located above the main entrance of the Lubyanka Prison, overlooking Dzerzhinsky Square in the heart of Moscow. He was in charge of all the borders of the Soviet Union, its coastlines, ports and airports. The Admiral's wife was one of Viktors' patients. She did not need a joint replacement, but I consulted her on her leg deformity, and in the course of this encounter met her husband. He was a nice man, pleasant, quiet, seemingly self-effacing, and even though all of our communication was through interpreters - Viktor, Iveta, his granddaughter and my fellows - we spent a fair amount of time together and he referred to me as his best foreign friend. It was hard to imagine his past history and his immense responsibilities, but having seen him at work in his Lubyanka office there was no question about self-effacement. He was one of the tough major powers in the Soviet hierarchy, with deferential assistants, multiple telephones on the desk and a loud "command voice." All of this in sharp contrast to his mild manner outside of the office. He was a good friend, yet unimaginable in so many different ways as I think about Communism, its terror, our flight out of Latvia, my godfather Janis and his brother Ludis dying in Communist hands and my time in the Vietnam war. He was a good friend, and the future of the world depends on the type of friendship we had in spite of our past histories.

Above and beyond the simple satisfaction of an interesting friendship, he was also helpful with our academic exchange programs, the fellows' visas and my own travels throughout the Soviet Union. Under his KGB watchful eye I felt as safe there as anyplace in the world. We had some interesting and fun times. He always carried a small briefcase, for instance. It may well have contained the most secret of documents, but its only content I was familiar with was the bottle of brandy that once opened had to be liquidated to our mutual health. He was always driven in a KGB limo by a man with bulging armpits (guns) who spoke some English and whose dashboard was decorated with hippie-type peace stickers, in sharp contrast to his license plates that identified its high-ranking passenger. The limo travelled in special traffic lanes, and if they were slower than expected he would activate a blue light that allowed him to pass anybody anywhere. In the Admiral's limo the trip from the Sheremetyevo Airport on the outskirts of Moscow to the center of town was a matter of 15 or 20 minutes – and an hour or more for an ordinary citizen. The Admiral could also park anywhere, and I was with him on a special occasion when he took advantage of this right and privilege. It was a Sunday morning and I was due to fly back to New York. The Admiral wanted to take me to the airport and arrived at my hotel at the scheduled time – but something was wrong. He looked haggard and told us about his night. His deputy had been promoted to "Full Admiral," and he had been at the event celebrating the occasion, where the custom apparently requires the consumption of a bottle of vodka for each star on your shoulders. The Admiral with his four stars was now suffering the effects of those toasts the previous night. He wanted a drink before going to the airport and his briefcase did not have the "usual." We went to some restaurants and bars, but they were closed. The situation was getting more and more frustrating, but then I remembered the bottle of some very special Armenian brandy given to me by one of my Moscow patients. The Admiral could not have been more pleased and stopped the car in an area forbidden to all traffic - the middle of Red Square just a few yards from Lenin's Tomb. We retrieved the brandy from my suitcase, got back into the limo and from its beginning to its end had a delightful time with the appropriate toasts to families, friendship, health, peace, Russia and America. I am sure the guards of this sacred ground and Lenin's Tomb were wondering about us, but I am equally sure they got the message we were to be left in peace and without unnecessary confrontations. The Admiral revived and I was ready for the flight home in a pacified frame of body and mind. If I were running for political office, I am certain this special, secret limo meeting would have required a Congressional investigation.

On another special occasion the Admiral was giving me and our eldest daughter Katie a ride from Riga to Moscow on his private KGB jet. It was still an early, dark morning when we arrived at the Riga Airport. We were driven through several security gates and pulled up to the waiting jet on one of the main runways. The Admiral was helped out of the car by a uniformed guard. Katie and I followed. Much to my surprise there was a line of at least eight high-ranking generals waiting to say farewell to the Admiral, with formal salutes, handshakes and a few hugs. The officers were the High Command of the entire Baltic Region. They knew their duty and recognized an opportunity to be exposed to my friend Aleksy. For the two of us who followed there were no salute or handshakes, just puzzled looks. It was an impressive military show. On the plane, we were the only passengers and were seated at a small table for what was to be an inflight breakfast. As soon as we were airborne, the Admiral opened his briefcase, pulled out an old newspaper which he spread out as tablecloth on which he put a hunk of cheese, a loaf of bread and the brandy. He produced his pocketknife and corkscrew, sliced the bread and cheese, poured the brandy – breakfast was on, in the simple manner of the old Russian peasant that he was. The flight took about an hour and is one of the most memorable Katie and I ever had.

Travel with the #2 of the KGB was easy. I have talked about arrival in Moscow under his guidance and in his shadow, but the departures were equally unique. He would pick me up in my hotel and drive to the airport where we would go directly to the VIP lounge. Several of the Admiral's comrades, in their dark leather coats, would take my suitcase, passport and ticket and return in quick time with the passport appropriately stamped, a boarding pass and luggage tags. In the meantime, we would be in the lounge doing our toasts and waiting for flight time. Typically, I would get somewhat anxious when that time arrived or passed and would question the Admiral, but his reply was to relax and have another toast to friendship. Finally, he would get a signal from one of the attendants and would indicate that the time had come to go. He would then lead me without any stops through all the inspection points and gates, up the ramp and into the plane. All the seats would be full except for my favored one, on the aisle in the second row. The other passengers on these nonstop Pan Am flights were mainly businessmen who had just spent a significant amount of time being "processed" at the airport, all of them eager to get out of Russia. My late arrival in the company of the Admiral, typically dressed in a non-descript jacket, was greeted with a hushed silence and all eyes on us as Aleksy

Stepanovich would send me off with a kiss on the lips, a Russian gesture of ultimate friendship (a custom I'd been familiar with since my childhood exposure to some of my older family members).   Who is this guy? Who is the one that brought him? Who knows? I am sure there were those who were convinced I was a special agent of some type, but no matter what people thought, the Admiral made travel in and out of Russia convenient and painless. I also wonder if I would have continued to do the work I did and the visits I made if I had to spend too many painful hours in the Sheremetyevo Airport. Perhaps the Admiral knew that, too.

I had been running our academic exchange for at least two years and had been to the Soviet Union at least 10 times when, without warning, I got a call from the FBI. My initial response to them was one of surprise that they hadn't reached out to me sooner, but we arranged to meet to discuss our activities with my Soviet fellows. A few days later, two agents came to my office to tell me they were aware of our academic activities and travels but wanted to tell me about the Russian Secret Police (KGB) and how they functioned. They were certain I was being watched and followed no matter where I went in the Soviet Union. They were also felt that if I had two fellows at Waterbury, one of them was certain to be reporting to the KGB or might even be a full-time agent. I told them I had been familiar with their ways since childhood, knew I was under constant surveillance when in Russia and was aware that some of our fellows had definite connections with the KGB and were providing them with reports about us. At the end of the meeting, I assured the agents that I would call them immediately if I became aware of anything unusual or of potential interest to our security services.

That moment came a year or so later. On one of

my visits to Moscow, the Admiral told me he would be coming to the United States and, while there, meet with me. That sounded exciting and I wanted to start planning for a good visit, but he did not know the dates of his stay in America. It was against KGB rules to give out, prematurely, specific dates of the travels of high-ranking officials, and even he was not privy to them until a few days before departure. He did however assure me I would be notified, and we would meet in Washington. That seemed fine. A few weeks later I had a late-night telephone call that was short and rather vague. It was a voice with a heavy Russian accent:

"This is Sergei. Admiral Shindjajev is coming soon. We will call you again."

Two or three weeks later came the second call from Sergei.

"The Admiral is in Washington and wants to see you Monday night."

I was given the name of his hotel. Monday night was only a couple days away and I had some scheduled operations in the morning, but I told Sergei I would be there. I had a Latvian and a Russian Latvian as fellows at the time and was planning to take them along as interpreters. The simplest way to make the meeting without cancelling and rescheduling the operations was to charter a small plane. The morning of our flight and planned meeting, it occurred to me the situation was unique enough to notify the FBI agents who had come to see me. I called them and told them of the planned visit and expressed the opinion that if they, the FBI, were doing their job, they would find me that night having drinks and dinner with the #2 man in the KGB. When we got to the Admiral's hotel room, he could not have been happier. It was a joyous occasion complete with the hug and kiss. He really was glad to see us, having had a long and frustrating trip with a group of Russian fishermen on their way to America to discuss offshore fishing rights. Eight hours on a plane to Vladivostok, several days on one of his Coast Guard ships to Alaska, followed by another endless flight to Washington. He had not been recognized by anybody and had already spent some days in what he described as boring meetings about fishing. We had a great evening at one of the finest Georgetown restaurants and I am almost certain that, between the Admiral, myself and our two fellows, we may well have liquidated most of their brandy supply. Yet the most interesting aspect of the visit was the following day and the remainder of his stay in Washington. Suddenly, thanks to my heads-up, he had been identified as described, drinking and dining with a Latvian-born Connecticut surgeon and Yale professor. From then on, he was visited by American admirals and high officials, and he was spared from more meetings with fishermen. I hope my two Connecticut FBI agents were appropriately rewarded for a job well done.

In the course of our friendship and meetings, the Admiral had also given me a Russian colonel's uniform with its star covered shoulder boards, and I have been photographed at some of our resident and fellows parties wearing that outfit. I am sure that in the eyes of any Congressional committee or CNN these pictures would be proof positive of my membership and status in the KGB. It did not last very long, since I resigned from the Red Army by giving my uniform to Cameron Price upon his graduation from West Point - thus he became a second lieutenant in the U.S. Army and a Russian colonel the same day. Cameron is the son of Jack Price one of my 173rd Airborne lifelong friends whose wounds I treated in Vietnam. Anyway, since "one good turn deserves another," I thought "commissioning" the Admiral would make sense during our Washington encounter. I was able to find a military jacket and the appropriate general's stars in one of our old Army-Navy stores, and with all solemnity presented it to him as we entered his hotel room. He was ecstatic.

He may have been a simple fisherman in Washington, but he could do anything in Moscow. The most amazing example of it was the trip he arranged for his granddaughter, who wanted to spend some time with us in Connecticut. Her father, the Admiral's son-in-law, was also in the KGB. He was a colonel, who at one point in his career had been in charge of the bodyguards of Libya's dictator Gaddafi. Within hours of the Soviet collapse, he was back in Moscow, where he became president of one of the largest banks. His daughter was 17, attractive, bright and fluent in English and German. I met her at the Admiral's apartment and was pleased to invite her to spend some time with our family, assuming it had to be arranged and would probably come to pass in a few months. I could not have imagined the events that followed. My flight back to New York was the following day, and much to my surprise she was on that plane in the first-class seat next to mine. Her passport, visa and all other documents were ready to go. It had all been arranged in less than 24 hours. Before boarding, her father, whom I had not met before, assured me that I need not worry about any financial issues with her and should she decide to enroll in a private boarding school in America, she could do so at any time, even without returning to Russia beforehand. She was with us for about a month. We all enjoyed her company and, as her father had said, money was not an issue as she would produce any amount of dollar bills to buy anything she desired. I have not heard about her since that visit, but I am sure she has been successful and has not lacked material support from her father, who is probably one of the oligarchs in Putin's regime.

My last visit with the Admiral was a sad one. The Soviet Union had collapsed, but he still seemed to be leading a privileged life with such benefits as a limousine and driver. Unfortunately, he had had a stroke, was partially paralyzed and had difficulty talking. He was a good man, good friend and was of great assistance in our academic work in Russia and the former Republics of the Soviet Union.

There are so many ways of looking at the Admiral and our friendship. There are those who would say that I was being used by the KGB, and that the Admiral was trying to learn as much as possible about our work in Latvia and thoughts about its independence. I am also sure there were agents in the Soviet Union who probably considered me a CIA operative. Ridiculous! You can think anything you want, but my absolute belief is he wanted to be a friend, wanted to reach out to us and the West. He was a Russian, like so many others I met, who wanted to be with us on common ground, in peace, in thought, in life. I am certain he had never had a relationship with a Westerner that would come close to the one we had. The future of the world depends on more friendships of this type and we have to encourage them, we have to support them, we have to understand each other, we cannot spend years breeding unnecessary paranoia. The Russians are not the enemy. They are of Judeo-Christian background and beliefs. Their musicians, ballets and literature are part of the Western canon. We have much more in common with them than with the Chinese or Muslim nations. We have to be strong, we have to be respected and we have to respect them. The Admiral and I understood that. The future is in the hands of those of us with similar hopes for a life of peace and collaboration in all areas of human endeavor. Russia and America are on common ground and we should make every effort to live together. Leaders change and new generations with new ideas come to pass. We should try to make friendly contacts at every level of our societies and be ready to move away from our present level of confrontation.

MISSIONS TO MOSCOW

S hortly after the operation on Minister Neilands, I was back in Riga for some more surgery at the Latvian Institute of Orthopaedics and Traumatology. On one of these trips, while I was passing through Moscow, Victors took me to the apartment of the president of the Russian Academy of Science, Valentin Ivanovich Pokrovsky, to examine his wife who was totally disabled with bilateral arthritis of the hips caused by congenital dislocations of the joints. We discussed the possibility of surgery and the potentially greater complications with hips as severely deformed as hers.

Professor Pokrovsky felt the risks were worth taking and we agreed to do the surgery in Riga. When I came to do the operation, I brought some extra prostheses from the States, donated by the Richards Company, that might be needed in her particular case. It was a complex operation, but it went well. We finished and came out of the operating room to speak with Prof. Pokrovsky. I explained that everything had gone well, and we could expect a good result. He was extremely pleased and immediately pulled out his bottle of brandy and insisted we drink a couple of toasts. I explained to him I couldn't possibly be drinking since I had another operation in a few minutes. He did not understand that and seemed disappointed, but we made up for it at dinner that evening. It was yet another complex operation performed in a foreign setting that with a wiser mind perhaps should have been left untouched, but Southwick's "You can do it, Kris!" prevailed.

Her right hip result was excellent, but she still had the left that was giving her problems. After some further discussions during another trip to Moscow, we decided to proceed with its replacement. This time, Prof. Pokrovsky and Viktors Kalnberzs did not think it was necessary to go to Riga. The political climate had continued to change, and it was arranged for me to do her operation at the "secret" Kremlin Hospital in Moscow. I would be the first western surgeon to operate in this special institution. The Kremlin Hospital was located close to the center of Moscow, surrounded by 12-foot walls. The hospital itself was a beautiful building in the middle of well-kept lawns and gardens. There was also a secondary building for recuperation and rest that could be used by high-ranking members of the party to recover from a night of excessive toasts. It had a swimming pool; indeed, the entire complex was totally out of context with the rest of the city. The hospital was not crowded, the operating rooms were large, clean and properly ventilated. When we arrived, they showed us a variety of total hip replacements, primarily of the Swiss Schweitzer type, but they were not to be used. The orthopaedic director, Doctor Abelcev, was in his mid-forties, well mannered, a descendent of the Volga Germans. He and Victors Kalnberzs assisted at the operation. The only amusing part of the entire process were the Kremlin nurses who were extremely put off by the Latvian nurses who had come with me and were my primary helpers in their operating room. I also brought with me some of my American instruments and some special prostheses from Waterbury to accommodate the particular problem we faced with Mrs. Pokrovsky. I operated in that Kremlin

Hospital once more, a few months later, on the top anesthesiologist of the Soviet Union, a member of the Soviet Academy of Science and major official within the Communist healthcare system. That operation also went well, and the Russian nurses did not seem as insulted as they seemed to be during Mrs. Pokrovsky's operation.

During the rest of my travels in the Soviet Union, I had frequent encounters with Valentin Ivanovich Pokrovsky and several major dinners, one of them at a former Czarist palace, the official headquarters of the Russian Academy of Science. It was at one of these dinners I had the pleasure of meeting Prof. Ilizarov, whose external fixator was being introduced into the western world by the Richards Company. We only had a short conversation. He apparently was not very happy about Viktors Kalnberzs, whose external fixator was major competition to the one he had designed and was now being promoted in the West. It was interesting to meet him, but he was not too keen on having extensive conversations with one of Viktors' friends. He did not seem to be in good health and shortly thereafter was taken to Memphis for medical care arranged by the Richards Company.

Mrs. Pokrovsky recovered nicely and was also able to come visit us in the United States during a trip to Disney World. At another time, Prof. Pokrovsky came to Washington for the presentation of my membership medal in the Russian Academy of Science. The ceremony took place within the Russian Embassy complex. I drove down from Connecticut with several friends and it was fascinating to be there with the Russian staff.

My last meeting with the Prof. Pokrovsky was in 2008, when I was invited to Moscow and presented with a special medal honoring me for medical work throughout

Russia. It is a medal that at any one time is in the possession of only 13 individuals. Only upon the death of one of the 13 could another be awarded. It was a major honor and the award ceremony was followed by a wonderful celebration. My relationship with Prof. Prokovsky was a very happy one, and he, too, was one of the Russians that I felt in the long run would do anything to establish peaceful, cooperative relationships with the western world.

It was also interesting to receive a sudden call to fly to Moscow to consult on the care that Soviet Minister of Health and Nobel Laureate Yevgeniy Chazov was getting for a broken humerus. I have no idea who thought a Western joint surgeon should fly to Moscow to participate in the management of a relatively simple fracture, but there I was, being driven to the Kremlin Convalescent Hospital in the countryside, several miles beyond the outskirts of Moscow. As we were approaching the hospital there were armed guards along the roadside. The access road itself was about a quarter of a mile long, perfectly straight with a guard house and entrance gate at the end of it. The guard house had a big red light on top of it, which turned green as we approached. The gate swung open at the same time and we were in a wooded parklike environment with several homes that were the rehabilitation centers or convalescent homes. We were directed to the one housing Minister Chazov and led to his room. He was a pleasant man of approximately 60 years, sitting up in bed with this left arm bandaged to his chest. He did not seem to be in any pain and his X-rays showed a minimally displaced fracture of the proximal humeral shaft. In the United States a few years later the standard treatment would be an open reduction and fixation of the fracture with plate and screws, but he was being treated in a manner tried and tested for centuries if not millennia before. It made sense to me and we discussed it with him and his treating physician in those terms. They had a well thought out plan. He was going to do well without surgery and did not need me. There was no brandy at this meeting, but as I remember it, we did have some tea and crackers. After the consultation and brief socializing, we were in our limo on our way back to Moscow and New York. After that visit I would occasionally hear about him. As far as I know, his fracture healed, and he continued to practice cardiology at the highest of medical and political levels. Minister Chazov certainly seemed like a reasonable man who was also known for his participation in a variety of international anti-nuclear weapons committees and programs, but in his official statements he was always very negative about the United States. I hope our consultation mollified his views. In any case it was another unusual/educational encounter with the Communist elite.

Another encounter with this elite was when I was invited to operate on the last surviving World War II Russian Army Marshal at the First Army Hospital in Moscow. The hospital had been founded and built under Peter the Great in the early 18th century. The building dating back to the beginnings of the institution were of solid brick construction, precise in alignment with straight floors and solid staircases. The modern additions of the Soviet era were a different matter. The hallway walls had unusual curves, the floors had undulations and the steps on the staircases were each of a different height. Where visible, the bricks in the walls were uneven, in sharp contrast to the precisely laid ones in the old buildings 300 years earlier. It was interesting to see it and think of it in historical and political terms. The chief of the orthopaedic service was pleasant, seemed very competent, had served in the Russian-Afghan war and was an expert in the use of external fixators in trauma and reconstructive surgery. Several years later, I was able to send my nephew, John Keggi, to spend some time with him and learn the finer points of external fixation.

Our patient, the Marshal (whose name I do not remember), was a delight and anything but the image of a medal-bedecked symbol of military power reviewing the Red Army, standing by Lenin's tomb. Viktor and I met him the night before the operation as he was preparing his own tea, in old pajamas and wool slippers. He did have a bad hip and was eager to have it fixed. The next morning, we performed the replacement, and all went well. That night we had the appropriate Russian celebration and I was awarded an Honorary Burdenko University Doctors Degree. The next morning, on the way to the airport and home, we stopped by to see my patient. He was happy, starting to walk and headed for a rapid recovery - confirmed in subsequent communications.

The care we provided to Mrs. Luchev, the wife of the commander of all the Warsaw Pact forces, is also a good memory. Viktors had seen her and evaluated her very osteoarthritic hip. The general and his wife had consented to the operation at the Latvian Institute of Orthopaedics and Traumatology, and I was to be performing her replacement. I had no objections. I flew to Riga with the appropriate Richards Company implants. On the day before the operation I was introduced to a very sharp looking Russian colonel, the senior surgeon under Luchev's command, who had come with the patient with orders to make sure everything went well. He was a general surgeon but had been told to assist at the operation. He seemed very rigid and aloof. He had many questions about the operation and was not friendly. I was able to communicate with him without interpreters since he, having spent many years in Germany, spoke the language I had learned as a child with our German governess near Riga and close to the spot where we were meeting 45 years later. He was adamant about being the first assistant at the operation. Viktors and one of his junior surgeons were to be the second and third assistants. I had no objection, nor could I have had any.

We proceeded with the operation the next day with the Colonel across the table from me, watching my every move with severe intensity. As the procedure was going smoothly, he seemed to relax, and I could not resist to play a few "games" with him by pretending to extend the incision or cut the femur. At the end of it he was a happy camper and immediately disappeared to communicate to General Luchev that all had gone well. I did another operation and the following morning, after visiting Mrs. Luchev, Viktors and I flew to Moscow and Tashkent (as I remember) to do some more operations. Four or five days later we were back in Riga to find our patient in great shape, walking well and pain free. The Colonel was a changed person, smiling, talkative and presenting me with a large bottle of brandy. Shortly after his work with us he was promoted to general rank, went on to be Surgeon General of the Soviet Army and eventually served as one of first Ministers of Health of the Russian Federation. The patient continued on a course of excellent recovery and we were able to visit her in the family dacha outside of Moscow a few months later. It was a house dating to pre-revolutionary days, with nice gardens, surrounded by a high wooden fence and patrolled by fully armed, uniformed guards. We were served a very nice luncheon but only one or two vodka toasts.

In Moscow I also had a visit at the Central Orthopaedic Hospital with Viktor Nuzhdin, their main joint surgeon, who eventually spent three months with us in Waterbury and at Yale. Nuzhdin was a superb surgeon and cultured individual with frank opinions on many subjects. He was a devoted Russian, but amazingly outspoken on the failures of the Soviet regime. Once we had established our friendship, I was invited to his apartment for dinner and an evening of lengthy conversations on surgery, Russian history, literature, families and the world. It was a true honor to be in his home and experience the ultimate in sincere Russian hospitality. He was not a member of the Party elite and the food and drinks he and his wife served us may well have cost him a month's salary. A good man, and, like so many others, ready to work for a better world with better Russian/Western relations.

Another Russian who must be remembered was one of Viktors Kalnberzs' patients with whom I spent an evening in his Moscow apartment - a general in the Soviet Army Nuclear Weapons and Missile Branch who had designed and built the largest hydrogen bomb ever, which if dropped on Philadelphia would destroy everything between New York and Washington. This "Rocket Scientist" was amazing. Tall and well-dressed, he could easily be mistaken for an American engineer or university professor. He spoke excellent English and was devoted to reading Shakespeare. He also knew German and liked Goethe. We talked about atomic weapons, but he was quick to point out his favored task had been their deactivation under a recently signed Reagan/Gorbachev treaty. To emphasize that point, he presented me with a metal shard of a missile deactivated (destroyed) under his command. The piece of metal was mounted on a card with a photograph of the missile, its identifying markings and the date of its destruction. His story is almost hard to believe, but it is once again an example of a member of the Russian intellectual and power elite seeking a world of Shakespeare, Goethe and Tolstoy - not nuclear annihilation of New York, Philadelphia and Washington.

Vladimir Kuzmenko was the chief traumatologist of the Soviet Union. He was supportive of our work, and, with perestroika under way, eager to establish better relations with his counterparts in the West. Viktor thought it important to arrange a visit for him to the United States, so we invited him to the annual meeting of the American Academy of Orthopaedic Surgeons, which was taking place in Washington, D.C. that year. While at the meeting he, jokingly at first, thought it might be constructive to visit the White House and President George H. W. Bush. John Barrasso, one of our former Yale residents and good friend, was also in Washington at the time. John was involved in Republican politics and close to Dick Cheney, who in turn became a very active Vice President of the United States under George W. Bush. I told John about Kuzmenko and wondered if it would be possible to arrange a visit to the White House. John took action, and with Cheney's help we had an appointment with Doctor Burton J. Lee, President George H. W. Bush's physician, the next morning. We were to be met in front of our hotel by a young Navy lieutenant who was to take us to the White House. All of it was similar to our travels in Moscow under the Admiral's command. We got to Lee's office in the basement of the White House as scheduled, and our appointment, which was to be a short one, turned into a good two-hour visit. Lee was Yale graduate, glad to meet Kuzmenko, and interested in our work in the Soviet Union. We had a tour of the White House, everybody was pleased, and it was a great morning in line with our hopes of helping to establish better relations between Americans and Russians. My understanding of the Russians mentality has been fairly good, and time with Doctor Kuzmenko added a few more vistas on the subject. He was an intelligent man with an excellent clinical reputation, but somewhat cynical of life in general and the Soviet regime in particular. He was also a chain smoker who left the odor of cigarettes in our Middlebury guest rooms that lasted for weeks after his departure. He and Julie got along very nicely because he loved ballet and was the physician for the major Russian ballet companies. While he stayed with us in Middlebury, I also learned about his drinking habits. Like all of my Russian friends he would be described, by most Americans, as a heavy social drinker, but after his stay with us I had to re-classify him into a much higher category. Our breakfast table was next to the pantry, where we kept bottles of various alcoholic beverages. While getting ready for our eggs, bacon, toast and coffee, I showed him where the liquor was and told him to help himself if he felt like a drink. I left the room to get something upstairs and when I got back Vladimir was sitting at the table with a water glass full of vodka. By the time we were finished with the meal, he had polished off another full glass, ready to get going without any ill effects. I saw him in Moscow on a couple of other occasions and it is my understanding he died within two years of our Washington White House visit. I have seen alcoholism in some sad friends in America, but his frank and unabashed consumption of the vodka with our breakfast was in line with behavior thought to be acceptable by many Russians, in line with their anecdote about a Russian's ideal life – "Get up hung over in the morning, go to work, feel better by eleven, work a few hours, go home, kick the dog, beat the wife, drink a bottle of vodka, go to bed and repeat it all the next day."

OTHER RUSSIAN
PEOPLE AND PLACES

V ladivostok, the remote city near North Korea and the terminus of the historic Trans-Siberian Railway from St. Petersburg, has always been a city of special meaning to our family. My maternal grandmother's brother, Fricis Smidhens, had been the Lutheran chaplain with the Czarist Army during the Russian-Japanese War (1904-1905). Vladivostok was central in that war and Uncle Fricis was there, stationed in a military hospital where one of the Lutheran Red Cross nurse volunteers was a noblewoman from Prussia, Princess Eleonore Caroline Gasparine Louise Reuss-Koestritz. Our uncle was the only one with an early camera and was able to record in photographs some of the activities and people at the hospital. Eleonore returned to Prussia and shortly thereafter was selected to be the wife/consort of the gay Tsar/ King of Bulgaria. She did not have a family and her life as the Queen of Bulgaria was devoted to helping the poor and wounded during World War I - work she knew well from her previous life as a nurse volunteer in Prussia and Vladivostok.

After returning to Latvia, my uncle sent her an album of pictures from their joint service in Vladivostok. She, in return, rewarded him with a gold watch engraved with her royal crest, the crowned letter "E." This watch has long been an important and proud possession of our family. It also facilitated the opening of the first boarding school in the Russian Czar's Empire outside of Riga by my grandfather and uncle Fricis, my godfather's godfather. In the administrative swamps of the era they had difficulty getting permission to start this school and equal difficulty getting loans to fund it. The process, however, was resolved by a visit to the Russian governor of the Baltic region who, when shown the royal watch, immediately consented to the project. The school was created in Jurmala, on the shores of the Gulf of Riga, but its success was short-lived because of World War I and the region's total destruction during the major battles that raged from 1914 to 1918. During its short existence it did however educate future leaders of the Independent Republic of Latvia, among them Paulis Stradins, the professor of surgery and my father's mentor at the University of Latvia. Uncle Fricis died in the 1918 flu epidemic. The watch was passed to his godson, my mother's bother Janis Berzins, who was my godfather. Janis was one of the most highly decorated officers in the Latvian units fighting the Russians with the German Army World War II, near Stalingrad, throughout Russia and finally in Latvia itself. We do not have the exact facts of his death. He was either executed in the Riga KGB central prison or died in a concentration camp in Siberia. The watch, however, was passed to me, his godson. The story of "The Watch," Eleonore and Fricis, the Trans-Siberian Railway, the Vladivostok hospital, the Russian-Japanese war and the gay King of Bulgaria could well make a historic book of romance with many Doctor Zhivago undertones.

When Viktors Kalnberzs talked about the possibility of visiting Vladivostok to lecture and operate in that remote city, I was very enthusiastic even though the trip would be an extremely long one. The distance from Moscow to Vladivostok is approximately twice the distance from New York to Los Angeles, and if you are trying to get there from Connecticut you come to the realization that it takes approximately the same amount of time to reach it whether you go east through Moscow or west by way of Alaska. I was there on two occasions, once reaching it from the west and the other time having reached it from the east. I got a good "feel" for the distances involved on my first night flight from Moscow to Vladivostok, sitting there for nine hours, flying over Siberia without seeing any lights or cities below. A flight from Anchorage, which I took after a Thanksgiving in the Arizona sunshine, was equally long and required a refueling stop somewhere in Siberia, in a remote airport covered with feet of deep snow.

The senior orthopaedic surgeon in Vladivostok was Igor Kuzmin, who was eager to learn about joint replacements with the latest of western prostheses and equipment. He was very serious and had the reputation of being an excellent surgeon. It was fascinating to be with him, to see the city, the monuments to the Russians, who had reached it several centuries earlier, and to work in their hospital. With all due respect to Igor and his staff, that experience was also somewhat unusual since halfway through the operation I noticed the Russian nurse assistant who was passing me instruments had a tear in her gown exposing her hairy axilla. Every time she reached for an instrument, this part of her anatomy was overhanging the operating table and it was certainly a reminder that most of the operations I was performing in the Soviet Union were potentially contaminated and had to be treated with more prophylactic antibiotics than usual. The nurse was a very nice woman, eager to help, and the operations we did went well both times I was there. It was also good to have Igor come to Waterbury/ Yale and expose him to some other American orthopaedic institutions. He was very attentive, and the work he was going to do in Vladivostok and Russia was going to be of the highest order.

Igor had a son by the name of Roman, a very bright, young man. As far as I could determine, he had led a very sheltered life, living at home with his parents, but we invited him to join us in the States, far from Vladivostok, and treated him like any of our other of our fellows. His father was very enthusiastic about that invitation, and Roman, definitely a leader in Russian orthopaedics and no doubt headed for a great future., more than deserved it.

When he arrived in Waterbury to stay in our fellows' house, there was a nurse from Latvia who was also spending some time with us, Karina Kurtiss, a bright young woman in line to be one of the leaders of Latvian nursing. She was single and later told us her relationship with Roman was love at first sight. Their stay overlapped for approximately two months, and soon she was sending messages home, telling all concerned that she had fallen in love with this wonderful Russian, a bright young surgeon with the most beautiful brown eyes. Eventually, we also learned she was pregnant by this wonderful young Russian and was going to have his child under any circumstances. She returned to Latvia before Roman was scheduled to leave for Vladivostok. He was left alone in our fellows' house and started going out with some fun-loving Lithuanian Russians. One evening, they were leaving a store on the edge of Interstate 84. The exact details are not clear, but Roman apparently set off an alarm as he was leaving the store and was so frightened that he started running toward the highway. It was dark, and by the time he reached the road he'd lost his glasses. People around him were screaming at him not to run onto the highway. He ignored the screams, ran through a ditch and some bushes, and then was immediately struck and killed by a car driven by a middle-aged woman. The spot where he was killed is such that it would have been impossible for her to stop in time. It was dark, she had just come around a curve and was going at a speed of approximately 50 miles per hour. Roman was dead on the spot. I had the sad task of identifying him in the morgue of Waterbury Hospital, calling his father, Igor, and arranging for him and his wife, Tatanya, to fly to Connecticut for a Russian Orthodox service, the cremation and the paperwork required to take the ashes back to Russia.

Another sad part of the story is that Igor somehow felt I was responsible for Roman's death. Roman was 24 years old, an educated physician, in possession of all his mental capacities and without any history of excessive drinking, drug abuse or psychiatric problems. The only way I could have prevented his death was by not allowing him out of the house without me or one of my associates. It was truly sad. A month or so later, Igor even contacted a lawyer in Connecticut to see if he had a legal claim against me, which obviously was not the case. Igor and I have seen each other at some meetings since then, but he has remained uncommunicative and angry at me. The happier side of the story is that Roman's baby was born in Riga and has been brought up by a very caring mother and her family. During the summer of 2017 when I met him in Riga, he was 16, doing extremely well in school, and spoke Russian, Latvian and almost perfect English. He has sent some e-mails telling me about his progress and perfect grades in school. When he was first born, Igor and his wife came to Riga to visit and made tentative plans to spend time there, but in recent years they have abandoned all thought of that and have not had any contact with their grandson.

While writing about Vladivostok, the Far East and

Siberia it may be of interest to relate the story of the Diamond Miner, another fascinating "character" in charge of diamond mining in Siberia, near China. As I was told, diamond mining in that part of the world was a relatively simple process of blowing up acres and acres of land and forests, followed by rummaging through the debris in search of the diamonds that would have been brought to the surface with the rest of the rocks, pebbles and sand. The man in charge (whose name I do not remember) had had an arthritic hip which, at the recommendation of some Chinese contacts, had been replaced at the First Chinese Army Hospital in Beijing. This device had failed in a short time, leaving him totally disabled and in severe pain. Somehow, he showed up at the other end of the world, in Riga, for a revision of his implant. He arrived in the company of his "private physician" bodyguard with handguns bulging in the armpits of a loose-fitting jacket - not a physician to mess with. The patient himself was a sullen man with a sense of entitlement or paranoia. His "physician-guard" had to be close to him at all times, as if he were expecting sudden assassination. It was interesting, but, as planned, I performed his operation, removed the handmade Chinese implant and replaced it with an American one. I was rewarded with the usual bottle of excellent brandy, but there were no diamonds under my pillow, even though I was fairly certain his road from Mongolia to Riga was paved with an occasional diamond along the way. The primitive, historic, handmade Chinese implant, which we still have at Yale, is however worth its weight in academic gold.

Irkutsk is close to 3,000 miles from Moscow, north of the diamond mining operation in Southeastern Siberia. For at least two centuries, it has been a city of exiles from the Czars' regimes and the Communists after their revolution. It is in this area that Viktors Kalberzs' family survived Stalin's purge of the old Latvian Bolsheviks in the 1930s. Latvians had been among the first to support the Communists in 1905, and their World War I military units, the Latvian Rifles, sided with Lenin when he promised them an independent Latvia. Lenin's climactic 1917 October Revolution in Saint Petersburg was won on the bayonets of these battle-hardened Latvian troops. Officers from these Red Rifle Regiments became the first commanders and the core of the Communist army, air force and political police. Fifteen years later, however, they seemed to represent a major threat to Stalin, and he gave the order to eliminate every Latvian male of military age in Russia. His will was done, and the few, like Viktors' father, one of the early Bolsheviks who escaped this purge, ended up in remote places like Irkutsk.

Irkutsk is also known for its proximity to Lake Baikal, the largest and deepest freshwater lake in the world. I was invited to come to Irkutsk to give some lectures and to perform some hip replacements. Academically it sounded like a constructive move, and the ancient trading town, with Lake Baikal only a "few" miles away, would be a unique sightseeing expedition. Daughter Katie seemed to have the time to join Viktors Kalnberzs and me, which made the venture even more exciting.

We were to fly from one of Moscow's southern airports. We got there via one of the KGB limos arranged by Admiral Sindjajev, only to find our flight cancelled. With the Admiral's help, we were scheduled on another plane and were off on our six-hour flight to Irkutsk. All was well until we were landing. Instead of the usual Aeroflot planes on the ground, we saw bombers and fighters along each side of our runway. This was not the civilian airport where we were supposed to be met; we were at a military installation. Once on the ground, Viktors was able to reach our host, the chief of orthopaedics in Irkutsk. He apparently was at the civilian airport and had called the military one to ask if his American guest might be there. He had been told no foreigner had ever been, nor ever would be, allowed onto their airbase - but we were there and were advised to be as inconspicuous as possible while waiting to be rescued by him. Viktor and I communicated as usual in Latvian, but Katie was to avoid any conversation in English and to act as Russian as possible. Our host arrived and we left the airbase in his car, passing all the guard posts without being stopped, compliments of the well displayed Hero of the Soviet Union Medal on Viktors' chest in the front seat.

The next surprise was a change in our schedule. My lecture was still on, but the operations had been cancelled because of an outbreak of gas gangrene at the hospital. That was unfortunate, but it gave us some extra time to visit the ancient town with its churches and to visit Lake Baikal. The trip to the lake, on dirt roads, over hills and through forests was fascinating, the meadows and the wildflowers along the lakeshore were spectacular. We also saw some Buryats, the indigenous inhabitants of the region, thought of as "inferior" human beings by our Russian friends.

We were also taken to a very unusual hospital in the woods outside Irkutsk. It was a facility that housed Russian veterans of the Afghan war with residual psychological problems and severe deformities - veterans who were obviously kept out of sight of the general Russian population, thousands of miles away in remote Siberia, the historic land of exiles.

I was happy about having had the opportunity to visit Irkutsk, and even happier we had not been taken there in a cattle car.

On one of my Moscow visits I was introduced to a Soviet Army colonel, Vitaly Dedushkin, who had been one of the senior orthopaedic surgeons in their war in Afghanistan. We talked about our experiences with war wounds in the Soviet and American armies and decided we should publish an article together. He was not interested in joint replacements but was interested in witnessing orthopaedic surgery in the United States. He was a very energetic man and was about to leave the army to practice and teach hand surgery in Leningrad-Saint Petersburg. We arranged his visit with us at a time when the Latvian Professor Haralds Jansons was planning on doing some research for his History of Biomechanics at the Yale Medical School Historical Library and would be able to help with the project. We spent several days talking about it and did write our article dealing primarily with the Russian approach to the management of severe extremity wounds in the remote mountains of Afghanistan and were able to get it published. Our basic principles of dealing with severe contaminated war wounds were the same, the differences were in the details.

Getting to know Vitaly and working with him was instructive. We had had so many similar experiences and the very real bond of having had the privilege of helping the young men who had given their all in places like Afghanistan and Vietnam. Back to thoughts of history, back to Plato, back to "The good die young."

Novosibirsk is on the Trans-Siberian Railway, 1,700 miles east of Moscow and said to be in "southern" Siberia, but there is nothing southern about it when you hear the stories of snow from September till May. It was developed as the Scientific Capital of Russia, in the middle of nowhere, remote and safe from attack from foreigners by land, by sea or by air, at least until the age of satellites and intercontinental missiles. It has the cathedral from czarist times, and an opera house, museums and ballets to accommodate the intellectual and scientific elite who called Novosibirsk their home in the days of Communism. The hospital and its staff were also of a high intellectual caliber and had great interest in the work we were presenting. Their most active orthopaedic surgeon was Valery Prokhorenko, an athletic looking man in his forties. It was satisfying to be with him in Novosibirsk, and he was one of our best foreign fellows when he came to Connecticut. His stories of life in Siberia were also fascinating. He was not a fan of the short, hot and insect infested summers, his love was the ice and the snow of the long winters, the ice fishing, the trapping and the hunting in deep, frozen forests. It was fun to hear his stories and to see some of photographs that went with them - all with a vast, white background.

My story would not be complete without mention of Saint Petersburg (Leningrad during the Communist era), the Imperial City in many ways similar to the Imperial Austro-Hungarian Vienna, with its parade grounds, palaces, churches, museums and parks. When questioned about how to spend one's time in Russia my answer has always been to spend a day in Moscow and devote the rest of the available time to Saint Petersburg. Viktors Kalnberzs did not have the same professional connections there as he did in the rest of the Soviet Union, and our first visit was a sightseeing one without any medical contacts. The second visit was at the invitation of their head of orthopaedics, who did not seem to have much interest in our work but was eager to show us his direct anterior approach to the hip. It was amazing to watch as he reached the hip with a single anterior incision through the skin and all the muscles. In my experience only an AK-47 fired at point blank range had exposed the hip faster than the professor's dramatic cut through all tissues. I was impressed, glad to have seen it, but not too eager to repeat it on my patients.

The sights of Saint Petersburg, however, are worthy of multiple repetitions. The palaces in the city and surrounding countryside compare with Versailles in France. The parks and gardens could be in Holland. The fortresses and the parade ground were where, in October 1917, the Latvian Red Rifle Regiments, bayonets fixed, put Lenin in power – a revolution won "on Jewish brains, Russian stupidity and Latvian bayonets." The story of this Imperial Russian Capital, its palaces and museums, its creation by Czar Peter the Great and Empress Catherine the Second in the 18th century must be understood to understand anything about Russia and Russians. It is also the ultimate cultural connection between Russia and the West. The Hermitage Museum is one of the best of European art in the world. Visiting two of their Leonardo da Vincis at close quarters, displayed in simple glass cases, in a room under the watchful eyes of two guards sitting in the corners with loaded AK-47 automatic rifles on their laps, was in major contrast to a visit to the Mona Lisa, on a distant wall at the Louvre in Paris. I am certain that winter evenings in Saint Petersburg have their charm, but it is a city best visited during the summer and its days without nights. All of it is a reminder of our common heritage and the need to understand it for the sake of mankind (big words, thoughts worthy of endless discussions).

As I write about Saint Petersburg, the Trans-Siberian Railway, Siberian gulags and cousin Ludis Smidhens all come to mind. My maternal grandmother's father remarried after his first wife died, and Ludis is one of the children of that second marriage. There are several other Smidhens who have had productive lives as university professors, world-class architects and engineers after escaping from Latvia, but the Ludis' story is one of Communism, Latvia, Siberia, love and survival. During their first year in Latvia (1940-1941), the Russians started mass deportations to Siberian slave labor camps. Ludis' wife was not home when the NKVD (predecessor of the KGB) came to the Smidhens' home. She escaped the deportation, but Ludis was arrested and put, with thousands of others, on one of the cattle-car trains to Siberia. He was a university-educated civil engineer, which probably saved his life since the commander of the camp used him extensively in a variety of construction projects in the camp and the surrounding area. In 1956, when Stalin's successor Nikita Khruschchev initiated an amnesty program of political prisoners still alive in various camps, Ludis was one of a few survivors among those thrown into the cattle cars 20 years earlier. Upon his release from the camp he decided to stay in Siberia, thinking he would be safer there than in a Latvia still in turmoil, with NKVD in control of all life, Russification and an aggressive, brutal Communism that included continued executions and imprisonment of "undesirables." He was able to contact his wife, who had survived, and she joined him in Siberia, where they built a small house and lived in it before eventually returning to Latvia as the Soviet world was changing into the more liberal form of "perestroika" and "glasnost."

Some of the stories Ludis told about survival in Siberia were amazing. He was more than willing to go with me to Siberia to show me which trees had edible barks, which bushes had edible roots, how to catch some small animals and how to stay warm in the coldest winter temperatures. We were considering a joint trip on the

Trans-Siberian Railway, but those plans did not work out. I was however very happy to be in a position, with my Russian friends, to get him a visa to visit us and some of his other relatives in the United States. One of the most interesting survival stories is that of his wife. When she did get to Siberia, she immediately got a live chicken, the ultimate survival animal – first you eat its eggs, then you eat the chicken after saving its feathers for stuffing blankets or pillows and when there are only a few left-over bones, you boil them to make the proverbial chicken soup to cure all ills. Some of these survival lessons were also handy when, after Latvia had once more become independent, he was able to reclaim the Smidhen farm and lands outside of Talsi and had to deal with the ruined farmhouse and its mismanaged lands. Upon his death, he was put to rest in our beautiful, 200-year-old Smidhen family cemetery, close to Uncle Fricis of Vladivostok and Queen Eleonore fame.

Kiev is a spectacular city of cathedrals and chestnut tree-lined streets on the Dnieper River. It is the river the Vikings used to reach the Black Sea, the Byzantine Empire and points beyond. It is the capital of Ukraine, but a major center of the early Russian Empire. Vladimir the Great, a descendent of Norsemen-Vikings, was one of its major kings and his son Yaroslavl the Wise was born there. It is Vladimir who made the decision to adopt Christianity for his Russian people, as long as he was allowed to keep his three wives and the hundreds of concubines he is said to have had. His choice of Christianity was interesting and based on his belief that his people could not live without their vodka, barred by Islam. Those are some of the details of Kiev history we heard during our visit to its orthopaedic surgeons. All went well and I was able to do three total hip replacements with the assistance of two of their junior surgeons while their chief was sipping brandy in the nurses' lounge. One of these younger surgeons, Alexander Kosiakov, after visiting with us at Yale/Waterbury has become a professor of Orthopaedic Surgery and has written a major book on hip surgery, giving us credit for his start in that specialty. It was also in Kiev that I was invited by a chubby general to a full Russian sauna treatment in his special officers "club." It was the dry sauna, the jump into a small spring-fed pool of freezing water, followed by the steam treatment, the switching with birch twigs, the massage and the inevitable socializing sitting, stark naked, around a table in a cloud of steam, toasting the occasion with ice cold vodka. I survived, but our naked chubby friend got the best of one of the Richards salesmen who had provided the hip implants. The poor man was the victim of the best of Russian hospitality, a tradition dating to the days of Peter the Great, under the table, lost wallet and passport, time at the U.S. Embassy the next day and a lesson learned about avoiding some of the toasts to country, wife, children, the president, etc. It was a great visit to a spectacular, historic town and wonderful people of Slavic, Norse, Lithuanian and probably invading Mongolian descent.

Yaroslavl is considered by many to be Russia's birthplace, founded more than 1,000 years ago by Yaroslavl the Wise, son of Vladimir the Baptizer, in the wooded wilderness along the Volga river, 100 miles northeast of Moscow. It was said to be a refuge from the Mongolian hordes who were riding roughshod over the Slavs and Russia, destroying among others the city of Kiev. It is a town known for the large number of churches and monasteries built by the descendants of Yaroslavl. Many were destroyed by the Communists, but they are still a major presence, the largest of them having been restored to its ancient glory. It was a wonderful to see them and to hear some of their history.

Academically speaking, it was also good to meet Doctor Kluchevsky, the head of orthopaedics in that part of Russia and to work with him in Yaroslavl. He was very enthusiastic about the anterior approach to the hip and was willing to leave his family and work to spend some time with us at Yale. He was sincere, bright, a good surgeon and administrator of a major orthopaedic center. Somewhat disheveled, in an ill-fitting suit and his tie always askew, he would on occasion, be it at dinner or in the midst of a conversation, break out into sad sounding songs. We loved him and arranged to participate in a joint-replacement course he was organizing in Yaroslavl. The course was a success. It was really cold when we got there in late fall, but, according to the rules of the local government, too early to turn on the heat in our residence and lecture halls. Kluchevsky was enthusiastic about having one of our Yale residents, Preston Phillips, spend some time in Russia. Preston, a great resident – six-foot-six inches tall, African-American - spent a January with them. I lent him my long down coat for his stay, which as expected was in deep snow and continuous below-zero temperatures. Preston had a great time, did some surgery he could not have been able to do at his level of training at Yale and thinks of his month in Yaroslavl as a high point in his career. Yaroslavl and Kluchevsky were another experience to make us think about common heritage and the need to live together in productive peace - in creative work and song.

As I look back at the more than 20 years of work and travels through Russia there are many thoughts that come to mind.

What a privilege it was to see this country almost twice the size of the United States, hear about its unique history, and recognize its ties to Christianity and Western culture. Establishing friendships with some of its political and military leaders was beyond anything I could have imagined on my first trip to Moscow and the Goodwill Games of 1986. Meeting some of the brightest minds in the world in this land was an education in itself. Reliving their years under Communism and its collapse, followed by the present resurgence of a dictatorship in the hands of a political police officer from the old state, has been sad. I am hoping for better days ahead and hope to do my part to achieve them.

It was a great honor to be elected to the Russian Academy of Science, to receive the Silver Star for Medical Service to Russia and an Honorary Doctorate from the Burdenko Academy.

The academic ties we established should also help with the future of the international education we have in mind at the Yale University Department of Orthopaedics and Rehabilitation with the Keggi Kimball Fund for International Orthopaedic Education. It is a satisfying feeling to have had so many capable Russian fellows pass through our operating rooms, sit in on our lectures and return to their homes with positive academic memories, the potential seeds of orthopaedic innovations, future cooperation and good will between our countries.

Those trips to Moscow, Novosibirsk, Saint Petersburg, Yeroslavl, Vladivostok, Irkutsk and all the Russian encounters there have also made it easier to move forward and come to terms with the horrors perpetrated on Latvia and our family by the Russian Communists during the Stalin era. There is great concern with Putin and his era, but he too should pass and behind him come all the "good" Russians I was privileged to meet.

There is hope and it is good to promote it.

There is also an amusing side to my medical work in Russian that could be told as story of spies, international intrigue and adventure. My Yale classmates working for the CIA, one as the Director of Clandestine Operations, the other in charge of the Far East, should make me a major suspect for my links to the KGB. My extensive contacts with the high-ranking KGB admiral, the commanding officer of the Warsaw Pact Forces and other Russian officials obviously make me one of their operatives. I should write up my orthopaedic work in those terms, have a bestseller book and make millions on movie rights. Something to think about.

BACK TO VIETNAM

Ace Barnes was one of my best friends in our Yale Medical School, Class of 1959. Ace came to Yale from the South and was very much the southerner in demeanor and accent. He was a wonderful man, married to an equally wonderful wife, Jean, and we have been good friends since our first days in medical school. We were commissioned on the same day as second lieutenants in US Army Medical Service Corps, went to weekly active reserve meetings for 2.5 years while in school, attended summer camps together and continued with service in the Army after receiving our medical degrees. Ace became a pathologist, served in Vietnam, had a very successful academic career and continued on active reserve status for his entire professional life. In Vietnam, he had the unbelievably responsible job of being in charge of blood and blood banking for all of our wounded soldiers. As I've written, I stayed in the reserves after medical school but had signed up for active duty at the end of my five years of orthopaedic training. After serving two years on active duty, one in El Paso and the other in Vietnam, I remained in the reserve until I moved to Waterbury and went into private practice. At that point, after 13 years of reserve and active-duty time, I resigned my commission since sudden reactivation would have been a major complication in my private practice, family and finances.

Ace, in addition to his work as a pathologist and his

duty in the army, was a very devout Christian who, during his entire life, participated in missionary work. For years, he went to Africa to work as a pathologist in remote hospitals and started going to Vietnam with a Christian medical/missionary group as soon as it was possible after the war. Officially, they were doing medical work, but it was combination of medicine and Christianity. Ace knew all about my activities in Russia and the foreign fellows' program we were running through the Keggi Orthopaedic Foundation at Yale/Waterbury. He was constantly reminding me I should be doing something in Vietnam and that he would arrange it through his missionary group. For several years, I was uncomfortable with the idea of having Vietnamese fellows. The horrors of the war, the Viet Cong and the North Vietnamese were heavy on my mind. I kept remembering the missionaries in Buan Ma Thuot in the Central Highlands of Vietnam and the patients I treated there - all killed by the North Vietnamese during the Tet Offensive in 1968. It was difficult to imagine and difficult to forget. Then I was involved in John McCain's presidential campaign and met him at a reception in Greenwich. We exchanged a few words on our Vietnam experiences and he "thanked me for my service." It was very embarrassing. I was back without a scratch and he had spent six years of torture as a prisoner of war. After our meeting, I read his book and was amazed how he had come to terms with the Vietnamese and his history with them. The conclusion was that I could be doing the same, so I accepted Ace's suggestion of taking Vietnamese orthopaedic surgeons into our foreign fellows' program. Ace and his missionary group were very helpful. They arranged for a relatively young academic orthopaedic surgeon from Hanoi to be the first to come. When he arrived, he was accompanied by Ace Barnes, the Vietnamese ambassador to the United Nations, and the Vietnamese Minister of Health. I have a very nice photograph of all of us at their bed-and-breakfast. During the next few years, we had five more come spend time with us. The initial visit was fascinating, historically interesting and also amusing. These Vietnamese functionaries and our orthopaedic fellows thought of the war in Vietnam as "ancient" history and made a point of telling us that they were trying hard to be as American as possible. Thus, they explained to me that if you had a bicycle in Vietnam, you were hoping to soon have enough money to buy a motor scooter. If you had a motor scooter, you were hoping to have enough money to buy a car, and so on and so on. The Minister of Health had some interesting stories to tell. The contact with the Minister had been through his wife, a devout Christian known to Ace's missionary friends. The Minister also thought of himself as a Christian. His father had been Ho Chi Min's private physician, which did not seem to affect his faith.

All of it came to a high point when we arranged for a welcome luncheon at Mory's in New Haven. We had reserved the Whiffenpoof table, the Whiffenpoofs being a Yale singing group that came for dinner every Monday and serenaded all their fellow diners. They certainly did not have a very "Christian missionary" image. As we sat down for our midday meal, I was at one end of the table and the Minister of Health at the other. We had poured some wine and I started to lift my glass to propose a toast but was interrupted by the minister saying, "Now just a moment. Haven't we forgotten something?" I looked at him, obviously wondering what he was talking about, but his reply to his own question was, "I would like to say Grace." We were all stunned since I could not possibly imagine anybody at the Whiffenpoof table having said grace at any time before, but Grace was said by our Vietnamese Communist and we proceeded with our meal, toasts, greetings and good hope for the future. The Lord obviously intervened on behalf of the minister and we now have professors of orthopaedic surgery in Hanoi and Hue. One of them, Nham, who is a professor at the University of Hue, has written a very nice book on hip surgery and gives us credit for some of his academic achievements. We can take pride in having had a small part in his work and life. As our program of international orthopaedic surgery continues, we have been in touch with Nham, and bright young Vietnamese surgeons will certainly be on the list of future fellows at Yale.

We have moved on, we have come to terms with the war. I thank Ace Barnes and John McCain for helping me do the same.

ONWARD

LITHUANIA. Under the USSR regime, Lithuanian orthopaedic surgeons had been training under Viktors Kalnberz's tutelage in Riga at the Latvian Institute of Othopaedics and Traumatology. Very soon after establishing our program of academic exchange, I was lecturing and operating in Vilnius, the capital of Lithuania. One of their most promising young surgeons, Norunas Poverneckas, was among the first of our fellows at Waterbury/Yale. He had spent several years training in Riga, spoke perfect Latvian and some English, which made communication with him a much simpler process than with a monolingual Russian.

Latvian and Lithuanian are the only two remaining languages of the Baltic tribes that lived in the territories of present-day northeastern Germany, Latvia, Lithuania and Belarus. They are old Indo-European tongues, close to Sanskrit and intriguing to philologists. Some ancient Prussian had survived until the end of the 19th century, and my grandfather, Ludis Berzins, who as a young man collected folk songs along the Baltic coast, had heard it spoken by old fishermen, but only at sea. They apparently thought of it as the language of the fish, and it was interesting to hear grandfather talk about it. As a Latvian more than a hundred years later, I can vaguely follow a conversation in Lithuanian. Deciphering a newspaper is easier, since so many of their written words seem like pure Latvian, but when spoken by Lithuanians are less comprehensible. Estonian belongs to the Ugro-Finnish group of languages without any similarity to Latvian. Even though the languages are completely different, Estonians and Latvians are culturally closer, having been conquered by the German Teutonic Knights in the 13th and 14th centuries, with a common history since then. The Lithuanian tribes were able to unite themselves, hold off the Germans, create a Kingdom that extended from the Baltic to the Black Sea and within kilometers of Moscow itself. They allied with the Poles and remained Roman Catholics while, at the time of the Reformation, Latvians and Estonians were converted to Protestant Lutheranism. Most of the churches in Latvia and Estonia also look like their Swedish and Northern German counterparts – the ones in Lithuania tend to have an Austrian Baroque look.

Vilnius has some spectacular Baroque churches and a university with buildings dating back to the Middle Ages. As was the case in Moscow at Burdenko University, these solid, ancient buildings were of no comparison to their Soviet-era hospital, with its bumpy floors, meandering walls and uneven staircase steps. Vilnius is also of interest as a city Napoleon entered in glory on his march to Moscow and then passed through, on his way out of Russia, defeated - in ice and snow, with Cossacks in hot pursuit.

I lectured and operated several times in Vilnius and Kaunas, the second largest city and capital between the two World Wars. We have hosted more than twenty Lithuanian fellows who enjoyed a very warm reception in Waterbury with its large percentage of people of Lithuanian descent.

ESTONIA. Visits to Russia, Ukraine, Georgia,

Uzbekistan and Lithuania were all instructive, but with an Estonian great-grandfather, whose family name we still bear, Estonia was "special." Its university in Dorpat (German name) or Tartu (Estonian name) was also attended by members of our maternal side of the family in the second half of the 19th century. Dorpat was known as the Heidelberg of the North and had many academic connections with universities in Germany. The teaching was in German and many of its traditions such as student corps (fraternities) were identical to their counterparts in German institutions.

Since earliest childhood we were exposed to the stories of our relatives who were the founders and early members of Lettonia, the first Latvian corps at Dorpat University, whose members played major roles in rekindling Latvian culture and the founding of an independent state at the end of World War I. The green, blue and gold student caps and chest ribbons were among our proudest family possessions, and when initiated in New York, I became a fifth generation "Lettonis." Our maternal grandfather, Ludis Berzins, studied theology at Dorpat and went on to be prominent in Latvian education, literature, the study of its language and folk songs. As a young boy I was most impressed by his stories of Dorpat and how he would get there from western Latvia by train, horse-drawn carriage and walking long distances barefoot. I did not get to operate at the Tartu Hospital, but had a nice visit with their surgeons. I was delighted to see the medieval town, the old university buildings where grandfather had studied and the Emajogi River, an ancient trade route used by the Vikings on their way in and out of Russian territories, the Black Sea, the Ottomans and lands beyond them.

In Estonia, most of my professional contacts were with the orthopaedic surgeons in Tallin, the capital city, in the North, on the Gulf of Finland. Their surgeons seemed very active, had a strong history of the treatment of musculoskeletal problems and were under the academic leadership of Professor Rein Raie, who had been the chief of pediatric spine surgery in Leningrad before returning to Estonia. Ivar Kask, a young surgeon from Tallin, was in the second or third group of our foreign fellows. Ivar eventually emigrated to England, where he has had an outstanding career in joint-replacement surgery. Ivar was typical of some of the other Estonians with his excellent English and familiarity of American customs, acquired by watching Finnish television, which the Russians were unable to block.

Ivar was also my guide to the northwestern corner of Estonia and the island of Saarema, the ancestral homeland of the Keggi side of the family. We went there shortly after the Russians had left, but to make certain we would not be detained at any of the old frontier posts, Ivar had brought along liquid refreshment for potential obstructive guards – a couple of liters of lab alcohol, strong enough to open any gates or to facilitate dealings with any Russian bureaucrat. As it turned out we did not need it for any of the guards, but it was most welcome to our hosts on the island of Saarema. Saarema was the home of the last Vikings, or pirates as they were called by the Germans, Danes and Swedes who Christianized them in the 13th century as the climate cooled (possibly in line with what was happening in Greenland at about the same time), freezing the Baltic Sea and allowing the German Knights to ride across the ice and proceed with their "Christianization at sword point." Previous attempts to take over the island by sea had failed because of the sailing and fighting skills of these hardy last of the Eastern Vikings.

The locals are also proud of a large meteorite crater

in the middle of the island where it is said Thor, God of the Norse, had come to earth in a spectacular flash of light and thunder still vivid in the islanders' collective memory. The castle built by the conquering Germans in the 14th century is spectacular and well preserved, and we, as a family, were able to visit it once more, several years later on our cruise from Stockholm to Riga. There are many ancient Viking settlements and artifacts throughout the island, and it is my understanding more and more of them have been found during the last 30 years of a renewed independent Estonian Republic. The folk costumes had anatomical fascination with their short skirts and knee-length socks that were made to look bulky around the calves. Big calf muscles were said to be a sign of beauty to the Vikings, who might be gone on far away expeditions and were looking for wives who in their absence would have the strength to take care of family, home, the fields and fishing. That DNA has definitely survived in our family as we run, row, hit golf balls, play volleyball or basketball, with calves doing a good job of it. It was also interesting to partake of their beer. Each male head of a household is expected to have a special brew for his family and guests. I had never had beer in its raw form, looking like hot chocolate and of a different taste in each family. It was good to partake of this ancestral brew, but on the whole, I will stick to the wines of Tuscany or Spain.

SWEDEN. When I started going to Latvia in 1987, there was a Swedish professor there who had previously demonstrated cemented Charnley hip replacements. On one of my visits to the Latvian Institute of Orthopaedics and Traumatology, he witnessed the anterior approach I was using and invited me to Stockholm to present it at Saint Goran Hospital. I was to give lectures on the anterior approach for hip replacements and my experiences with war wounds in Vietnam. I was also to perform a hip replacement with the orthopaedic residents to show them the procedure in vivo. I accepted the invitation with enthusiasm and arrived as scheduled for a dinner, a tour of Stockholm, the operation and the lectures to follow. It was an exciting experience for me, but the Swedes, even though expressing interest in my work, were restrained and almost sullen. It was also interesting to experience the totally organized and regimented lives they were leading. As I was performing my operation, the resident first assistant, who was across the operating room table from me, suddenly, and much to my amazement, without saying a word, walked away to be replaced by a male nurse. I was told it was nine o'clock, and, according to their rules and regulations, the young doctor assistant had to take a 20-minute break. He did return 20 minutes later as I was finishing the operation and looked so "refreshed" that I thought we should institute similar rules in our American operating rooms immediately - to save our residents from excessively long exposure to older teaching surgeons, add years to their training and to live happily ever after, all in the mold of Swedish socialism.

In the afternoon, as I was in the middle of my lecture on war wounds, all of a sudden half of my audience got up and walked out of the lecture hall. I was told not to take it personally since it was three o'clock and if they stayed longer, they would accrue overtime, taxed at a higher rate that they could not accept. Some of them also had such obligations as picking up their children from kindergartens that closed at precise hours or get home to their spouses at a designated time. It was an educational experience to see such regimentation in action. I am happy to have been there, to have worked with the Swedes and seen their country, but there was little excitement or fun. I imagine those traits were beaten out of the Swedes when they lost the Great Northern

War to Peter the Great some 300 years ago and made them wise enough to cooperate with both the German Nazis and the Russian Communists in order to be on the winning side during World War II.

AUSTRIA. Having written about the dour Swedes, the opposite end of the spectrum in Austria comes next to mind – not quite like my extraordinary trip to Bologna, where orthopedics and joint surgery were barely mentioned between multiple courses and wines at the best of restaurants, but close. In Austria I spent some time with Professor Franz Endler, a major figure in Austrian and German orthopaedics, at his weekend home in the Burgenland, a province east of Vienna known for its many castles, built to protect Christian Europe from the Muslim Ottomans. It was sightseeing, lessons in general history and the history of orthopaedics, fine cuisine, the best of Austrian wines, good humor and fun. My second visit to Vienna was with Karl Zwymueller, an example of the best of pioneers in hip replacement surgery in Austria and the world. I visited him at a relatively early stage in his career, having read about his unique non-cemented prosthesis and having heard it discussed by some German surgeons. Professionally, it was extremely satisfying to sit with Zwymueller in the basement of an old Viennese hospital where he kept his X-rays and review some of his cases without any formalities. It was also good to watch him operate. In doing so, I learned not only about his prosthesis, but also some special tissue releases, use of instruments and the preparation of the bones for the insertion of the implant. He was and is a "Master Surgeon." The dinners we shared were memorable from an academic perspective and enjoyable with the fine food, service and wine. I made a point of stopping in Vienna on my way home from Russia a few more times to exchange ideas with their surgeons and to be in their Imperial City.

They were productive and fun visits.

GERMANY. The Germans have always played a major role in precise science, medicine and surgery. I was exposed to their sense of order ("Ordnung muss sein") as a child in Latvia and later in Germany itself. In medical school we also learned that anything we might think of as new and revolutionary had already been published in the 19th-century German literature. In 1983, as Americans were experimenting with a variety of devices with minimal clinical follow-up, I discovered the precise laboratory and clinical work of Professor Heinz Mittelmeier. He had studied non-cemented implants and ceramics for many years, and I decided to use his devices in my younger patients. I had success with them, and they have a definite place in the history and evolution of joint surgery. A visit to Hamburg in Western Germany to see Mittelmeier work was another encounter with a "Master Surgeon" and his peculiarities. He was able to insert his hips with only a few primitive (in the eyes of American surgeons) instruments and felt you should be able to do the same. The Swedes may have been sullen and the Italians bon-vivants, Mittelmeier the German was precise, strict, pedantic and blunt. If you could not do it as he was showing it, he did not mince words and made it clear you should be a gynecologist (his words). Having success with his implants and writing about them qualified me in his eyes as a "good surgeon." It was complimentary, but somewhat embarrassing since he dismissed most American surgeons, who were having difficulties with his operation and the screw-in acetabulum from the posterior approach, as less than competent. It is unfortunate that Mittelmeier, in his Germanic manner, was unwilling to change a procedure that worked well in his hands but needed adjustments of instruments and approaches to work for the majority of others. As a result, the ceramic-on-ceramic implants acquired a negative image that has been difficult to overcome in spite of their superb performance in the young and very active patients.

One of the most amazing examples of the durability of the Mittelmeier joint is a compulsive runner whose hip I replaced in the 1980s. He has completed four full Iron Man Triathlons, has logged more than 30,000 miles running, probably 50,000 miles bicycling and 3,000 miles swimming. At the age of 76, he gave up long-distance running, but continued to play tennis, jogs without pain and zero evidence of ceramic wear. It has been a privilege to be an advocate of the Mittelmeier ceramic-on-ceramic hip and to teach it in this country and throughout the countries I have visited. It remains controversial but following in Mittelmeier's Germanic footsteps I am willing to show its benefits in any manner and at any level of academic debate.

The Germans were also among the first to use robots in total hip surgery. Initially I was very intrigued by that idea and continue to think in the long run there will be more and more of this technology in all fields of surgery. I had been in Sacramento to visit the American company involved in the promotion of "Robodoc," the first of these devices, and was encouraged to visit a German surgeon using it in Frankfurt. Thus, on one of my trips to Russia I flew back to New York via Frankfurt and spent a day watching the robot in action. It was interesting, but at the end of it I saw no use for it in my practice of total hips through the anterior approach. I am sure many of the problems I witnessed have been or will be resolved, but at the time of my visit it took the entire morning to complete the operation.

It was a two-stage process. The first stage consisted

of inserting metal markers, under general anesthesia, in the patient's thigh. The patient was then awakened to have a CAT Scan, which was assessed by the surgical team and programmed into the robot for the mathematically planned preparation of the femur. The patient was then re-anesthetized, strapped to a futuristic operating table attached to the robot. The surgeon then exposed the hip with his hands and old-fashioned instruments, implanted the acetabulum and attached a reamer to the robot's "arm." For the next 30 minutes the surgeon stood there while the robot reamed the proximal femur - brrr, brrr, brrr, brrr - to the predetermined dimensions. Once done, the wound was irrigated in an old-fashioned manner and the femoral component inserted into the cavity prepared by the robot. It was a perfect fit, but I saw no reason to subject my patients to two anesthesias, long surgery with the wound exposed to bacterial contamination and potential infection, for the sake of having absolutely perfect looking X-rays. Our record of a perfect fit in approximately 95 percent of cases, with the rest in the satisfactory range, seemed good enough and we were doing the operations in a quarter of the time. The German surgeon was very pleased with the absolute precision, but I thought we were doing well enough with our "Kentucky windage" approach and gave up the thought of robots in my practice at that time. The world and surgery are changing. In the long run, robots, computerized navigation and devices we have yet to imagine will be doing more and more of the operations, but we cannot forget how to do operations with simple instruments as taught by surgeons such our "Chief," Wayne O. Southwick of Korean War surgery experience.

ENGLAND. Julie and I met in London and traveled through England on our European bus tour in 1956. We had been back to London and had enjoyed a golf cruise around Scotland, Ireland and Wales. I had also rowed in Veterans Regattas, watched daughter Mara row in a World Championship in England and caddied for daughter Caroline in a British Open Championship. But I had not visited any of their hospitals until I was working in the Soviet Union/Russia with our Keggi Orthopaedic Foundation. We had been able to get special funding from the Smith & Nephew Company to help our foundation establish a nurses' exchange program between the Baltics, Russia and Oxford/Nuffield in England, above and beyond the program we were running at Waterbury/Yale. It was established and administered by our assistant in Waterbury, Laurene Zatorski, Iveta Kelle in Riga and the Oxford orthopaedic head nurse. It was a very successful academic program that exposed at least 100 Russian, Estonian, Latvian and Lithuanian nurses to western medicine and orthopaedic surgery. I was very happy about the funding we had been able to arrange for it, but the day-to-day operations were in the hands of the three nurses mentioned above.

I did however make a visit to Nuffield as we were getting organized to see the Oxford Institution and its director Robert Duthie. I was interested in Oxford, but was especially eager to see Professor Duthie, whom I had previously met with Doctor Southwick at one of our Academy meetings. He had been the chair of the University of Rochester Department of Orthopaedics, and I had once come very close to filling his vacated chair. As mentioned earlier, I had been selected by the university search committee for the appointment, and Julie was looking at houses in town, but at the last minute the major private practice group in Rochester voted me down as being "too liberal" for their community. That turned out to be very fortunate as I proceeded with my career in Connecticut, but it is the first and last time I have been marked with not only the "liberal" label, but as being "too liberal." Doctor Duthie and I had a great meeting in England. He was amused by the "liberal" story and had a few Rochester stories of his own. He was enthusiastic about our nurses' program and supported it for as long as we were able run it

VENEZUELA. When Viktors Kalnberzs was invited to Venezuela, I was asked to join him. It was primarily to promote Viktor's external fixator, but I gave a lecture on total hips and war surgery. I was made a Member of the Venezuelan Orthopaedic and Trauma Society and we talked about setting up an exchange program with them, but the country was in its early phases of disorganization and nothing came of those discussions. It was an opportunity to meet briefly with my mother's sister, Irene Ebersteins, who was very active in Caracas as the director of their National Choir, music teacher and church organist. She and her husband, Harrijs, an outstanding portraitist, had emigrated to Venezuela hoping to paint the portraits of the generals and officials who were running the country in the 1950s. The era of generals and dictators, however, had come to an end and Harrijs instead made a living painting Venezuelan wildlife and teaching his craft, which had much earlier reached its pinnacle with the painting of a portrait of the Queen of Belgium.

LATVIA

The travels to multiple countries and the programs for orthopaedic fellows and nurses we were privileged to teach at Waterbury Hospital and Yale all took time, but only a fraction of the hours we devoted to Latvia and its people in a variety of efforts.

Following my first visit in December 1987, I became devoted to the teaching of orthopaedics in Latvia. In the course of 20 years, I gave multiple lectures and performed more than 120 hip replacements in Riga. Some of these patients were high ranking Soviet officials, as I have chronicled, but most were Latvians. Some of them were well known, such as Valdis Muiznieks, the winner of two Olympic silver medals in basketball. He had earned these with the Soviet team, which on two occasions had come in second to the United States. He was so pleased with the result of the operation that he gave me the medal he had won in the Rome Olympics in 1960. It was a magnificent solid silver medal attached to an elaborate, decorative silver chain. We displayed it in a special glass case in the conference room of the Keggi Orthopaedic Foundation in Waterbury until Latvia regained its independence and established a sports museum. There was no question in my mind that that was where the medal belonged. It was received with enthusiasm and there it remains

All the operations I performed in Latvia and in the

other Soviet Republics were on a goodwill basis, and, even though I occasionally thought about the hours, days, weeks and months of my time I was devoting to this work, I could not imagine a fee-for-service arrangement. It is possible some of the people who arranged these operations were compensated in dollars or rubles, but I never questioned it. I was happy and felt more than rewarded for being there, to be able to do the surgery and the teaching. But for the occasional bottle of the best of brandies, the silver medal was my highest material reward.

The medals, honorary degrees, memberships in scientific academies and other awards are priceless as I think of "rewards" - priceless to me and my family, Yale University and Yale Orthopaedics. Financially, the operations, lectures, academic exchange programs and related activities were sustained by my personal monetary contributions and those of a long list of orthopaedic companies, friends and patients. The Keggi Orthopaedic Foundation, under the administrative leadership of Laurene Zatorski and supervision in Latvia by Attorney Krevolin and Accountant Teplitzky, was the official and legal entity that made all of this work possible.

In Latvia, most of my time was spent in the capital city of Riga and Jurmala, the beach community west of it, where our grandfather had started his boarding school before World War I. It is where he had settled after that war and where, as a family, we had spent many happy days. I was, however, driven in Viktors' car (limousine), to many other areas of the country, among them Aluksne in the northeast, where we lived from 1938 to 1944. Seeing it again more than 40 years later was a special privilege, arranged by some of Viktors' friends and the KGB Admiral Shindjajev. It was normally a forbidden city because of its location near some major missile sites. The town, the house we had lived in, the lake and the ruins of the old island castle, built by the Teutonic Knights in the 14th century, seemed unchanged and brought back many memories. The Lutheran parish house where, in the late 17th century, the German Reverend Ernest Gliks had translated the Bible into Latvian, was intact along with the two oak trees he had planted to commemorate the event – at the completion of the Old and New Testaments. It was also there, in Gliks' household, that a bright young servant girl grew up to marry Peter the Great and became Catherine the First, Empress of Russia. A story of romance, marriage, mistresses, legitimate or illegitimate children and amazing love between the Czar and a peasant girl who grew up less than a mile from our childhood home in a remote corner of Latvia. The old hospital next to the house we lived in had been closed and a new hospital had been built to replace it. It was a relatively small institution but was functioning with a professional staff that seemed well educated, modest yet efficient. I was very pleased to meet them; later, their orthopaedic surgeon and chief anesthesiologist spent time with us in Waterbury. The orthopaedic surgeon was born in Siberia, where his parents had been deported in the 1940s. He considered himself a devout Christian, but apparently had never been baptized and, while he was with us, I had the unusual duty of bringing him to the altar for baptism in our Middlebury Congregational Church. It was a heart and soul lifting experience for all of involved in the ceremony.

Cesis, a medieval town with its castle built by the German Knights in the 13th century, is approximately halfway between Riga and Aluksne. It is there that our paternal grandfather owned a shop to dye the linen and wool brought in by the peasants of the surrounding region. Father Janis Keggi grew up in Cesis, with the exception of the years the family had fled to Russia to escape World War I and the fighting raging in Latvia. The shop and house were still owned by the family. The buildings were not habitable, but the gardens were maintained for their flowers and vegetables by my four lady cousins. It was a nice visit, especially with cousin Ruta, who is of my age, with a good sense of humor, blunt talk and whom I remembered playing with on the roof of the old house 60 years earlier. All the cousins, their husbands and children were doing well, and a few years later I was able to bring two of them to the States to babysit Catherine's and Mara's children, and learn English.

Dzukste, approximately 60 miles west of Riga, was the birthplace of our maternal grandfather, Ludvigs (Ludis) Ernests Berzins, the youngest of 10 children. The farm where he was born and brought up had been totally flattened by successive tank battles during Christmas of 1944 – only a few piles of rocks were left to mark the site of the family farmhouse. His son, Janis Berzins, my godfather, was there as the commanding officer of the Latvian/German light artillery unit that stopped the Russian tanks. The details of these Christmas battles were related to us by a second (or third) cousin who still lived in Dzukste and had heard them from Uncle Janis himself while he was still free before his arrest, wandering around the countryside, working with the anti-Communist guerillas in the deep woods of the surrounding area. Janis' artillery unit had been across the road from our family homestead, in a farmhouse that had belonged to another relative. At the end of the fighting there were, on our great grandfather's fields, a dozen burnt-out Russian tanks blown up by Janis. He was an extremely cool-headed man and highly decorated officer, but even for him it must have been an emotional experience to be fighting on these ancient family fields. Those Christmas battles were said to be especially difficult because by this time the Russians had drafted many Latvian men and boys from the parts of the country they controlled, who were now fighting with the Red Army and encountering their "brothers" on the German side.

Uncle Janis' last letter was from Dzukste in which he wrote about the church's historic altarpiece painting and also about some of the Berzins relatives still in the area. On my first visit to Dzukste and the bombed-out ruins of its church, I made a point to inquire about this painting - to no avail. Who knows, it may well turn up in California, the same way that a famous painting of Ivan the Terrible, missing for a Ukrainian museum for more than 70 years, turned up in a Connecticut home. It was fun to meet a few of our distant relatives, but on my first visit to Dzukste, it was still under Communist rule and most of them were very cautious about talking to me for fear of being labelled enemies of the state, or spies. A few years later, after Latvia had become free again, we planned a family visit to Dzukste and announced our plans ahead of time. We were met by over 100 relatives and cousins, probably a fraction of Grandfather's nine siblings' children, grandchildren and great-grandchildren. Many of them were also there when we reburied my grandparents' ashes in the family lot next to the ruins of the church that had been there since the Middle Ages. Over the years I helped Dzukste to establish a museum where many of Grandfather's works and accomplishments are well displayed.

Ventspils is a port city west of Dzukste that has a well-run hospital. I was able to bring two of their physicians to Connecticut. One of them went back home to practice medicine, but the other, Gundars Daudze, became involved in national politics as the longstanding speaker of the Latvian General Assembly in Riga. He is a good friend. I have had the honor of visiting him in the

Assembly and we exchange messages on a fairly regular basis. Ventspils has been for over 1,000 years a port of entry into what is now Latvia and the territories to the East, the Dnieper River on the way to the Black Sea and distant points beyond. It was conquered by the German Knights in the 13th century and the castle they built is still there in amazingly good condition. It is where Uncle Janis, of Dzukste artillery fame, found himself in May of 1945, at the time of the German surrender to the Soviets. One of his best friends had been able to escape to the West via submarine, but Janis elected to stay in Latvia, stating that if destined to die he would want to do so in his native land rather than foreign soil. As the commanding officer of a major German artillery unit, he then proceeded to write an official document releasing himself from "trench digging duty." With this official German military document in hand, he went to the Soviets, who accepted it and issued him documents allowing him to return to his farm. Thus freed, he then wondered around Latvia, working with the anti-Communist guerillas until his arrest on the streets of Riga six months later. We gathered this information from his friend who got on the submarine, the cousins he had visited in Dzukste and the KGB files when they became available after the collapse of the Soviet Union. The details of his ultimate fate are unknown. He was condemned to death and was either executed in Riga's infamous Central Prison or died in a Siberian Gulag.

Liepaja, south of Ventspils, is also a major port connected to a direct railway to Russia. Iveta Kelle, our longstanding assistant with all of our activities in the Baltics and throughout the former Soviet Union, was brought up in Liepaja and went from there to work as the equivalent of an American nurse practitioner in Riga, where we were fortunate to recruit her to work with us. Initially the physicians in Liepaja were not too involved with the program we had started with Viktors Kanlberzs at the Latvian Institute of Orthopaedics and Traumatology, since they had established academic contacts with a Swedish university and hospital (in Upsala, as I remember). Eventually that changed. I lectured at their hospital and performed a total hip replacement for a woman of my age who had been deported to Siberia as a child but had survived to return to Liepaja in her middle age. It was a somewhat emotional experience since I could easily have had her fate. The surgeon from Liepaja, who came to us as a fellow, was by far the most involved in exploring all cultural activities, such as museums, lectures and concerts, available at Yale. He too had been deported to Siberia as a child, but upon his return to Latvia had completed his education to become an orthopaedic surgeon. He was an active member of a Baptist Church, somewhat unique in a land of Lutheran majority and had a brother who for many years, single-handedly, maintained the grand organ in the Riga Doms Cathedral and deserves recognition for that task.

The northern part of the Western Baltic coast is beautiful with its white beaches, dunes and pine forests, and was worth a visit. It is where, as children, in the middle of the night we sat in the forest waiting for the boat to Sweden. Iveta made arrangements for our excursion, which also included a visit to Talsi, and the Smidhens family homestead (Renci), where our maternal grandmother, Minna Charlotte Wilhelmina Smidhens, was born and went to school to become a writer of folk tales and history. It is a beautiful farm with the family cemetery in a grove of oak trees on a small hill which I remembered from the summer of 1944. It is an image of a great family and a loving grandmother.

Riga is of course the capital of Latvia with a population close to 700,000. It is on the Daugava River, which had a trading post on its banks long before the arrival of German Crusaders in the late 12th century. It was already one of the major Viking entry points into what is now known as Russia more than 1,000 years ago. Over the centuries, it has maintained its role of a major port and trading center between the Western world and the East. It has been a city of great wealth, and, since the re-establishment of Latvian independence, is flourishing again. It is a town with a well-preserved medieval castle and cathedral in its Old Town surrounded by parks, museums and an opera house dating to its 19th century prosperity, a time when Richard Wagner was living there. It is the home to the University of Latvia, two medical schools with excellent hospitals and the Latvian Institute of Orthopaedics and Traumatology. The institute, at the time of my activities in Latvia, was under the clinical leadership of Professor Viktors Kalnberzs and its biomechanical research division under Professor Haralds Jansons. The clinical work and scientific research had the reputation of being the best in the Soviet Union. The institute was my overseas professional "home," and it is there that I was able to perform, without major problems, more than 100 hip replacements, give lectures and run seminars.

Riga is where I was born. It is where my grandfather was a professor of education, philology and folklore at the University of Latvia. It is where my mother went to school and where my father studied medicine. It is where my father had his surgical training with Professor Paulis Stradins, a student of the best Russian surgeons in Saint Petersburg and the Mayo brothers in Minnesota. It was also saved from some unnecessary destruction by my Godfather Janis Berzins in the summer of 1941. As mentioned earlier, the German army had arrived on the western shores of the Daugava and was getting ready to start an artillery barrage before entering the city. That potentially destructive attack was stopped by Uncle Janis and one of his Lettonia fraternity brothers who rowed across the river to inform the Germans that the Russians had retreated, and the Latvian inhabitants of the city were awaiting them as liberators from a year of "terror" under the Communists.

I heard this story from the fraternity brother who was in that boat with Uncle Janis and somehow survived more than 10 years in Siberia. It is a delight to think of grandfather Ludis Berzins as a professor at the University of Latvia, but to be standing on the banks of the Daugava and imagine his 23-year-old son in a small boat with a white flag, rowing across the wide river to face an army with machine guns and artillery, is a dramatic vision.

My excursions through Latvia and Estonia were wonderful, and as we visited ancestral homes and lands it was easy to imagine the lives our grandparents and great-grandparents led there as Latvian farmers 100, 200 or 1,000 years ago. As you visit the castles built 800 years ago, learn about the ancient traditions of the Baltic tribes kept alive in their folk songs through more than 600 years of foreign rule, you suddenly have a sense of belonging to all that history. I am very much a Latvian, identify with my ancient Baltic/Indo-European tribes of South Asia and speak their tongue, but also feel affinity to the sturdy Saami and Estonian tribes of northeastern Siberia, whose DNA has come to me through my father's side of the family. My DNA is also from northern Germany, my Teutonic heritage. I have been attacked by them and the Vikings but know I have been down the Dnieper to the Black Sea as one of them. It is a feeling expressed by

General George S. Patton in his biblical poem, "Through a Glass, Darkly," based on Corinthians 13:12. I cannot say it with Patton's tone, but it is worth quoting:

> So as through a glass, and darkly
>
> The age long strife I see
>
> Where I fought in many guises,
>
> Many names, but always me. . .

It is a wonderful feeling of belonging to this land of my Latvian parents and grandparents whom I knew, whose ancient genes I have lived with and am passing to our children and grandchildren. It was good to be in northwestern Estonia and the island of Saarema, where the "Keggi" family name was common as far back as the early 17th century. It is from this area that my paternal great grandfather left to marry a Latvian, to become a Latvian, yet keep his family name for us to carry on. As I pass through the fields, homes and castles of those ancestors in Dzukste, Talsi, Cesis, Riga and Estonia, I feel this continuum of life now flowing in America.

So, when I was given the opportunity to contribute to the work and hopes of my parents, grandparents and their parents to reestablish a free Latvia, with its culture and traditions, it was a responsibility I owed them. I enjoyed the work throughout Russia and the medical education I was able to provide to all the foreign fellows at Yale and Waterbury, but my activities in Latvia reached well beyond the hip replacements I was performing and the young doctors and nurses I was bringing to the States.

The 1989 Latvian Physicians Congress was an amazing event, and I was somewhat involved in getting it authorized and outlined. My previous two years of various activities in Latvia and the operations I performed on high ranking officials in Riga and Moscow probably helped, but the majority of the effort and work for the event was in the hands of American/ Latvian Bertrams Zarins and the leaders of the Medical Community in Latvia, Professors Haralds Jansons, Viktors Kalnberzs and many others. It was an amazing and truly historic event attended by hundreds of Latvian Physicians from all over the World as well as almost every local Latvian physician, medical student and nurse. The highlight of the Congress was the march of all participants through the streets of Riga, on a beautiful sunny day, to lay flowers at the Freedom Monument. At the head of the parade were Kristaps Zarins (Stanford University), Bertrams Zarins (Harvard), Viktors Kalberzs (Latvia) and me from Yale. We were followed by several thousand Congress participants carrying the flags of their towns, hospitals and schools and the red-white-and-red flag of Latvia - the flag that had been banned under the Communist regime but now authorized to be shown in public for the first time in the memory of most. The streets were lined with thousands of cheering people. I was approached, hugged and given flowers by hundreds of them. After every two or three blocks I had been given so many flowers I could not get my arms around them and had to pass them to someone else in the parade hoping they would reach the Freedom Monument to honor Latvia and its fallen heroes. In the course of the Congress, I was also one of five members of the Lettonia fraternity from America and Canada to raise the Latvian flag, for the first time in 50 years, on the Tower of the Riga Castle. It was an "unofficial" event, we were very proud of it, but it was avoided by the local organizers of the Congress. It went well, no ill came of it, the flag was removed soon after we had raised it, but it was of great symbolic meaning.

The Ludis Berzins Museum was of great importance. My grandfather, a well-known educator, theologian and folklorist, had been declared a "non-person" by the Communist regime. Now, encouraged and helped by Viktors Kalnberzs and his friends, I found myself in a position to bring his works and thoughts back into the history and culture of Latvia. His house in Jurmala was scheduled for demolition, but I was awarded its ownership by the Communist government and converted it into a museum of his works and life. It was a major attraction to all those interested in Latvian folk songs, hymns and education. It was a gathering point for his former students. Initially it was funded by the Latvian government, but after 1991 the costs were all mine. I handled them as best as I could, but after more than 10 years they were beyond my reach and the house was bought by my cousin Juris Berzins, who was planning to establish it as an English language school. The historic contents of the museum were transferred to the National Archives in Riga and the Rundale castle in the countryside south of Riga. The money I received from the sale was transferred to Yale University and the establishment of an endowed Keggi Berzins Fund for Baltic Studies. It remains active and has been supplemented by a major gift from Juris Padegs. It has sponsored conferences and fellows from Latvia, Estonia and Lithuania at Yale. These endowed funds will continue to accrue in value and assure a permanent program of Latvian studies at Yale.

A Berzins Prize for the best essay by a Latvian teacher was also established and awarded yearly in the Jurmala Museum and has continued under the leadership of Anita Smite, the chief editor of the Teachers Journal ("Skolotajs").

Having brought Ludis and Minna Berzins' ashes from the Latvian Cemetery in Upstate New York to Latvia, we had a funeral service in the Riga Doms Cathedral, complete with a Lettonia Honor Guard, followed by reburial in the family plot in Dzukste, next to the ruins of the old church, destroyed during the Christmas battles of 1944 - battles fought by their son, my godfather, Janis Berzins, whose last letters to his parents in Germany were written from Dzukste.

Grandfather Ludis had also bequeathed me an interest in books and libraries, which I pursued at Yale College, Yale Medical School and over the years as member of the Yale faculty. I was also fortunate to be in a position to sponsor 10 Yale Library interns, primarily from Latvia. This led to the recognition of the Yale Sterling Library as a major repository of Latvian books and historical materials.

There is also a Keggi File in the Yale Medical School Historical Library with materials from the Vietnam War, letters, lectures, images, initiation into the Rhade Tribe (in the mountains of central Vietnam), movies on the management of war wounds, etc. It has all of my presentations on the management of war wounds, the photographs and Schlossberg paintings that were in the original scientific exhibits in the late 1960s. On a personal level, it has all of my letters from Vietnam to Julie in El Paso and her letters to me. They have been catalogued by granddaughter Julia Hunter and tell the story of our year in a combat zone, a mobile surgical hospital and life at home with three young daughters without a father. They are also a diary of the first year of America's commitment of regular combat troops to the War in Vietnam.

Having received honorary doctorates from Stradins University and the University of Latvia, I decided to leave the original copies of all my academic diplomas, honorary degrees, other citations and the West Point Military Academy saber awarded to me by the Class of 1961 for taking care of them in Vietnam (as an "Honorary Member" of their class) to the Stradins Medical Historical Museum in Riga.

A few years after Latvia had regained its independence, I was approached by one of the political parties to be a candidate for the presidency of Latvia. It was definitely a flattering honor, but I could not possibly consider it, not with an American wife, children and grandchildren in American schools and a very active orthopaedic career in Connecticut and at Yale. I also explained that even though I had been to Latvia multiple times, I did not have an understanding of the country's politics and lacked the written language skills required of the job. In the course of the years, I have had extensive contacts with the presidents and have enjoyed all of these encounters. President Vaira Viksne–Freiberga was the most interesting, since her background was similar to mine. She was a professor at the University of Toronto and prior to emigration had gone to a French high school, but instead of a native Canadian her husband was a Latvian willing to return with her to Latvia. I felt honored by her visits to our Ludis Berzins Museum but could not imagine myself in her job. It was also a wonderful experience to have President Andris Berzins visit Yale University, its library and have lunch with him at Saybrook, my residential college. He came from a region of Latvia close to Dzukste and had a very familiar (in the true sense of the word) look. There also was a very solemn visit to Riga Castle to receive a special citation from President Raimonds Vejonis. It brought back memories of our flag raising ceremony during the First Latvian Physicians Congress in the summer of 1989. Last but not least is our good friend and former fellow at Yale/Waterbury, President Valdis Zatlers. All of them are special people whose work and responsibilities deserve my respect and gratitude.

In 1991, as the Soviet Union was collapsing, there was some fighting between the Latvian independence group and some of the Communist special forces. A well-known journalist, Zvaigzne, was badly wounded and went into renal failure. He was in a very critical condition and needed help. I was able to bring to Riga hospital, on a rushed emergency basis, a dialysis unit from Waterbury Hospital in the hopes of saving his life. Unfortunately, it got there too late, but the dialysis unit was given to the Aluksne Regional Hospital for future use.

At the family level, I was able to bring two Keggi cousins for babysitting duties and to learn English with Katie's children in New Orleans and Mara's in Connecticut. It was a fun "win, win" situation for all involved and even more fun to see the children of these cousins speaking perfect English.

Under Viktor Kalnberzs leadership we had, in Riga, an annual orthopaedic symposium called "Keggi Days." It was always a well-attended event with physicians and students primarily from the Baltic States.

We organized a bicycle race from Aluksne to Riga in honor of my father, who rode that distance in the summer of 1944 to escape the advancing Russians. We, Mother and the four of us boys, had left Aluksne in the early spring of that year and were staying in Jurmala, west of Riga, with our grandparents. Father, as the only surgeon in Aluksne, had not left his post, but when the Russians were within a few miles of town he got on his bicycle, to ride it some 220 kilometers (approximately 136 miles) to join us in Jurmala. The Keggi Velo was a very successful event in those early days of independence, and the watches contributed by the president of the Timex Company were accepted with great enthusiasm by the participants. Latvia has had some world-class bicyclists, and some of them, who had also ridden in the Tour de France, were in these races. It was a relatively simple event in those days, and it is a pleasure to see the advances that Free Latvia has made in bicycling and all other sports.

Rowing is another sport I was able to promote in Latvia as the Soviet Union was collapsing and during the first years of independence. My involvement in Latvian orthopaedics and Latvia in general started with the Goodwill Games in Moscow. During my first academic visit to the Latvian Institute of Orthopaedics and Traumatology in 1987, I was introduced to a group of rowers, some of whom had competed in the Olympic Games in Mexico. Viktors Kalberzs' son, Konstantin, was also a rower and had friends who were very interested to hear of my participation in veterans rowing in America and at the International Regattas. One thing led to another and a year later we had organized a veterans' regatta between the United States and the Soviet Union. The American group consisted primarily of my fellow members of the New Haven Rowing club and Yale alumni, with two Harvard exceptions. The Soviet rowers were from Latvia, Lithuania and Estonia. We had a great time in special uniforms and rowing gear organized by Jim Elting one of our Yale rowers and orthopaedic surgeon. The Regatta was also in conjunction with a symposium on sports medicine. It was the best of all worlds. It was the beginning of Latvian Veterans Rowing which has continued to this day. Another year later, we were able to sponsor a Latvian crew to come to New Haven and then row in the Head of the Charles Regatta in Cambridge. Good fun for all.

In Latvia I gave multiple interviews to the press and on television about all of our activities in Latvia and the United States. In the United States I also promoted the cause of Latvian independence and academic exchange programs. As a result of these activities I was invited to the White House as Hillary Clinton's guest to participate in some discussions related to the Baltic States. It was nice to meet her, especially at a time when her husband was involved in his sexual scandals and the press was reporting them on a daily basis. One of his former partners, Jennifer Flowers, had just been featured as the "Centerfold" in *Penthouse*, and upon my return to Connecticut I was asked by my politically incorrect friends to comment on both of these ladies. The comparisons were difficult verbalize. Hillary was well informed about Latvia, charming and somewhat flirtatious. Jennifer looked good.

My activities were officially rewarded with the

Latvian Order of Three Stars and honorary doctorates from Stradins University and the University of Latvia. These were very meaningful since my grandfather Ludis Berzins had an honorary doctorate from the University of Latvia and had been awarded the Order of Three Stars twice, for his work on the Latvian language and folk songs.

Finally, there was the publication by Laima Poga of my biography in the form of multiple interviews she conducted with me. It is in Latvian and at some point in the future may be worth a translation into English.

The work for Latvia that started in 1987 has been rewarding in a thousand different ways. It presented itself very unexpectedly. I was able to do it and continue doing it years later. It is work members of my family had been doing for more than 100 years. I had the opportunity to carry it forward and did so with joy as its greatest reward.

CONCLUSION

We have come to the end of this story, which started with a brief outline of my Baltic ancestry. There are many more happy stories that could be told of my marriage to Julie and our family. The stories of Catherine married to Howard and their two children, George and Julia; Mara, her husband Chip and their twin sons and daughter; Caroline and her companion Connie, could be a book by itself. Their lives, their work, their achievements and relationships are exciting recollections.

I have written my memoir primarily for my family and friends, but it may be of interest to a larger audience. It is a story of one boy surviving WWII, growing up and living in America after the escape from Europe in 1949. Some of these recollections of this life should be of interest to historians studying WWII, Latvia, American Latvian immigrants, a Yale education, the evolution of orthopaedic surgery, the Vietnam War and the collapse of the Soviet Union.

Most of my life has been surgery and the teaching of orthopaedic surgery. Since 1984, these surgical activities centered around the hip joint, its replacement and correction of failed primary implants. It has meant the teaching of Yale residents working with me in the operating rooms of Waterbury Hospital and Yale. It has meant spending time with foreign fellows and nurses, attending conferences, clinical research, writing, publication and presentations of our work at national and international meetings. Orthopaedic surgery and lectures throughout the Baltics, Russia and former republics of the Soviet Union were also a large segment of this life.

It meant long hours in the operating room, working on high-risk cases requiring both mental and physical stamina. It meant getting up every morning, doing some exercises, then working until dinner and frequently beyond. It has been challenging but rewarding, professionally and personally, has allowed our family to live well and "give back" to Yale University for taking in 17-year-old World War II refugee, Kristaps.

My four honorary doctorates, medals from Latvia, Estonia and Russia have been wonderful, but none of them compare to the sudden, unexpected letter of thanks from a patient whose hip problems were a struggle 10 years earlier.

The evolution of the anterior approach to total hip surgery and its benefits to the patient we introduced to the American orthopaedic community in 1977 has been very rewarding. Having our foreign fellows in Vietnam, Russia, Latvia and Ukraine publish books on total hip surgery which they learned with us at Waterbury Hospital and Yale, has also been satisfactory from every educational perspective. The book on this approach, with most of the hard work involved with its publication carried out by Lee Rubin, one of our residents and fellows, has been a great success and benefitted many surgeons and their patients.

There are so many individuals who have made possible my life and work. It obviously begins with basic education and some inspiring teachers at schools in Latvia, Germany, Brooklyn, Greenwich and Yale. It is based on the teachings and spirit inspired by Dr. Wayne O. Southwick. It has been helped along the way by untold other individuals during my time in training, work in the army at Beaumont General Hospital in El Paso, the 3rd Surgical in Vietnam, Yale and Waterbury.

The love and support of my wife Julie and our children is beyond simple words.

None of the work we accomplished would have been possible without assistants such as Marjorie Santore, Suzy Napoli, Lisa Rettalick, Sarah Pabst, Diane Reilly, Kathleen Lucey and many others. Laureen Zatorski deserves a special place in our life and work with the untold contributions she made to the Keggi Orthopaedic Foundation, our foreign fellows and nurses. Iveta Kelle has been an alter-ego in Latvia and all the other former Soviet republics. Peggy DelGatti has been with me for more than 40 years and remains a friend, assistant and member of my family.

Such individuals as Attorney Sherman Krevolin and the accountants Earl Jacobs, Marvin Teplitzky, and his sons Josh and Jeff, have led us through the real world of rules, regulations and taxation.

There were many orthopaedic colleagues who have been part of our efforts beyond Dr. Southwick - Gary Friedlaender, Ben Bradburn, Jack Raycroft, Jim Elting and the 150 residents I was privileged to work with. Many of them have become major figures in orthopaedics. We also, once again, take pride in the work of our former Yale orthopaedic surgery resident, John Barrasso, of the U.S. Senate, and Valdis Zatlers, one of our Latvian fellows, who became President of Latvia.

There has been joy in all these activities and human relationships. As I am completing this account, I also feel privileged to be still spending every day as a somewhat productive member of our society, Yale and my family.

Even though I have frequently used the word "work" on these pages, I have not thought of my career in medicine and orthopaedic surgery as work. It has been a way of life. Work, to make a few dollars to buy a shirt, was digging ditches in Colorado at age 16.

POSTSCRIPT

Most of my life has been in peace, as an orthopaedic surgeon with a wonderful family and friends. But wars have been a part of it, too.

War has been with us since time immemorial. Plato, the Greek philosopher, summed it up 3,000 years ago: "Only the dead shall not see war." Plato saw it and we continue to see it daily around the world.

World War II was my childhood from 1939 to 1945 - a life of flight, bombing, strafing, hiding, escape from fatal danger, hunger and a dark future. We survived to live in peace, yet had Americanized Latvian friends, just a few years older, who were drafted to fight and die in Korea.

Vietnam was my turn to be in the ranks, caring for the wounds of our fighting men as taught by my Yale Chief, Doctor Southwick, who had served as an orthopaedic surgeon with the Marines in Korea and made sure all of our young surgeons knew the basics of war surgery. It was Dr. Southwick's belief and continues to be mine as we face the potential horrors of war.

Doctor Southwick and I are the authors of an American Academy of Orthopaedic Surgeons instructional course on the management of these wounds. All of my students have received it and I have lectured on the subject throughout the United States, Europe and Russia. It has also brought me into another war - Ukraine 2022.

Olafs Libermanis is a Latvian orthopaedic and micro surgeon who spent four months with me learning joint surgery, but he heard my lectures on war wounds. He thinks of these lectures as having been "life changing," and has talked about them to a paramilitary group of surgeons in Latvia who also invited me to lecture on two occasions.

As soon as the war in Ukraine started, Olafs drove down to the battle zone and has been there ever since, taking care of the severest of severe wounds. He keeps me informed about the operations he is performing. He is doing amazing work and will show it to the next generation of surgeons. I am with him - in war again, 83 years after the German invasion of Poland and the start of war for "young Kristaps."

"Old Kristaps" feels proud of the work Olafs is doing, and feels privileged to have been one of his teachers at Yale. Olafs is a Yale presence in the Ukraine War of 2022. All of us can take pride in that, in keeping with the distinguished lineage of Southwick, Cushing, Halsted and the rest.

September 2022

Made in the USA
Middletown, DE
28 June 2023

33904874R00209